McGRAW-HILL's

CONQUERING SAT WRITING

McGRAW-HILL's

CONQUERING SAT WRITING

Second Edition

Christopher Black
College Hill Coaching™

New York / Chicago / San Francisco / Lisbon / London / Madrid / Mexico City
Milan / New Delhi / San Juan / Seoul / Singapore / Sydney / Toronto

McGRAW-HILL's Conquering SAT Writing

2 3 4 5 6 7 8 9 10 11 12 13 14 15 QDB/QDB 1 9 8 7 6 5 4 3 2

ISBN 978-0-07-174913-8

MHID 0-07-174913-6

Library of Congress Control Number: 2010933209

McGraw-Hill books are available at special quantity discounts to use as premiums and sales promotions, or for use in corporate training programs. To contact a representative please email us at bulksales@mcgraw-hill.com

*SAT is a registered trademark of the College Entrance Examination Board, which is not involved in the production of, and does not endorse, this product.

College Hill Coaching™ is a registered trademark under the control of Christopher F. Black.

Contents

Contents

About the College Hill Method

Much of the material in this book is based on the College Hill Method, which I have been using with my students for 15 years. It focuses on developing reasoning skills, and so provides a sound basis for preparing for reasoning tests like the SAT. It is based on seven principles.

1. **Good students work to understand how their minds work.** For instance, you should know that your brain has evolved to solve some problems naturally, but not others. We learn to speak and to gesture without being taught, but we can't learn to write essays without instruction. This is because speaking and gesturing helped our ancestors to survive and reproduce, but writing did not. Therefore, there is no "natural" way to write. It is an unnatural process that requires us to think differently than we do when we are simply talking.

2. **Good students work to improve their reasoning skills.** We use many different reasoning skills to solve tough problems, and all of them can be improved with practice, just as a baseball player's skills can be improved with practice. These reasoning skills include the ability to conceptualize problems, to analyze problems, to find patterns, to manipulate mental images, to simplify problems, to recall information, and to use logic. Good students work to improve these skills, and pay attention to how they are used in solving tough problems. To become a good writer, for instance, you must learn to analyze your audience, your task, your essay, your paragraphs, your sentences, your clauses, your phrases, and your words. These are not natural skills, so they require focused practice.

3. **Good students focus on the questions that concern the disciplinary experts.** In school, it's easy to get caught up in the task of getting good grades and lose track of the questions that concern the real disciplinary experts. A good student should not merely be interested in getting a good SAT Writing score, but also with solving the problems that a good writer must solve, like *How do I write something that is worthwhile? How do I convince an antagonistic audience? How do I keep their attention?* and *How do I analyze a difficult topic?*

4. **Good students build disciplinary understanding through mental models.** A mental model is a set of interrelated concepts that work together like a mechanical device in your mind. You can manipulate these concepts to test hypotheses and make deductions. For instance, the "balanced scale concept" helps students to understand how to manipulate equations in a logical way. A good writer understands the craft of writing with mental models also. For instance, writers tend to conceptualize paragraphs as "stepping stones" on a journey, and examples and reasoning as the "foundation" of a building.

5. **Good students break bad thinking habits.** The bad habits we develop as writers usually come from our habits as speakers. A good writer understands the difference between having a casual conversation and writing a formal essay. Different assumptions must be made, and different rules must be followed.

6. **Good students constantly seek new challenges.** Life will present you with many opportunities to take the easy way out. If you want to be happy with yourself, avoid them. You're on the right track because you've chosen to prepare for the SAT Writing with the method that works best, even though it's not the easiest.

7. **Good students work to make the world better.** Okay, so getting a 750 on your SAT Writing won't really make the world better. But the skills you develop in getting it just might, if you put them to good use.

I'll try my best not to hit you over the head with these principles as we work together. I'll try to work them in only as necessary. It might benefit you, however, to think of these principles as you go about your business of being a student.

Acknowledgments

Deepest thanks to Elizabeth, Sarah, and Anna for their love and support and to my students at College Hill Coaching for their inspiration and hard work. Special thanks to Jennie Nevin for her energy and inspired words.

McGRAW-HILL's

CONQUERING SAT WRITING

Part 1
Introduction

Lesson 1—The importance of good writing skills

Lesson 2—The SAT Writing

Lesson 1—The importance of good writing skills

Writing: a tool for success

The ability to write well is perhaps the most important learnable skill in academics and business.

In a 2004 report by the National Commission on Writing,[1] executives at 102 major American companies employing 8 million people estimated that these companies spend over *3 billion* dollars annually correcting writing deficiencies. "People unable to express themselves clearly in writing limit their opportunities," said Bob Kerrey, former U.S. senator, president of the New School University, and chairman of the Commission. The survey also concluded that "people who cannot write and comunicate clearly will not be hired and are unlikely to last long enough to be considered for promotion." According to Joseph M. Tucci, president and CEO of EMC Corporation, "one might think that [because of technologies like grammar and spell checkers] the value of fundamental writing skills has diminished in the workplace, [but actually] the need to write clearly and quickly has never been more important than in today's highly competitive, technology-driven global economy."

Colleges are no less adamant about the importance of good writing skills. In a 2003 College Board survey,[2] 1,044 college professors rated persuasive writing as the "most important" academic skill and as the "most often assigned" means of evaluating students. However, this survey also indicated that high school students were not being adequately prepared for the challenges of college writing. College professors consistently rated their students' writing skills substantially lower than high school teachers did, and assigned substantially more essays than did high school teachers, who gave more multiple-choice tests. Furthermore, although teachers and professors rated practically all of the grammar and usage skills included on the survey high in importance, the survey indicated that high school classroom work did not focus on these skills.

Good writing ability, it seems, is a precious commodity. It is not surprising, then, that writing has now become a very important part of the SAT. In a College Board survey, 74% of college admissions officers said that they would use the SAT Writing in their admissions decisions, and 68% said that they would download and read their applicants' essays.

Why students are not being prepared for college writing

If business executives and college professors value writing skills so highly, why don't high schools focus more intensely on teaching good expository writing skills? There seem to be several reasons. First, teaching writing skills is demanding and time-consuming. To do it well, teachers must first master the difficult art of clear and cogent writing themselves. Then they must teach this art to their students. But most high school English teachers are responsible for more than 100 students at a time, each of whom thinks and writes differently and so needs individualized instruction. Ever try to give useful feedback on 100 essays? It's enormously taxing, if it's possible at all. Second, many high school English teachers consider themselves more teachers of literature than teachers of writing and grammar. They prefer exploring the mind of Holden Caulfield to exploring the techniques of cogent writing. It's hard to blame them; Holden is a fun guy. Third, a small minority of teachers actually work against the goal of teaching good expository writing skills.

Beware the pitfalls of academic-speak

Ironically, English teachers include not only some of the greatest champions of clear persuasive writing, but also some of its greatest enemies. Some of my best friends—like me—are English teachers, but a small minority of us tend to value empty and flowery writing over clear and logical writing. They prefer abstract, vague, and intellectual-sounding language to straightforward expression, and assume that if an essay is hard to decipher, it must contain profound ideas. Smart students usually figure out how to please such teachers; they learn to write floridly to get a good grade. On the SAT, however, you don't want to confuse pompous writing with good writing.

This situation arises when teachers confuse expository writing with literature. The purpose of literature—novels, stories, and poems—is to expand human experience by evoking emotions and thoughts in the reader through imagery and other suggestive literary devices. The purpose of expository writing, on the other hand, is to instruct through clear and logical prose. Good expository writing is always precise, but good literature is often deliberately imprecise.

---

[1] Writing: A Ticket to Work...or a Ticket Out, *Report of the National Commission on Writing*, September 2004.
[2] Curriculum Survey on Reading and Writing, found at www.collegeboard.com/highered/ra/sat/sat_research.html.

Don't try to make ideas seem more profound than they are; pretentions serve no good purpose in persuasive writing. Denis Dutton, editor of *Arts and Letters Daily,* sponsors an annual Bad Writing Contest in which he solicits published prose that epitomizes pompous and deliberately vague academic-speak. Here is an example.

> This book was instigated by the Harvard Core Curriculum Report in 1978 and was intended to respond to what I took to be an ominous educational reform initiative that, without naming it, would delegitimate the decisive, if spontaneous, disclosure of the complicity of liberal American institutions of higher learning with the state's brutal conduct of the war in Vietnam and the consequent call for opening the university to meet the demands by hitherto marginalized constituencies of American society for enfranchisement.

> —William Spanos, *The End of Education: Toward Posthumanism*

Read this sentence over until you can decipher it. Be patient; it may take a few days. Surprisingly, this is not a casual first draft. It is the final draft of the first sentence of a book written by an English professor. Good writers craft their first sentences carefully to draw readers in. This sentence, it seems, has been crafted to keep readers out, or at least to make them feel less brilliant than the author. Writers of such sentences often defend them by saying that profound ideas require dense and difficult language. Untrue. Let me offer this revision.

> The Harvard Core Curriculum Report of 1978 attempted to undermine the movement to reveal how American universities contributed to atrocities in Vietnam, as well as the consequent movement to give disenfranchised minorities more power in American universities. This ominous report deserves a critical response.

This revision conveys all of the relevant ideas lurking in the original sentence, but makes them accessible to every intelligent reader. No thoughtful person can claim that the first version conveys more subtle reasoning than the second. It doesn't. It is merely more pompous and vague.

This example, and perhaps your own experience with some English teachers, might lead you to believe that clear writing is not valued in college. Fortunately, only a small minority of professors value pompous writing more than clear and cogent writing. Simply know that this minority is out there, and avoid such professors if you can. Even more fortunately, the SAT essay graders are trained to give higher marks to clear writing than to pompous writing.

Good persuasive writing is clear, instructive, and respectful conversation, not an opportunity to show off. The teachers who grade SAT essays are trained to reward clear and logical writing, not vague and pompous writing.

Beware the salespeople

There are a lot of people with different opinions of what will get you a good score on the SAT essay. Some say that you must write according to a certain "formula," cite Shakespeare, avoid personal examples, or use big SAT words. When you hear such things, be careful. Sometimes the opinion comes from someone selling a test-prep program.

In my 15 years of preparing hundreds of students to take the SAT Writing, I have learned to be very skeptical of simple-sounding formulas. The SAT is a reasoning test. If you are serious about improving your SAT Writing score, learn to think like a writer. My students have had a good deal of success with this approach, improving their scores, on average, over 115 points on the Writing SAT alone. Success on the SAT is not simply a matter of memorizing some tricks.

The real "secret" to acing the SAT essay

Those who score highest on the SAT Writing are those who have learned to think and write clearly, logically, and creatively. You can't become a millionaire by swallowing a pill, and you can't ace the SAT just by memorizing a formula for writing an essay. Things that sound too good to be true usually are. But that doesn't mean that writing a good essay is terribly difficult. You simply have to learn to think a bit more like a good writer.

If you learn the craft of gathering, analyzing, and expressing your thoughts in writing, you will enjoy a great deal more success in college and beyond. Oh, and you'll ace the SAT Writing.

Lesson 2—The SAT Writing

What does the SAT Writing test?

The SAT Writing assesses your ability to identify and correct errors in sentences and paragraphs, and to write a clear and cogent essay about a general topic. The multiple-choice portion of the SAT Writing assesses your knowledge of the two dozen or so fundamental principles of standard written English. These rules represent the widely accepted standards of good writing. The essay portion assesses your ability to reason persuasively and communicate clearly through writing. The SAT Writing also measures, to a degree, your ability to work under pressure, an important skill in college and beyond. You will have 25 minutes to complete the essay and 35 minutes to complete the multiple-choice portion.

What's on the SAT Writing?

The SAT Writing has three parts: an essay and two multiple-choice sections. The first section of the SAT asks you to write an essay in 25 minutes in response to a question about human behavior, experience, or values. It also gives you a quotation representing a particular point of view on the question. You do not have to respond to the quotation directly; it is simply an example of one of many valid perspectives. Your task is to present and support your own unique point of view in response to the question.

> The right of any human being to speak his or her mind must never be abridged. Suggesting that certain ideas are too "offensive" to be voiced is to commit the vilest of tyrannies. Societies that do not allow unpopular ideas to be expressed seal their own demise.

Assignment: Is censorship ever justified? Write an essay in which you answer this question and explain your answer with reasoning and examples from literature, the arts, history, politics, science and technology, current events, or your experience or observation.

The SAT also includes one 25-minute multiple-choice writing section and one 10-minute multiple-choice writing section. These multiple-choice sections contain three types of questions. Each Improving Sentences question gives you a sentence with one underlined portion which may or may not contain an error in grammar, diction, or idiom. You are to choose the best revision from among the choices. The original sentence may be correct, in which case the correct response is (A), which repeats the original phrase.

<u>Having finished dinner</u>, the waiter brought us a dessert menu.

(A) Having finished dinner
(B) Finishing dinner
(C) Being done with dinner
(D) After we had finished dinner
(E) In our finishing dinner

The answer here is (D). In the original sentence, the participle *having* dangles. That is, it is not close to its subject. Who finished dinner? The original sentence suggests it was the waiter, but this is illogical. Choice (D) is more logical.

Each Identifying Sentence Errors question gives you a sentence and asks you to identify which underlined portion, if any, contains an error in grammar, diction, or idiom. If the sentence contains no error, choose (E).

Our instructor <u>suggested</u> that we move <u>more closely</u> to one another <u>so that</u> we might
       A   B   C
<u>communicate</u> more effectively. <u>No error</u>
   D   E

The answer here is (B). The phrase *more closely* should be replaced with *closer*, because it is an adjective modifying the pronoun *we* rather than an adverb modifying the verb *move*.

Each Improving Paragraphs question follows a draft of an essay that needs revision. The question will ask you to improve the essay by rewriting, rearranging, inserting, removing, or combining particular sentences, often taking into account the context of the essay as a whole.

Which of the following sentences contributes the least to the unity of the second paragraph?

(A) sentence 4
(B) sentence 5
(C) sentence 6
(D) sentence 7
(E) sentence 8

To answer this question, you must determine the overall purpose of the second paragraph and then figure out which of these sentences contributes least to that purpose.

What is the experimental section?

Every SAT has one 25-minute experimental section. This section, which may be a writing, math, or critical reading section, does not count toward your score, and is simply used to field test questions for future SATs. You will not know which of the sections of your test is experimental, so you must do your best on every section. If your SAT contains, for instance, two 25-minute multiple-choice writing sections, you will know that one of them was an experimental section (because only one 25-minute multiple-choice writing section counts toward your score), but you will not know which one is experimental.

What will I be asked to write about on the essay?

You will be asked to answer a general question, most likely about human behavior, experience, or values. It will not require you to have advanced knowledge of any particular subject. It will also be broad enough so that you can choose from many possible perspectives on the issue and from many possible examples to support your perspective. Examples of questions include *Is patience always a virtue? Is competition important in a society?* and *What rule or law would you change if you could?*

How is the essay scored?

Two high school or college English teachers will read your essay and score it from 0 to 6. These scores will be combined to produce a score from 0 to 12. If there is a disparity of more than one point between the two scores, a third reader will determine the final score.

The readers are trained by the ETS to score the essays on the basis of how clearly you present a point of view, how well you support and develop this point of view, and how effectively you use language throughout your essay. The essays are scored holistically, that is, in terms of their overall effect, rather than in terms of specific features. They are urged to reward you for what you do well rather than punish you for small mistakes like misspellings and grammatical errors.

After considerable training, readers are given 40 sample essays to score. If they do not score at least 70% of the essays exactly as the ETS's expert graders do, they do not qualify as graders. Although there is of course some degree of subjectivity in scoring, the scores given by qualified graders are remarkably consistent. In fewer than 8% of the cases do the two readers' scores differ by more than 1 point.

There is no right or wrong response to the essay question. You are not graded on what you say so much as on how well you say it and support it.

How will colleges use the SAT Writing score?

Most colleges look carefully at your SAT Writing score as an indication of how well prepared you are to do college-level writing. In college, as on the SAT, you will be evaluated in good measure on your ability to write timed expository essays. Many colleges will not only use your SAT Writing score to evaluate you for admission, but will also use it to place you in an appropriate English class once you've been admitted. Many college admissions officers will even download and read your essay for themselves.

Isn't it true that Ernest Hemingway would have failed the SAT essay?

Some expensive test-prep companies use a marketing trick called "Hemingway would fail the SAT essay" to sell their services. They present a short piece by a great writer, and then tell you that it would receive a low score on the SAT. They would like you to think, "Well, if Hemingway would fail the essay, I certainly need special help to pass it." They'd also like you to think, "What kind of dopes at the ETS would write a test that even Hemingway would fail!" If you can be convinced that the SAT is dumb and irrational, you will probably think that you need the special help that these companies sell.

These companies conveniently neglect to tell us three important things. First, they, not Ernest Hemingway, chose the excerpt and decided where it would begin and end. Second, Hemingway did not write the excerpt in response to an SAT assignment. In fact, he wrote it for a very different purpose. And third, the test-prep companies, not trained SAT readers, scored the essay. Their goal is to make the SAT scoring system seem as irrational as possible, so that you believe you need their help.

Don't be fooled, The SAT is not biased against good writing and toward mindless formulas, although some test-prep companies would like to convince you that it is. Before signing up for a class or tutorial, find out whether it teaches you to master the persuasive writing process, or merely to memorize "insider's tricks" that supposedly apply only to the SAT.

Don't the essay graders give scores based primarily on length and number of paragraphs?

No. Many long essays get low scores, and some short essays get high scores. Of course, there is a correlation between length and score: high-scoring essays tend to have four or more paragraphs and over 300 words, and low-scoring essays often have few paragraphs and fewer than 200 words. It's easy to see why. To conclude that longer essays automatically get better scores, though, is to make a basic error in logic. Correlation does not imply causality. A correlation exists in professional baseball between weight and home runs: heavier players tend to hit more home runs. From this, a narrow-minded coach might conclude that heaviness leads to good hitting, and make his players eat more rather than practice their hitting skills. As you might imagine, this plan would fail miserably. Similarly, anyone telling you that a good essay score comes from merely writing a lot of words and indenting as often as possible, is not going to help you to ace the SAT essay.

The SAT readers are not dumb. They know the difference between empty prose just written to fill two pages and well-reasoned prose that just *happens* to fill up two pages.

Will colleges see my SAT essay?

When you submit your SAT scores to a college, the college will have the option of downloading a copy of your essay to read. In a recent survey, 68% of admissions directors said that they were likely to do so.

How is the overall Writing score determined?

Your overall Writing score, which ranges from 200 to 800, is determined by combining your essay score and your multiple-choice score. The essay counts for about 30% of the overall score, and the multiple-choice portion for the other 70%.

Are some SATs easier than others?

All SATs are "equated." That is, they are graded on a scale so that getting any given score is just as difficult on one test as on another. Therefore, every SAT is just as hard as any other (or, at least, if one is any harder than another, it will just have a more generous curve). Although the difficulty of the SAT doesn't change from administration to administration, your readiness might. Therefore, the best time to take the SAT is when you are best prepared for it.

If I take the SAT, will I also have to take the SAT II: Writing?

In the past, many competitive colleges asked applicants to submit both SAT I scores and SAT II Writing scores. Since the SAT I has incorporated the writing section, you can expect that the SAT II Writing will be phased out. If you submit your SAT scores, you will almost certainly not be requested to submit an SAT II Writing score.

Part II
The Essay

Lesson 3—Lay the groundwork

Lesson 4—Analyze the writing task

Lesson 5—Gather your ideas

Lesson 6—Organize the essay

Lesson 7—Write the essay

Lesson 8—Practice your essay writing skills

Lesson 3—Lay the groundwork

1. Know what the readers are looking for

To write well, you must know your reader. On the SAT, your readers are two English teachers who are trained by the ETS to read and score these essays. They are looking for the five basic elements that all good humanities professors expect of good writing: an interesting, relevant, and consistent point of view; good reasoning; solid support; logical organization; and effective use of language. These are precisely the qualities that the SAT essay readers are trained to look for. These—not grammatical perfection, big words, or number of paragraphs—are the qualities that earn high scores.

Writing for a college professor is not like writing a story or a letter to a friend. On the SAT essay, your job is not to entertain but to persuade. You may be funny and creative if you wish, but your primary task is to explain and support an interesting point of view, not to impress someone with flowery language or cute observations.

A good persuasive essay respects the reader's intelligence, but still explains an argument carefully. Although you can assume that your readers are smart and well-read, you cannot assume that they think exactly as you do, or that they will fill in logical gaps for you. You must show your reasoning.

The qualities of a good persuasive essay

Interesting, relevant, and consistent point of view. Do you take a thoughtful and interesting position on the issue? Do you answer the question as it is presented? Do you maintain a consistent point of view?

Good reasoning. Do you define any necessary terms to make your reasoning clear? Do you explain the reasons for and implications of your thesis? Do you acknowledge and address possible objections to your thesis without sacrificing its integrity?

Solid support. Do you give relevant and *specific* examples to support your thesis? Do you explain how these examples support your thesis?

Logical organization. Does every paragraph relate clearly to your thesis? Do you provide logical transitions between paragraphs? Do you have a clear introduction and conclusion? Does the conclusion provide thoughtful commentary, rather than mere repetition of the thesis?

Effective use of language. Do you use effective and appropriate vocabulary? Do you vary sentence length and structure effectively? Do you avoid needless repetition? Do you use parallelism, metaphor, personification, or other rhetorical devices to good effect? Do you use strong verbs? Do you avoid needlessly abstract language? Do you avoid cliché?

2. Read good persuasive prose

What is the best essay you've ever read? If nothing comes easily to mind, then you should change your reading habits. Good writers learn their craft not just by writing, but also by reading. Start by reading one good persuasive essay every day from the opinion page of a national newspaper.

The best modern newspaper columnists include Tom Friedman, Maureen Dowd, and Paul Krugman of the *New York Times*; Paul Gigot and Dorothy Rabinowitz of the *Wall Street Journal*, Colbert King of the *Washington Post* and Leonard Pitts of the *Miami Herald*.

Also, pick up a copy of *The Norton Reader,* published by W. W. Norton & Company. It compiles much of the best persuasive prose ever written in the English language. It includes essays that every good writer should read, by writers like E. B. White, Mark Twain, Thomas Jefferson, and Maya Angelou.

3. Learn to read like a writer

When reading a good essay, you shouldn't settle for being entertained or even understanding the arguments. Good writers read differently from other readers. They read to find out how essays work. When they read a good essay, they try to find things that they can use—not just information, but rhetorical tools—in their own writing. They ask questions like

Does the author choose words carefully?

How does the author treat his or her audience?

What kinds of evidence does the author use, and how well is it presented?

What kind of reasoning does the author use, and how effective is it?

How does the author address opposing viewpoints?

How does the author uses devices like anecdotes, statistics, authority, metaphor, and hyperbole?

Does the author persuade me?

An example: The Gettysburg Address

Let's examine a good example of persuasive prose, Lincoln's Gettysburg Address, from the perspective of a writer. (My apologies to my southern friends who are still bitter about the War of Northern Aggression.)

> *Four score and seven years ago our fathers brought forth on this continent a new nation, conceived in Liberty, and dedicated to the proposition that all men are created equal.*

> *Now we are engaged in a great civil war, testing whether that nation, or any nation so conceived and so dedicated, can long endure. We are met on a great battlefield of that war. We have come to dedicate a portion of that field, as a final resting place for those who here gave their lives that that nation might live. It is altogether fitting and proper that we should do this.*

> *But, in a larger sense, we can not dedicate—we can not consecrate—we can not hallow—this ground. The brave men, living and dead, who struggled here, have consecrated it, far above our poor power to add or detract. The world will little note, nor long remember what we say here, but it can never forget what they did here. It is for us the living, rather, to be dedicated here to the unfinished work which they who fought here have thus far so nobly advanced. It is rather for us to be here dedicated to the great task remaining before us–that from these honored dead we take increased devotion to that cause for which they gave the last full measure of devotion–that we here highly resolve that these dead shall not have died in vain–that this nation, under God, shall have a new birth of freedom–and that government of the people, by the people, for the people, shall not perish from the earth.*

Let's begin with the first sentence.

> *Four score and seven years ago our fathers brought forth on this continent, a new nation, conceived in Liberty, and dedicated to the proposition that all men are created equal.*

Everyone remembers the *four score and seven years ago* part, but what follows is much more significant. Good sentences are driven by verbs. Lincoln begins with five powerful verbs (or, more precisely, two verbs and three participles) in the first sentence. The first two participles, *brought forth* and *conceived,* evoke the ideas of birth and hope, important ideas to inspiring a young nation. But these words can also evoke the idea of immaturity, dangerous to a nation at war and struggling for its survival. So he uses the weighty verb *dedicated* as a counterbalance, evoking the sense of a noble drive and a profound responsibility. The final clause, *all men are created equal,* not only reinforces the hopeful participles we just heard, but more importantly echoes the most powerful clause in the Declaration of Independence, the document that inspired the birth of our nation. The force of this clause impels the listeners to realize that the most basic ideal of our country has not been realized. Lincoln does not mention *slavery* by name; the issue is too volatile. Instead, Lincoln reminds the nation of its commitment to equality and liberty. That is enough.

Lincoln's choice of nouns is no less masterful than his choice of verbs. By mentioning *liberty* rather than *slavery*, he elicits hope rather than division. By choosing *fathers* over the more distant *founding fathers* or *forefathers* and *nation* over *country* or *government,* he employs the language of family. Most wartime language demonizes the enemy. (Compare this address to recent wartime speeches.) Lincoln wisely chooses not to. He speaks only of a single nation of noble people, because he knows that if the North is successful, it must welcome the South back into the fold.

> *Now we are engaged in a great civil war, testing whether that nation, or any nation so conceived and*
> *so dedicated, can long endure.*

The verb in this sentence, *are engaged*, is in the passive voice. Good writers know that the active voice is stronger than the passive voice. Lincoln could have easily used the active voice, *Now we engage in a great civil war…*or even a more forceful verb, *Now we fight a great civil war…* Instead, he chooses the weaker verb to convey reluctance rather than belligerence. (Many citizens of the South, to be sure, doubted this reluctance, but there is no doubt that this is the effect of his diction.) The battle at Gettysburg and many other battles have persuaded Lincoln that war is horrible. The rest of the sentence repeats the participles, and hence the ideals, of the previous sentence. Lincoln is saying that this is not a war against an evil; it is a war for nobility.

> *We are met on a great battlefield of that war.*

This seems to be a simple declarative sentence, but it is noteworthy for the poetic repetition, echoing the previous sentence: *we are engaged in a great civil war…we are met on a great battlefield of that war.*

> *We have come to dedicate a portion of that field, as a final resting place for those who here gave their*
> *lives that that nation might live.*

Lincoln repeats the word *dedicate*, but now for a slightly different purpose. Some students think, and some teachers teach, that repeating words is always bad. Very untrue. Repetition without purpose is bad, but this repetition has purpose: it moves the listener to a new place. Every good war leader consecrates the deaths of soldiers in order to give purpose to the war. These soldiers must not have died in vain—such a possibility is too difficult for a nation to bear. Note the diction: the soldiers were not *killed*, they were not even *taken from us*, but rather they *gave their lives*. Their deaths were given willingly for a higher purpose—*that this nation might live.*

> *It is altogether fitting and proper that we should do this. But, in a larger sense, we can not dedicate–*
> *we can not consecrate—we can not hallow—this ground.*

If Lincoln had given this speech to a middle school teacher, he would likely have been told to combine these two sentences into one so as not to begin the second sentence with *but*. It's a good thing he didn't. This would have weakened the contrast between desire and reality. The period drops us into a warm pool of complacency: *we are doing the right thing*. The *But* is a splash of cold water. A comma would lessen the effect. The parallelism at the end of the sentence—*we can not, we can not, we can not*—is virtually hypnotic.

> *The brave men, living and dead, who struggled here, have consecrated it, far above our poor power to*
> *add or detract.*

Lincoln uses strong verbs—*struggled* and *consecrated*—to explain the strong claim he has just made. The predicate, too, catches us. We expect a predicate like *have consecrated it far more than we ever could*—a poignant idea, but a phrasing so common as to border on cliché. Instead, we hear a novel arrangement of simple words that show conviction: *have consecrated it far above our poor power to add or subtract*. Thoughtful words, used unpretentiously, move us.

> *The world will little note, nor long remember what we say here, but it can never forget what they did*
> *here.*

Lincoln was wrong: we have long remembered what he said. Nevertheless, this sentence humbles us, and focuses us on the sacrifices of war. To use grander, more intellectual language would have been to draw attention away from the task of dedication, and to the speaker himself. Good speeches don't show off. Note how simple the words are, but how powerful their effect.

> *It is for us the living, rather, to be dedicated here to the unfinished work which they who fought here have thus far so nobly advanced.*

After being humbled, we are quickly ennobled again. We are given an important task.

> *It is rather for us to be here dedicated to the great task remaining before us—that from these honored dead we take increased devotion to that cause for which they gave the last full measure of devotion—that we here highly resolve that these dead shall not have died in vain—that this nation, under God, shall have a new birth of freedom—and that government of the people, by the people, for the people, shall not perish from the earth.*

After so many concise, unpretentious sentences, we receive our orders. We are suddenly addressed by a bold leader, a field marshal. In concluding with a sentence more than twice as long as any other, Lincoln leaves us with much more than a mere tidy thought or hopeful note. Instead, he instructs us as a leader should. With the final echoes, we understand the nature of our nation and of our immediate purpose: *that government of the people, by the people, for the people, shall not perish from the earth.*

Even those who question the cause of the North cannot deny the power of Lincoln's words. They inspire. To hear someone speak these words aloud is to feel a swelling in the chest, building to the final word.

This exercise should give you a sense of what to look for when you read a persuasive essay. Of course, Lincoln's purpose in writing the Gettysburg Address is different from your purpose on the SAT essay. Since he is not addressing a potentially antagonistic audience, he does not need to support his claims with specific examples or to discuss an opposing viewpoint, as you will on the SAT. You will need to analyze an issue more deeply and give more support to your point of view than Lincoln does. Nevertheless, examining great persuasive prose like this helps you to understand the choices a good writer makes.

4. Be specific

Lincoln didn't need to support his claims with specific examples, but you will. Extraordinary claims require extraordinary evidence. Every good essay makes an extraordinary, or at least interesting, claim; otherwise, it would not be worth reading. To support an extraordinary claim about human experience, behavior, or morality, you need relevant and specific examples. SAT essay readers expect them.

Producing relevant and specific examples isn't always easy. For instance, if your assignment is to answer the question *Does wisdom always require great knowledge?* and you want to claim that *The wisest person is not always the most knowledgeable*, what examples would you give? Take a few minutes to think.

Good examples are not general or hypothetical. If you support this claim just by saying that *a leader of a company can be a good leader without having graduated from the top of his or her class*, you will not convince many people, because such a leader is general and hypothetical. Discussing a *specific* leader and explaining how he or she exemplifies wisdom more than intelligence, however, will convince more people. Discussing a second example, from literature or from another walk of life or era, will convince even more people. Specificity counts, but so does range. Choose widely different examples to show that your claim does not apply to only a narrow range of experience. For instance, using one example from a Dickens novel and another from current events shows that your thesis endures over centuries.

5. Prepare with Source Summaries

To pull out good examples for your essay, you must be prepared. But don't just memorize a few canned examples to shoehorn into the essay regardless of the assignment. Good preparation means consolidating the many lessons you've learned from the books, people, and events you've studied recently, so that you can connect the right examples to the right themes.

Students at College Hill Coaching prepare for the SAT essay by writing Source Summaries in the weeks before they take the SAT. If you complete about 10 good Source Summaries like the ones below, you will touch upon most of the common themes used in SAT essay assignments, and have a much easier time recalling examples for your essay.

A good Source Summary consolidates the key lessons from your study of a book, person, or event. It summarizes their major themes and connects each theme to a thesis and a set of details. Here are two examples.

Subject	*Jane Eyre* by Charlotte Brontë	
Themes	**Theses**	**Details**
Feminism	*Women should not accept a subservient role in society.*	Jane refuses to accept a lower station as a woman, and criticizes society's double standards for men and women.
Social status/ meritocracy	*In 19th-century England, one's status in society depended on breeding rather than ability.*	Jane is treated poorly by Rochester's house guests because she does not have noble status.
Love	*Love is blind and often irrational.*	Rochester marries Jane while literally blind. Jane overlooks Rochester's previous marriage.
Independence	*Independence can open one to new experiences, but can also lead to tragic isolation and inability to connect emotionally with others.*	Orphaned as a child, Jane learns that she must fend for herself, and that others don't necessarily have her best interests in mind. She doubts Rochester's love for her at first, and takes an assumed name to avoid revealing herself to Reverend St. John Rivers.

Subject	*D-Day or Operation Overlord* June 6, 1944, Normandy, France	
Themes	**Theses**	**Details**
Good planning	*Careful and smart planning pays off.*	Operation Overlord was a monumental achievement. Thousands of soldiers had to keep it secret. Not since 1688 had an invading army crossed the English Channel. Over 800 planes brought paratroopers and another 300 dropped 13,000 bombs. Within weeks, 20,000 tons of supplies per day were being brought ashore.
Loss	*Great achievements require great loss.*	By nightfall, 100,000 soldiers had landed, but over 9,000 were dead or wounded.
Bravery	*To accomplish great things, we must conquer our fears.*	Thousands went ashore fearing death and the unknown.
Persistence	*Victory requires persistence.*	From D-Day until Christmas 1944, Allied soldiers captured German prisoners at the rate of 1,000 per day.
Unity	*Unity emboldens individuals. We can accomplish more as a group than we can as individuals.*	American soldiers knew that they had the American and European people behind them, so they were willing to face great danger.

Source Summaries

Directions: Use the space below to summarize the major books, people, and events that you have studied in recent years. Try to generate as many interesting theses as possible, and support each one with specific details from your source. Use the examples on page 15 as a guide.

Subject

Themes	Theses	Details

Subject

Themes	Theses	Details

Source Summaries

Directions: Use the space below to summarize the major books, people, and events that you have studied in recent years. Try to generate as many interesting theses as possible, and support each one with specific details from your source. Use the examples on page 15 as a guide.

Subject

Themes	Theses	Details

Subject

Themes	Theses	Details

Source Summaries

Directions: Use the space below to summarize the major books, people, and events that you have studied in recent years. Try to generate as many interesting theses as possible, and support each one with specific details from your source. Use the examples on page 15 as a guide.

Subject

Themes	Theses	Details

Subject

Themes	Theses	Details

Source Summaries

Directions: Use the space below to summarize the major books, people, and events that you have studied in recent years. Try to generate as many interesting theses as possible, and support each one with specific details from your source. Use the examples on page 15 as a guide.

Subject

Themes	Theses	Details

Subject

Themes	Theses	Details

Source Summaries

Directions: Use the space below to summarize the major books, people, and events that you have studied in recent years. Try to generate as many interesting theses as possible, and support each one with specific details from your source. Use the examples on page 15 as a guide.

Subject

Themes	Theses	Details

Subject

Themes	Theses	Details

Source Summaries

Directions: Use the space below to summarize the major books, people, and events that you have studied in recent years. Try to generate as many interesting theses as possible, and support each one with specific details from your source. Use the examples on page 15 as a guide.

Subject

Themes	Theses	Details

Subject

Themes	Theses	Details

6. Practice

In the months before taking the SAT, practice your persuasive writing skills as often as you can. Since you will be reading newspaper opinion columns regularly, perhaps one will inspire you to write a letter to the editor in response. Give it to your friends, parents, and teachers to read before you submit it. Consider their responses and revise your letter carefully until you are satisfied that it is concise and persuasive. If it's published, you will have a satisfying confirmation of your persuasive writing skills.

When you write a persuasive essay for a school assignment, go through the same process. Solicit comments from your friends, parents, and teachers. If it helps, ask them to focus on the questions listed on pages 15 and 16.

Lesson 8 contains 10 SAT essays for you to practice with. After reading the next four lessons, take out your stopwatch and give yourself 25 minutes to complete each essay. Pay attention to the process. Do you use your time well, or do you rush to finish? Do you make a good outline before you begin, or do you make it up as you go? Do you get writer's block at any point? Do you struggle to make your thoughts clear? Do you have trouble thinking of examples or connecting them to the thesis? Do you get off topic? The next four Lessons will discuss many of these issues, but you may find, as you practice, that you need to return to these discussions several times to work out your kinks.

The SAT essay must be handwritten. If you ordinarily write on the computer, you may want to practice your handwriting skills in preparation for the SAT essay. It has to be legible, and you don't want to cramp up!

Writing well isn't easy, but if you practice and approach the task the right way, you'll begin to welcome the challenge.

7. Know the instructions

On test day, you won't want to spend time reading the essay directions. Know them beforehand. Know that you're graded on point of view, logic, and clarity (not grammar and spelling); that you have to fit everything on two lined sheets of paper (no extra sheets allowed); and that you have to write legibly. Here are the directions exactly as they will appear on the test. Keep them in mind as you complete the practice essays in Lesson 8.

ESSAY
Time—25 minutes

The essay gives you an opportunity to show how effectively you can develop and express ideas. You should, therefore, take care to develop your point of view, present your ideas logically and clearly, and use language precisely.

Your essay must be written on the lines provided on your answer sheet—you will receive no other paper on which to write. You will have enough space if you write on every line, avoid wide margins, and keep your handwriting to a reasonable size. Remember that people who are not familiar with your handwriting will read what you write. Try to write or print so that what you are writing is legible to those readers.

You have twenty-five minutes to write an essay on the topic below. DO NOT WRITE ON ANOTHER TOPIC. AN OFF-TOPIC ESSAY WILL RECEIVE A SCORE OF ZERO.

Think carefully about the issue presented in the following excerpt and the assignment below.

---

8. Overcome perfectionism

As you practice, realize that perfectionism is the enemy of a good writer. Good writing is like sculpting in clay, not in marble. A sculptor of marble worries constantly about making a mistake, because one mistake can ruin the stone permanently. A sculptor of clay, though, can fix a mistake or start over at any time. Like the clay sculptor, be concerned first with getting a general shape, and only later with perfecting it. Concern yourself with saying something interesting and substantial, not with saying something perfectly. Get the shape of your essay first, and linger on the words later.

Lesson 4—Analyze the writing task

1. Give yourself time to think

By now you've learned what the SAT readers are looking for, you've read and written many persuasive essays, and you've completed your source summaries. Now you're sitting for the SAT and the proctor says, "Turn to the first page of your test booklet, where you will see your essay assignment. You have 25 minutes to read the assignment and complete the essay. Begin." What do you do?

Thankfully, this will not be the first time you've seen an SAT essay assignment. You will have practiced with the 10 practice essays in Lesson 8, so you'll know what to expect. Even so, you'll probably still have butterflies in your stomach, and might even panic a bit. Don't worry. Take three deep breaths to settle your nerves; then set aside at least 6 minutes to brainstorm and organize your thoughts.

> Don't start writing too soon. Set aside at least 6 minutes to read the assignment, brainstorm, and organize your essay. If you don't, your essay will likely be unfocused, weak, and redundant. Good planning makes your essay not only stronger, but much easier to write. Don't think that you must start writing right away in order to finish the essay on time. Good planning actually saves time.

2. Read the assignment carefully

On the SAT, your essay assignment is always to answer the question that follows the word *Assignment*. You do not have to agree or disagree with the quotation that precedes the question; the quotation simply represents one possible point of view on the topic.

Read the question carefully and underline the important concept or concepts. For instance, if the question is *Does wisdom always require great knowledge?* underline *wisdom* and *knowledge*. If the question is *Does every tragedy have a benefit?* underline *tragedy* and *benefit*. These concepts, and their relationship, must be the focus of your essay. There are many interesting points of view on these ideas, all of which are equally valid. You need to find just one, and show why it is valid.

3. Define your terms to show your point of view

Once you understand the question, think carefully about the concepts you've underlined. Do not assume that your reader interprets these concepts the same way that you do. For instance, *wisdom* means different things to different people. One person might think that it is a quality of an innocent mind, while another might think that it only comes from the experience of making mistakes.

> Think carefully about how you would define the important concepts in the question. In order to make your point of view clear, you may need to define these concepts specifically in your essay. Do not assume that your point of view on these concepts is shared by your reader. In fact, you should assume that you are trying to *change* the reader's point of view on these concepts, which may mean redefining the concepts.

Consider the question *Does wisdom always require great knowledge?* An author's unique point of view can be conveyed simply by defining terms.

> *Wisdom is rare because it requires two seemingly contradictory elements: hard experience and innocence. Adults become wiser having endured hardship and pain, but wisdom is not the exclusive domain of adults. One essential element of wisdom is a non-judgmental acceptance of others that only comes from the mind of a child.*

The reader immediately thinks, *Wow, there is a thoughtful and interesting point of view.* Of course, this point of view still needs specific and logical support, but these sentences represent an excellent start.

Defining terms practice

Here are several concepts that appear frequently in SAT essay assignments. Write your own definition for each concept, showing your unique point of view.

1. Power

Power is a very dangerous thing to chase. To have power over someone or something means to have authority over them. Yet power can serve to corrupt a person, making them demanding

2. Safety

Safety is interesting because while it is a necessity, focusing too much on oneself's security can lead to not fully living life. Overfocusing on being safe, can serve to result in living ones life in fear.

3. Trust

Trust is an interesting concept because it only truly works if the participation of two or more parties is involved. It is more easy to trust oneself than to trust others, because true trust requires vulnerability.

4. Courage

5. Happiness

Happiness is not yet just a fleeting sense of emotion, as many will suggest. Instead, happiness is merely coming to terms with

6. Liberty

7. Maturity

8. Discipline

4. Stay focused on the question

Your task on the SAT essay is not simply to define your terms in an interesting way. Your task is to answer the question. Don't get caught up in saying something profound but lose sight of the question. A good essay never loses sight of its central purpose.

For instance, in the example we just discussed, defining *wisdom* is only part of the task. The task is to discuss whether or not *wisdom requires great knowledge*. If you never get around to discussing the relationship between wisdom and knowledge, you won't get a very high score.

Lesson 5—Gather your ideas

1. Brainstorm examples before picking a thesis

Don't expect a great thesis to come to mind immediately upon reading the question. In fact, picking your thesis first is like putting the cart before the horse. Your examples are what support your essay and pull it forward, like a horse supports and pulls a cart. So think about examples first.

Don't pick your thesis right away. A thesis that is chosen too soon usually lacks uniqueness, nuance and substance. Instead, brainstorm examples first. Think about the concepts that you've just defined, and consider examples that relate those concepts in an interesting way. Don't worry if they seem to contradict each other at first. You won't necessarily use every example, and often very different examples make for a more interesting thesis. Think of as many examples that answer the question in as many different ways as possible.

For example, try to think of examples—pro and con—for the question *Does wisdom always require great knowledge?* A wise judge, like Solomon or Charles Evans Hughes, must have great knowledge not only of law but of the people and culture he or she serves. On the other hand, children who have yet to develop prejudices and embrace everyone they meet also show great wisdom. The Oracle at Delphi was considered wise, not because she was knowledgeable but because she could converse with the gods. Think of the books, people, and events that you've summarized on your source summaries. Who are examples of wise people, and how knowledgeable are they?

2. Keep your mind open

When brainstorming, don't censor your ideas or dismiss them right away. Just write them down. You don't have to use every idea that you brainstorm, so just be creative. The SAT will give you a bit of room to scribble notes. Use it. Write down examples. Connect them. Cross them out. Underline them. Do whatever your open mind tells you to do.

You may find that the ideas you were going to throw away are the best ones after all!

For instance, when brainstorming about people and things that are wise, you might think of owls. Owls are supposed to be wise, right? Then you might think, *no, that's stupid—this should be about people, not birds.* But if, instead of dismissing the thought, you explore it, you might hit upon a great idea. Why are owls the symbol of wisdom, anyway? Perhaps because they are patient and watchful, and only act when necessary. Perhaps this is the same with humans. So perhaps wisdom doesn't require knowledge; owls don't know very much.

3. Choose specific examples

I've said it before, but it bears repeating: be specific.

When brainstorming examples that illuminate the question, pick examples that are as specific as possible. For instance, the example *a child who has not yet developed any prejudices* is general and hypothetical, so it is not a very effective example. On the other hand, examples like *my 4-year-old niece Katherine, who holds no grudges or prejudices and gives a big freckled smile to every new person she meets,* or *Billy Budd, the Herman Melville hero who, despite his lack of knowledge and worldliness, is wise beyond his years, and even heroically accepts an unjust fate because he knows it is for the greater good,* are more powerful examples because they are more specific, and hence more real to a reader.

4. Choose interesting examples

The best writing begins with taking a chance, not applying a formula.

As we discussed earlier, SAT readers are generally intelligent and well-trained English teachers. (They are a far cry from the dunderheads that some test-prep companies like to portray them to be.) But knowing your readers means more than simply knowing how smart they are. It also means understanding what they like. Of course, SAT essay readers don't all love watching *Gilmore Girls* and eating Lucky Charms. They are a diverse bunch. But they are all smart readers, and smart readers like to be challenged a bit. Imagine yourself sitting in front of a big pile of essays that are supposed to answer the question *Does wisdom always require great knowledge?* (Actually, if you are an SAT essay grader, the pile will likely be a bunch of scanned and e-mailed files on your computer.) You have already scored a few dozen essays, and you are noticing that many of them are starting to sound alike. Most essays seem to discuss the author's parents or relatives and how wise they are, and many also try to discuss a wise literary character, like Atticus Finch in *To Kill a Mockingbird* or Gandalf in *Lord of the Rings*. Some of these will be excellent essays, because they will discuss these topics with an interesting and well-developed point of view. Nevertheless, you will probably start to hope for something *really* different.

Now let's get back to you the writer. Since the readers are scoring your essay on how well it develops an interesting point of view, you should get off the beaten path. Don't go crazy and spend the whole essay discussing your incoherent theory that wisdom is directly proportional to the amount of cosmic radiation one's body has absorbed, but think *interesting*. Perhaps a landscaper friend of yours is the wisest person you know. (*Being There* by Jerzy Kozinski follows this premise.) Perhaps you think a painting or a building is wise. That's a unique point of view.

Going off the beaten path will not only catch your reader's attention, it will keep you on your toes. Your score is based not only on your point of view, but also on how well you support it. When you take an easy, run-of-the-mill point of view, you will probably fall into lazy writing habits like cliché, redundancy, and vagueness.

5. Choose manageable examples

As you get closer to organizing and writing your essay, you must select examples that you feel comfortable discussing in some detail. Creativity is helpful, but a mind-blowing example isn't so mind-blowing if you can't explain how it supports your thesis. For instance, saying that a Mahler symphony is wise is an intriguing idea, but if you can't articulate *why* it is wise so that an intelligent reader will believe you, the creative example is pointless.

Select examples that are not only interesting, but manageable. Show your reader that you know what you're talking about. If you discuss a book, make sure that you know the author and the relevant details of the story. If you discuss a person, make sure you can give enough details about that person's life so that you can connect it clearly to your thesis. Good source summaries like those in Lesson 3 will help you to recall important details and connect them to your thesis.

Brainstorming Practice

Give yourself 6 minutes to brainstorm about each of the following questions. Write down all the words, ideas, associations, people, events, books, etc., that pertain to the question. Don't censor your ideas, and don't worry if some of them contradict each other. Just write them down. Try to think of lots of specific examples that each represent an interesting point of view on the question.

1. Should personal safety (always) be a priority?

- American Sniper   - Childish Gambino
- Sacrifice
- Asian
- Fiona Gallgher
- D-day
- War Veterans
- George Washington
- Man on subway
- Firefighters 911
- Union Soldiers (white ones) in civil war

2. What qualities must a person have in order for you to trust that person?

Lesson 6—Organize your essay

1. Craft your thesis

At this point, you should have about half a page of notes from your brief brainstorming session. You have thought of a few silly ideas, but also a few specific, manageable, and interesting examples that shed light on the question you've been asked to answer. Now you must craft a thesis. A thesis makes a claim that you will stand behind, but it is much more than that.

A good thesis is challenging and focused. It challenges and intrigues the reader with a unique point of view, and makes the reader want to keep reading. It also challenges the author to support it against the opposition. It is focused on the question at hand, and doesn't stray to easier topics. It is equally focused on the support it will be given; it doesn't get too big for its britches.

For instance, if you've brainstormed on the question *Does wisdom always require great knowledge?* you may have come up with examples like Atticus Finch in *To Kill a Mockingbird*, Gandalf in *Lord of the Rings*, King Solomon, your mom, Chance the gardener in *Being There,* the Oracle at Delphi, Franklin Roosevelt and the New Deal, and Kermit the Frog. You'll feel more comfortable discussing some than others. Some of these examples suggest that the answer to the question is yes; others suggest no. You can't discuss all of them in the 20 minutes you have left to write the essay, so you must pick the two or three that fit the most interesting thesis. You might pick Chance and Kermit to make the point that wisdom does not require great knowledge, and throw in Atticus Finch to demonstrate that wisdom also includes a willingness to uphold high moral principles. To encompass all of these examples, your thesis might be something like *Wisdom requires very little knowledge at all, but it does require a commitment to principles that are higher than one's self.*

When you take the time to craft a good thesis based on your examples, your essay will flow much more easily. Spend a minute crafting the language of your thesis statement. Write it out on your scratch paper and revise it until it is concise, interesting, and effective. This is the most important sentence of your essay, and the first part of your outline.

To give you a better sense of what makes a good thesis, consider the following responses.

Assignment: Has technology improved our lives?

Thesis 1: *Technology has improved our lives because it has produced fun video games and DVDs and computers which can be very educational as well as fun.*

Reader's evaluation: Dull, dull, dull. These are the easiest examples of technology, and the thesis is obvious and uninteresting. This demonstrates a nondescript point of view.

Thesis 2: *Technology has not improved our lives because nuclear weapons are very dangerous and cell phones are often very annoying.*

Reader's evaluation: This is only marginally better than Thesis 1. The examples are unoriginal, and the thesis is also somewhat obvious.

Thesis 3: *Technology has improved our lives because it has given instruments that allow us to peer not only into the outer reaches of space and into the inner sanctum of the atom, but even into the human mind at work.*

Reader's evaluation: This is a much more thoughtful, relevant, and intriguing point of view. I am intrigued to know what, specifically, has been discovered about space, atoms, and especially the human mind through technology. If the rest of the essay follows up on this thesis, I will probably learn something that I didn't know before.

Thesis 4: *In simplifying our lives, technology often dissociates us from our most fundamental human needs, like intimacy with other people and with our natural environment, creating an unhappiness that is barely masked by entertaining gizmos.*

Reader's evaluation: This is a very thoughtful and intriguing point of view. Since most people believe that communication technology connects us *more* intimately, I am intrigued by the argument that technology tends to dissociate us. The idea that the entertainment value of technology masks an unhappiness is also very interesting.

2. Write a manageable outline

Many students worry that they won't have enough time to write an outline for a 25-minute essay. Don't worry. With practice, you'll find it easy. A good outline does not have to include a lot of detail. A simple, manageable outline helps your writing to flow easily, and so you'll save time in the long run. I can always tell when a student has written an essay without an outline. The ideas are often redundant or don't connect smoothly, and the essay doesn't move forward as it should. To avoid these problems, write a brief outline.

Your outline should concisely summarize the four or five paragraphs of your essay. Paragraphs are the stepping stones of an essay; each takes the reader forward to a new place by discussing a new idea. Your outline should be a simplified map of the journey the reader will take. Use it to determine whether your essay moves forward, or merely spins its wheels.

Here are two assignment questions and a good outline for each.

Assignment: Does wisdom always require great knowledge?

Paragraph 1: *Wisdom requires very little knowledge at all; however, it does require a commitment to principles that are higher than one's self.*

Paragraph 2: *Kermit the Frog and Chance the gardener are examples of wisdom embodied in a humble, naïve persona. They are simply unselfish characters trying to understand their small world.*

Paragraph 3: *Atticus Finch is a more worldly example of a wise person, but he is equally innocent in his ability to see the good in all people, and he is committed to achieving real justice. He is wise because he is good, not because he is knowledgeable.*

Paragraph 4: *Wise people are not always the smartest people. They are the ones who learn to see the good in others, and commit themselves to bringing it out of them.*

Reader's evaluation: This outline represents a well-developed and interesting point of view. The examples support the thesis directly, and seem to be very carefully chosen. The conclusion does not merely repeat the thesis, but extends it by expanding on the principles that were mentioned in the thesis statement.

Assignment: Has technology improved our lives?

Paragraph 1: *In simplifying our lives, technology often dissociates us from our most fundamental human needs, like intimacy with other people and with our natural environment, creating an unhappiness that is barely masked by entertaining gizmos.*

Paragraph 2: *Instantaneous communication (cell phones and instant messaging) does not create a more intimate world. Rather, it encourages superficial communication that is easily misinterpreted because these technologies hide gestures and facial expressions.*

Paragraph 3: *Instant access to processed foods through technology dissociates us from the natural world, from which our food ultimately comes.*

Paragraph 4: *We can minimize the harm that technology does by writing letters, having more face-to-face conversations, and growing and making our own food.*

Reader's evaluation: The author presents a very intriguing point of view, and supports it with excellent analysis. Although the examples of technology are fairly ordinary, the analysis of each is excellent, and raises very interesting questions. The conclusion does not merely repeat the thesis, but rather offers a solution to the problem suggested by the essay.

3. Connect your ideas logically

A good essay shows good logical development. To make sure that your essay is logical and cohesive, keep the following words and phrases in mind as you write your outline:

> *for example*   *furthermore*
> *therefore*   *however*
> *because*   *although*

Every idea in your outline should connect to another idea by words like these. Look again at the outlines on page 30. Notice that the relationship between the ideas can be made clearer by including these logical key words.

Assignment: Does wisdom always require great knowledge?

Paragraph 1: *No, **however** it does require a commitment…*

Paragraph 2: ***For example,** Kermit the Frog and Chance show wisdom **because**…*

Paragraph 3: ***Furthermore,** Atticus Finch demonstrates that wisdom often involves…*

Paragraph 4: ***Furthermore,** wise people are those who learn to see the good in others…*

Assignment: Has technology improved our lives?

Paragraph 1: *Technology is harmful **because** it dissociates us from important things…*

Paragraph 2: ***For example, although** many think instantaneous communication creates a more intimate world, it does not **because**…*

Paragraph 3: ***As another example,** instant access to processed foods is harmful **because** it dissociates us from the natural world…*

Paragraph 4: ***Therefore,** we can minimize harm from technology **by** writing letters…*

4. Play devil's advocate

No, playing devil's advocate doesn't mean selling your soul to the devil for a good SAT score. It simply means addressing potential objections to your thesis. If you want to persuade a good reader, you must acknowledge and address at least one significant point of view that differs from yours. (If you can't think of an alternative point of view, then your point of view is not interesting enough.) For instance, if your thesis is *Competition for grades creates a bad learning environment,* a reader might object by saying that competition motivates students to do their best, much as it motivates athletes. Your argument will not persuade such a reader until you address this objection. So you might address it this way:

> *Although many claim that competition motivates students to do their best, much as it motivates athletes, this claim misrepresents real learning. A great artist creates art not to outdo other artists, but to express an understanding of nature, beauty, or humanity. Similarly, the best students don't study to outscore their fellow students, but to make themselves more competent human beings.*

Every worthwhile thesis must argue **against** something as well as **for** something. A good thesis should acknowledge the common objections to it, and address them thoughtfully.

As you write your outline, play devil's advocate. Address any significant potential objections to your point of view effectively, if briefly. Often, objections can be addressed in a single sentence or even a single clause within a sentence, but sometimes a response requires its own paragraph. When discussing potential objections, don't forget to come around to reinforce your own thesis. If done well, playing devil's advocate does not weaken your argument, but strengthens it.

Devil's Advocate Practice

To write a strong persuasive essay, you must take into account opposing sides of an issue. After each of the following questions, write two thesis statements, one for the pro position, and one for the con position.

1. Should criminal trials be televised?

   Yes, because

   criminal trials should be televised, not in order to humiliate those on trial, but to reassure the public the the justice system is proceeding with fairness, as well as to assure the public that criminals are being brought to justice.

   No, because

   the publication of these trials only serves to teach other criminals how not to get caught. By exposing the weakness of one criminal, ~~the~~ ᵀⱽ strengthens the others.

2. Is envy ever a constructive emotion?

   Yes, because

   envy can serve to inspire people to work harder in order to gain something they need or desire.

   No, because

   envy causes people to become captivated by material items, instead of focusing on how they can work to achieve their desires.

3. Does monetary wealth make people happier?

   Yes, because

   With monetary wealth, comes the ability to support oneself, and the people one loves, creating a more self sufficient happier person.

   No, because

Outlining Practice

Now that you have brainstormed about the following questions and understand the qualities of a strong thesis and a good outline, write your own four- or five-point outline for an essay answering these questions.

1. Should personal safety always be a priority?

2. What qualities must a person have in order for you to trust that person?

Lesson 7—Write the essay

1. Use natural language

If you have done a good job brainstorming and outlining, the rest of your job—actually writing the essay—is relatively easy and fun. Since you have already established an interesting thesis and know how you will support it, you can focus on simply articulating it. Once you have constructed the framework, the writing will flow.

Clear and natural language is more effective than pompous language. It's easier, too. Don't try to impress the readers with your ability to talk like a Nobel laureate. Just express your ideas naturally and clearly.

This doesn't mean that you shouldn't use good SAT words when they are necessary. The operative word here is *necessary*. If using an SAT word helps you to convey an important idea, use it. But remember that you are being graded more on your logic than your diction.

Here is an example of a wordy and pompous sentence.

> *An individual's lack of tolerance due to prejudice and an inability to appreciate different aspects of other individuals is something that negatively affects the ability of a society to avoid division and hatred and establish the environment in which the children of that society ought to be raised.*

This kind of language wastes space and time. The readers will appreciate it if you use clearer, more natural, and more concise language.

> *We can create a healthier and more peaceful society by learning to appreciate the differences in others.*

2. Use strong verbs

The verb drives the sentence. If your verbs are weak or unclear, your sentences will be weak and unclear.

The most common verb in English is *to be*. We use *to be* in sentences that simply define or describe, as in *Protists are single-celled animals* or *My ear was red and swollen*. But most ideas require more forceful verbs. Many writers, even good ones, overuse *to be* in their first drafts, because they are not thinking about words, but ideas. After they get the shape of an essay, though, most good writers revise their sentences to strengthen their verbs.

Take out an essay that you've written recently for school, and circle all of the main verbs. Count the number of *to be* verbs like *is, are, was,* and *were*. (Be careful. Don't count verbs that use *to be* as a *helping* verb, such as passive or progressive verbs like *was bitten by* or *were walking*. These are actually forms of the verbs *to bite* and *to walk*.) Next, divide this by the total number of verbs. (Don't worry; you can use a calculator.) Is this number greater than 0.5? If so, you probably need work on strengthening your verbs. Now look at an essay in the op-ed section of the *New York Times*, or in *The Norton Reader*, and do the same exercise. The best writers tend to have *to be* ratios of 0.3 or less.

Try to minimize the verb *to be* in your writing, but don't go overboard. Sometimes verbs like *is, are, was,* and *were* convey a thought clearly and forcefully, but often they don't. If a stronger verb is readily available, use it.

You won't have time, of course, to write a second draft of your SAT essay and perfect your verbs as a professional essayist would. However, if you have outlined your essay well, you can focus on your diction—your word choice—more carefully. Also, you can practice strengthening your verbs in your everyday writing, when you have more time to revise, and gradually develop your ability to choose strong verbs as you write.

A subject and verb should convey the central idea of the sentence as clearly and forcefully as possible. Often you can find a better verb lurking in a sentence. Find it and turn it into the main verb.

"Lurking" verbs aren't really verbs. They are nouns or modifiers that *could* convey the idea or action of the sentence more effectively if they were turned into verbs.

> *Outside the office were a dozen chairs filling the hallway.*

This sentence is clear, but not forceful. It becomes stronger when the adjective *filling* is turned into a verb.

> *A dozen chairs filled the hallway outside the office.*

> *We will not be tolerant of anyone who is insulting to the opposing players.*

This sentence also uses *to be* where stronger verbs are lurking as adjectives—*tolerant* and *insulting*. Uncover them.

> *We will not tolerate anyone who insults opposing players.*

Passive verbs are less forceful than active verbs. Use the active voice whenever you can. Not only does it make your ideas clearer, but it also forces you to fill in important details.

The **active voice** uses the *actor*—the person or thing *doing* the action—as the subject of the verb.

> *The boy kicked the ball.*

Here the subject of the verb is the thing doing the action. The *boy* is the subject, and he did the *kicking*. In contrast, the **passive voice** places the actor *after* the verb, as an object.

> *The ball was kicked by the boy.*

This sounds odder to the reader's ear than the active voice does. In general, you should use the actors as your subjects. This does not mean that the passive voice does not have its place. For instance, if you don't know—or don't want to reveal—the actor, you must use the passive voice.

> *The sneakers were stolen from the locker.*

Also, logical sequencing and parallelism of ideas often require the passive voice. However, if you become lazy and use the passive voice when it is unnecessary, you run the risk of omitting the actor altogether. Politicians have used the passive voice to avoid culpability.

> *Mistakes were made.*

> > —Richard Nixon, regarding the Watergate scandal

Don't hide important information from your reader by using the passive voice when you could use the active voice. Don't say

> *The company was established in 1903.*

when you know that

> *Theodore Bennington established the company in 1903.*

And don't weaken strong verbs by making them passive. Don't say

> *The bold maneuver was made by the army under the cover of night.*

when you could say

> *The army maneuvered boldly under the cover of night.*

Verb strengthening practice

Rewrite the following sentences to strengthen the verbs. Uncover any good "lurking" verbs.

1. *One thing that happened was that the players were getting taunts thrown at them by the spectators.*

2. *The industrial revolution caused an endangerment of the agrarian way of life.*

3. *The viewership of the championship game consisted of over 3 million fans.*

4. *The committee's response was to change the hiring procedure.*

5. *The workers had the need to form a union that could stand up to the ownership.*

6. *The fact that the governor ignored the questions of the citizens made them resentful of him.*

7. *This action is in violation of the company's own contract.*

8. *The village was affected to a devastating degree by the earthquake.*

9. *The mice have a tendency to overeat when they are in the absence of this hormone.*

10. *My failure on the test was reflective of the fact that I didn't study.*

11. *The movie was considered by the critics to be dull and hackneyed.*

12. *There is always a worry that mothers have that their children will get hurt when they are playing.*

See the answer key on page 49.

3. Write with personality and intelligence

When you are writing your essay, it's not enough to avoid mistakes. You must draw your readers in and encourage them to think by using lively and persuasive language. Persuade your reader not only with forceful argumentation, but also with an engaging voice.

The precautions in this lesson only help you to avoid offending, confusing, or turning off your readers. It's up to you, though, to make them want to read your words. Establishing a point of view means creating an intelligent and engaging voice on paper.

The right of a free press is a supreme entitlement that is necessary to securing the integrity of our government. Without the scrutiny that a free press entails, power will continue unchecked in the halls of power. This can only lead to oppressive conditions and severe injustice.

These sentences make intelligent points, but they sound as if they are coming from an automaton. Another writer might discuss the same topic but with more personality.

Okay, so the National Enquirer *isn't exactly the* New York Times. *Maybe what Paris Hilton eats for breakfast isn't going to cure cancer, but torching tabloid rags won't do anyone any favors, because a free country needs a free press. If we don't permit journalists to write and publish what they want, then sleazy politicians will just get away with their oily shenanigans in Washington, DC (which stands for "Definitely Corrupt").*

These sentences are alive with personality, but the language is flippant, unsubstantial, and self-indulgent. Cute but unsubstantiated language like *oily shenanigans* and *Definitely Corrupt* do not compensate for a lack of substantial analysis. A good writer writes with both personality and intelligence—creativity under control.

The right of a free press provides the foundation of a just society. Although unshackling journalists may lead to overindulgences in Paris Hilton's eating habits, it will also cast a necessary light on the halls of power. Stories about alien abductions and celebrity catfights are a small price to pay for an institution that can root out the mismanagement of public funds, the deception of voters, and the oppression of those with unpopular beliefs or lifestyles.

To create an intelligent voice in your essay you must write creatively, but under control. Writers without personality are dull to read. But writers who are too enamored of their own voices are perhaps even harder to read. A good writer strikes a smart compromise.

4. Use personal and concrete nouns

The following sentence was written as part of a debate about free speech.

> *My concerns in general center on numerous omissions of relevant facts and quotes which had the effect of diminishing the extent of the apparent support of free expression, and the force of the moral arguments for free expression, and of enhancing the support of those who are vigilant against danger- ous speech, and obscuring the more extreme arguments made on their behalf.*

Most readers would need at least several readings to make sense of this morass of words. It overwhelms us with too many abstract and vague nouns. We can begin to see the problem by underlining the nouns.

> *My <u>concerns</u> in general center on numerous <u>omissions</u> of relevant <u>facts</u> and <u>quotes</u> which had the <u>effect</u> of <u>diminishing</u> the <u>extent</u> of the apparent <u>support</u> of free <u>expression</u>, and the <u>force</u> of the moral <u>argu- ments</u> for free <u>expression</u>, and of <u>enhancing</u> the <u>support</u> of <u>those</u> who are vigilant against dangerous <u>speech</u>, and <u>obscuring</u> the more extreme <u>arguments</u> made on their <u>behalf</u>.*

How can someone keep track of the relationships among 19 nouns in a single sentence? A good writer doesn't put a reader through such torture. Furthermore, most of these nouns are **impersonal** and **abstract**, which makes them particularly hard to relate to. To make a sentence clear and easy to understand, use **personal** and **concrete** nouns. Personal nouns refer to the things in your readers' common personal experience. **Concrete** nouns refer to things that can be **seen, heard, smelled, tasted,** or **touched.** Of course, discussions about ideas require abstract nouns, but a good writer doesn't use any more than are necessary. Here's a revision of the sentence, with the nouns underlined.

> *Some <u>people</u> have ignored important <u>facts</u> in this <u>discussion</u>, and have not appreciated how much <u>people</u> support free <u>expression</u> and instead have emphasized how much <u>people</u> want <u>to eliminate</u> offensive <u>speech</u>. <u>They</u> have also ignored the many illogical <u>arguments</u> against offensive <u>speech</u>. In fact, the <u>majority</u> of <u>Americans</u> support free <u>expression</u>, and regard it as a moral <u>necessity</u>.*

The number of nouns has been reduced by nearly a third, and the percent of personal and concrete nouns has been increased from 11% to over 50%. Also, by breaking the sentence into three smaller ones, we have made the ideas easier to digest. We've reduced the number of nouns per sentence from 19 to under 5.

Minimize abstract and impersonal nouns. When they pile up, your thoughts become hard to follow.

5. Minimize jargon and slang

Jargon—specialized language—annoys good readers when it is used unnecessarily. Common jargon includes phrases like *win-win scenario, thinking outside the box, bulletizing the issues, targeting a goal, bottom line, downside, facilitate, prioritize, optimize, time frame, mutually beneficial, parameter,* and *utilize.* When writing to a general audience, avoid jargon when ordinary language will suffice. If you must use jargon to convey a specialized concept, define it carefully, and use it only when necessary.

> *If we think outside the box and prioritize our concerns, I'm sure we can facilitate a win-win scenario for all parties.*

Sometimes, specialized ideas require specialized language. Not here.

> *If we think creatively and set our priorities, I'm sure we can find a solution that everyone will like.*

Using standard English doesn't make you a standard writer. Writers can assert their personalities in myriad ways with- out using jargon or slang. Slang, like jargon, tends to differentiate the writer from the reader, which a good persuasive writer never does. Avoid slang expressions like *dude, Larry, kick it, squish, on the slab,* and *mugg,* because your reader is likely to be a fifty-something English teacher without a subscription to *The Source.*

Clarification practice

Rewrite the following sentences to strengthen the verbs, eliminate jargon, and make the nouns more concrete and personal.

1. *The concept of competition is an essential element with regard to the ability of society to encourage people to achieve excellence.*

   competition is fundamental

2. *The consideration of all ideas of our employees is done by our management with the goal that only the most quality concepts will elevate to the forefront.*

3. *A concern in the general population with regard to the ability of the government to optimize the positive use of federal funds has accelerated in recent times.*

4. *When placing the emphasis on the deterioration of personal moral responsibility, the role of social institutions is ignored by those who are commenting on the state of society.*

5. *(Bonus)* *The most aggressive of the new companies, whose priorities are characterized by their capital commitment to market share and name recognition, will be seen as the "players" in their niche, and may see an extension of share overvaluation, despite weak product development or business models.*

See the answer key on page 49.

6. Eliminate wordiness

Use no more words than necessary to convey an idea clearly. You won't impress readers by giving them superfluous words to read. Using wordy constructions makes your reader think that you're pompous or inarticulate.

> *Courage is a value that is very difficult to be found in and among individuals in the world today, even though it is clearly something that nearly everyone of every persuasion and creed finds to be an extremely important and valuable element of human morality.*

This can be said more forcefully in seven words.

> *Courage today is rare, and therefore precious.*

Here are some common wordy phrases to avoid, and the more concise alternatives.

Wordy	Concise	Wordy	Concise
has a reaction	*reacts*	*in the event that*	*if*
has a dependence on	*depends*	*regardless of the fact that*	*although*
provides enforcement	*enforces*	*in our world today*	*today*
is in violation of	*violates*	*in this day and age*	*today*
has knowledge of	*knows*	*being that*	*because*
achieves the maximization of	*maximizes*	*due to the fact that*	*because*
provides opposition to	*opposes*	*at this point in time*	*now*
is reflective of	*reflects*	*at the present moment*	*now*
give consideration to	*consider*	*are aware of the fact*	*know*
lend assistance to	*assist*	*make contact with*	*contact*

7. Minimize prepositional phrases

Avoid overloading your sentences with prepositional phrases. When you use too many, your sentences become awkward and unclear.

> *People in the media must keep sight of their responsibility to the public to remain impartial in their presentation for the sake of expanding their readers' trust in their representation of the issues.*

This sentence contains eight prepositional phrases. That's seven more than necessary.

> *Journalists must remain impartial to maintain the trust of their readers.* (one prepositional phrase)

8. Eliminate redundancy

When we speak casually, we often use redundant phrases like *protrude out* or *fall down*. In formal writing, eliminate words that convey ideas that have already been stated or implied.

> *The best elements of her previous works were combined together in this symphony.*

To *combine* means to *bring together into one*. Therefore, the word *together* is redundant.

> *The best elements of her previous works were combined in this symphony.*

9. Don't state the obvious

Many students have a fear of short sentences, so they throw extra words and phrases into their sentences to make them longer but not clearer. Usually, these words and phrases merely state the obvious.

> *There is always a fear of change that people have in the world. One thing that is constantly changing is technology, which is supposed to be a major force in making life for humans easier.*

A good writer respects the reader, and does not condescend by stating the obvious or repeating ideas unnecessarily. What do the phrases *in the world* and *for humans* serve in the sentences above? They merely state the obvious, and so they are unnecessary. These sentences also use weak verbs, but contain stronger "lurking" verbs. Good readers will appreciate your eliminating the obvious and strengthening the verbs.

> *People fear change. Even technology, which is supposed to make our lives easier, can be scary.*

Don't fear short sentences. In fact, short sentences are almost always more powerful than long ones.

Don't state the obvious. Needless filler makes your writing seem incompetent.

10. Eliminate clichés

Phrases such as *give it 110%, go for the gold, rip it to shreds, in the lap of luxury, keep at arm's length, pick up the pieces, cross that bridge when we get to it, go to town* are overused phrases otherwise known as **clichés**. Any phrase that you have heard more than five times in your life probably qualifies as a cliché. **The use of clichés suggests that the writer is lazy, unoriginal, or clumsy with words. Avoid cliché and use your own, original words to convey your thoughts.**

Cliché: *Believe me, I felt like a fish out of water giving that speech in front of the class, but I sucked it up and gave it my all.*

Better: *Although the prospect of speaking in front of the class intimidated me, I tried to focus on my words rather than my fear.*

Cliché sweeping practice

Rewrite each sentence to eliminate any clichés.

1. *Many adults these days are fond of saying that the youth of this day and age are lazy as dogs.*

2. *They say that kids are nothing but couch potatoes who sit like bumps on a log playing video games or listening to their iPods.*

3. *For all intents and purposes, this assumption is dead wrong.*

4. *As a matter of fact, many of my friends are thinking more about careers that will change the world as we know it rather than careers that will just chase the almighty buck.*

See the answer key on page 49.

Sentence tightening practice

Rewrite the following sentences to eliminate wordiness, redundancy, jargon, and the obvious. Prune mercilessly!

1. *In this day and age, people in the world are concerned about the prospects for the future because they are uncertain about what is coming ahead.*

2. *An effective manager who is good at what he or she does relies on sound, proven management principles that have worked in the past for other managers, even if those managers may be in similar areas of occupation or different ones.*

3. *A lot of students are aware of the fact that they need not only to become educated in order to become eligible for the jobs that they may want in the future, but also that they have to continue to become even more educated so that they can stay in the jobs because of the increasing need for education in the work force.*

4. *Parkinson's is a disease that people get and one of its features is that it gets progressively worse the longer some-one has it, causing them to degenerate, but a lot of current research provides the people who suffer with the disease of Parkinson's with some hope that treatments may sometime soon in the future perhaps alleviate the symptoms somewhat or even cure the disease completely.*

5. *Due to the fact that corporations endeavor to achieve the maximization of profit, they rarely put their focus on the achievement of environmental needs.*

6. *In the event that your boss provides opposition to your proposal at the meeting, consider having a head-to-head conversation with her about it privately to discuss the issue that you have concerns about because public confronta-tion might lead to resentment on the part of your superior.*

7. *It is certainly clear that too few people give consideration to the fact that economic strength is often reflective of the hopes of consumers.*

See the answer key on page 49.

11. Connect your thoughts logically

The SAT readers grade your essay on *logical development*, or your ability to connect your ideas in a logical chain. In order to develop a logical train of thought, you must connect your ideas clearly.

Use pronouns carefully, particularly when they refer to ideas mentioned in previous sentences. Make sure that any definite pronoun refers to a clear antecedent.

> *Lawyers often have the difficult task of representing a criminal who they know is guilty, knowing that if they refuse, they may suffer financially. This is what makes me question my decision to become a lawyer.*

What does the word *this* in the second sentence refer to? Are the writer's doubts stimulated by the difficulty of the task of representing a guilty person? the possibility of suffering financially? the difficulty of choosing whether or not to represent a defendant? some combination of these?

This lack of logical clarity makes your reader work harder, and your argument less forceful. Clarify your references so that your train of thought is easy to follow.

> *Lawyers often have the difficult task of representing a criminal who they know is guilty, knowing that if they refuse, they may suffer financially. I'm not convinced that I will be able to choose between money and my conscience.*

12. Vary your sentence structure and length wisely

Good writers vary the structure of their sentences as they write.

> *Medical interns are overworked. They are constantly asked to do a lot with very little sleep. They are chronically exhausted as a result. They can make mistakes that are dangerous and even potentially deadly.*

These sentences make a good point, but their structure is so unvarying that they nearly put us to sleep.

> *Medical interns can make dangerous and even deadly mistakes because they are overworked. Constantly asked to do a lot with very little sleep, they are chronically exhausted.*

Good writers vary the structure of their sentences so that their ideas flow smoothly and engagingly, not monotonously. Your readers won't appreciate your profound ideas if they are stupefied by unvarying sentences.

Good writers also consider the lengths of their sentences as they write.

> *Many people believe that "guns don't kill people; people kill people," a statement that, on its surface, appears to be true. However, some deep thought and analysis about this statement, its assumptions and implications, shows clearly that it is mistaken.*

There is nothing very wrong with these sentences, but consider an alternative.

> *Many people believe that "guns don't kill people; people kill people," a statement that, on its surface, appears to be true. It's not.*

The second version has a stronger impact because the second sentence is abrupt. A short sentence, particularly following long ones, hits the reader like a slap in the face and drives home an important point.

Good writers always think about the length of their sentences. Long sentences may be necessary for explaining complex ideas, but short sentences are often best for emphasizing important points.

13. Eliminate sentences to nowhere

Eliminate unnecessary sentences by crossing them out neatly.

Sometimes a sentence that seemed profound when you first wrote it turns out, on second reading, to be nonsensical, obvious, or unnecessary. If a sentence does not convey a fresh and interesting idea that moves your argument forward, eliminate it.

Don't worry about erasing it completely—your essay doesn't get extra points for looking perfect. Just cross out the offending sentence with one or two lines.

> *Life is characterized by the ups and downs one experiences while living from day to day.*

This sentence may have sounded profound at first, but it really doesn't say anything at all, because no rational person would disagree with it. Eliminate it.

> *Every country seeks a constant prosperity in its growth.*

This sentence is so vague and uninteresting that it's hardly worth saving. How can a country *seek* anything? Maybe the people can, but not the country. Saying that people seek prosperity is a pretty uninteresting observation. Do they really seek *constant prosperity*? What does that even mean? And what the heck is *prosperity in their growth*? Clearly, this is a sentence to nowhere.

14. Choose your words carefully

One well-chosen verb or noun is often worth six modifiers. Choose words that convey your ideas precisely. As you read good essays, pay attention to how good writers choose their words. You can develop your writer's vocabulary with a good guided vocabulary-building program such as that in *McGraw-Hill's SAT I*.

> *I walked through the finish line as if my legs were ridiculously heavy, and sat down exhausted.*

This sentence makes its point, but clumsily. Notice how more precise diction gives it punch.

> *I lumbered through the finish line and collapsed.*

Always keep in mind, however, the difference between a precise vocabulary and an overbearing one.

> *An astute scribe shall always eschew superfluous grandiloquence.*

The twenty dollar words don't make this sentence any more precise than good nickel words do.

> *Good writers use big words only when necessary.*

Sentence variation practice

Add punch to these paragraphs by shortening the sentence that is too long.

1. *Fiscal conservatives have long claimed that lowering taxes actually raises government revenue. Any rational examination of this claim demonstrates quite clearly that it is superficial and, in a fundamental sense, incorrect, or at least that the relationship is not as simple as they are claiming. In fact, the government's tax revenue depends on many things other than the tax rate.*

2. *My mother sat me down and explained to me how important it is to spend money wisely. After listening to her carefully, I'm pretty sure I understood the point she was trying to make because all in all it's a good point. I began keeping better track of my accounts and became a wiser consumer.*

See the answer key on page 49.

---

15. Explain but don't overexplain

Always remember that the SAT is a *reasoning* test. It is designed to assess how well you think, not how well you apply a formula. The essay readers, therefore, are trained to assess how well you *explain* your reasoning. Explaining is a subtle art. Explain enough to allow the reader to follow your argument, but not so much that you insult the reader.

Good explanations often follow the word *because*. Be wary, however, of using phrases like *because of* and *due to*, because they tend to produce weak explanations. To work grammatically, these phrases must be followed by noun phrases, which don't often provide much explanation. The word *because* (without the *of*), however, can be followed by a clause, which permits a more substantial explanation.

> *I am wet because of the storm.*

This sentence explains with a *because of* phrase. As a result, it does not explain very much. Notice that avoiding the *of* forces the writer to give a more substantial explanation.

> *I am wet because I was forced outside in the storm without my umbrella.*

> *I am wet because a car sped through a puddle and splashed me after the storm had ended.*

> *I am wet because the wind blew the rain so fiercely that my umbrella was of no use.*

Notice that each *because* is followed by an independent clause conveying a more substantial explanation.

Be wary also of overexplaining, because it insults the intelligent reader.

> *"I disapprove of what you say, but I shall defend to the death your right to say it." This is a famous quotation by Voltaire that shows how strongly he valued the idea of free speech and was willing to defend it.*

This writer earns points by citing a smart quotation (even though it seems Voltaire may never have said precisely those words), but then squanders them by overexplaining. There is no need to say that this is *a famous quotation* and that it *shows how strongly [Voltaire] valued the idea of free speech and was willing to defend it*, because this is manifestly obvious to any intelligent reader. A good writer lets the quote do its work.

> *Voltaire epitomized the proper attitude toward free speech when he said "I disapprove of what you say, but I shall defend to the death your right to say it."*

Logical connection practice

In each of the following paragraphs, the pronoun in bold makes an unclear reference. Rewrite the sentence to clarify it.

1. *The ceremony at the White House celebrated the service of the outgoing Secretary of State, whose policies and diplomacy elevated the status of the United States in the international community.* ***This*** *was a welcome development in a time when many citizens feared that the reputation of America was waning.*

2. *Many activists worked untiringly to make sure that donations continued to flow into the relief fund, and to fight the corruption that was diverting much of those funds into the hands of unscrupulous bureaucrats.* *Because of* ***this****, the tens of thousands of refugees were able to continue to get much-needed food and medicine.*

3. *My grandfather continues to remain active and learn new things even though he has been diagnosed with terminal colon cancer and must spend days at a time undergoing painful chemotherapy.* ***This*** *has been an inspiration to me.*

See the answer key on page 50.

Bargain word practice

Rewrite each sentence using more precise diction.

1. *Eleanor was very sad for several weeks because she missed her pet cat.*

    Eleanor was distraught for many weeks because she longed for her pt cat.

2. *David looked very closely at his test results.*

3. *The girls in the car talked on and on about meaningless things for hours.*

4. *The coach gave us a long, harsh, and critical speech about our lack of effort in the first half.*

Toning down practice

Tone down the fancy vocabulary in the following sentences.

1. *When a practitioner of medicine suggests an appropriate remedy for a malady, it is best that the person to whom it was offered utilizes it strictly according to the instructions.*

2. *Plebeians execrate prevaricators, while aristocrats lionize them.*

See the answer key on page 50.

16. Leave your reader thinking

A good conclusion does not simply summarize or repeat your thesis without developing it. Repetition shows laziness at best and condescension to your reader at worst. If you have already stated your thesis clearly and developed it well, you don't need to remind your reader of that fact in the conclusion.

A good conclusion does not summarize, but rather provides the reader with a resonant thought connected logically to the thesis. You can do this in many ways, but here are three general tasks that a good conclusion can accomplish:

- **Connect the thesis to a broader scope of experience.** In a short essay such as this, you can only discuss a few specific examples in the main body of the essay, but your conclusion can show that your thesis applies more broadly. You can connect your thesis to your own life, society at large, a particular problem, the future, etc.

- **Offer a solution.** Many persuasive essays discuss problems that need to be fixed. In your conclusion, you can leave your reader with a hopeful thought by offering some ideas of how to fix these problems.

- **Refine or clarify your thesis.** In the body of your essay, you may not have the opportunity to address objections to your point of view or to clarify important points. The conclusion provides an opportunity to do this.

17. Don't tell us what you're doing—just do it

Don't distract your reader by trumpeting what you are doing—just do it. Your reader knows that you are describing your own point of view, so there is no need to announce it with phrases like *I believe that*, *it is my opinion that*, and *the truth is*. Your reader also knows that your final paragraph is your concluding paragraph, so don't say *In conclusion*. Good transitions convey logical relationships between ideas, they do not trumpet intentions.

> *I believe that bullies are often people who are not truly happy. It's just my opinion, of course, and a lot of people say different things, but those who have to pick on the weak can't really feel good about themselves, as I can demonstrate with a few examples.*

This phrasing distracts the readers with questions of how you acquired your *opinion* and your *belief* and with the unnecessary announcement that you will actually try to support your claim with examples. It is much better to simply state your position.

> *Bullies are often people who aren't really happy. They may have what psychologists call "self-esteem," but those who have to pick on the weak can't really feel good about themselves.*

Likewise, avoid presumption. Don't tell your reader what you *have done*. If you've done it, the reader knows it. If you haven't, saying that you have is presumptuous. Don't use phrases like *as this shows* or *as my analysis demonstrates*.

Consider this conclusion to an essay that discussed some positive outcomes of war.

> *As I said in the beginning, every cloud has a silver lining, and this has been shown in this essay with the examples of some wars and individual diseases. Both of these are bad things overall but which sometimes can have good things come out of them. This shows that...*

This conclusion says "In case you weren't paying attention, here's what I just finished saying." It insults the reader. Instead, a good conclusion should present new and interesting thoughts connected to the thesis. This conclusion merely repeats the thesis and condescends to the reader

> *Of course, wars are among the most tragic of all human events. If wars can have beneficial outcomes, then surely we can see the good in lesser tragedies. Perhaps if we could take such a positive perspective on our everyday problems, we would live happier lives.*

This conclusion is more effective because it extends the thesis, offers a suggestion, and leaves the reader thinking.

Answer Key

Verb strengthening practice

1. *The spectators taunted the players.*
2. *The industrial revolution endangered the agrarian way of life.*
3. *Over 3 million fans viewed the championship game.*
4. *In response, the committee changed the hiring procedure.*
5. *The workers needed to form a union that could stand up to the ownership.*
6. *The citizens resented the governor for ignoring their questions.*
7. *This action violates the company's own contract.*
8. *The village was devastated by the earthquake.*
9. *The mice tend to overeat when they lack this hormone.*
10. *I failed the test because I didn't study.*
11. *The critics considered the movie dull and hackneyed.*
12. *Mothers always worry that their children will get hurt when playing.*

Clarification practice

1. *Competition encourages excellence.*
2. *Our managers consider all of the ideas submitted by our employees, and use the best ones.*
3. *People are increasingly concerned that the government is wasting their tax money.*
4. *When we focus exclusively on personal moral responsibility, we ignore the importance of social institutions.*
5. *Investors like aggressive companies that are committed to promoting themselves to consumers. As a result, these investors put a lot of money into these companies, thereby overvaluing them, even though the companies often have weak products or business models.*

Cliché sweeping practice

1. *Many adults today think that young people are lazy.*
2. *They say that kids spend too much time playing video games or listening to their iPods.*
3. *They are wrong.*
4. *In fact, many of my friends are choosing tough careers that are more helpful than lucrative.*

Sentence tightening practice

1. *People are worried about the future.*
2. *An effective manager relies on proven management principles.*
3. *Many students know that they need to become educated not only to get jobs but to keep them.*
4. *Parkinson's is a degenerative disease, but current research offers hope that it will be ameliorated or even cured.*
5. *Since corporations want to make money, they rarely focus on preserving the environment.*
6. *If your boss opposes your proposal at the meeting, talk with her privately about it because public confrontation might make her resent you.*
7. *Too few people realize that economic strength depends on the hopes of consumers.*

Sentence variation practice

1. *Fiscal conservatives have long claimed that lowering taxes actually raises government revenue. **It's not that simple.** In fact, the government's tax revenue depends on many things other than the tax rate.*

2. *My mother sat me down and explained to me how important it is to spend money wisely. **I got the message.** I began keeping better track of my accounts and became a wiser consumer.*

Answer Key

Logical connection practice

1. The second sentence does not make clear what the *welcome development* was. Was it the ceremony, the diplomacy, or the policies? The revision must make this clear.

    The ceremony at the White House celebrated the service of the outgoing Secretary of State, whose policies and diplomacy elevated the status of the United States in the international community. ***These policies*** *were welcome in a time when many citizens feared that the reputation of America was waning.*

2. The second sentence does not make clear what helped the refugees. Was it the work of the activists, the donations, or the corruption? The revision must make this clear.

    *Many activists worked untiringly to make sure that donations continued to flow into the relief fund, and to fight the corruption that was diverting much of those funds into the hands of unscrupulous bureaucrats. Because of **their efforts**, the tens of thousands of refugees were able to continue to get much-needed food and medicine.*

3. The second sentence doesn't make clear what inspires the author. Is it the grandfather's love of life, his ability to withstand the chemotherapy, his ability to live with cancer, or some combination of these? The revision must make this clear.

    *My grandfather continues to remain active and learn new things even though he has been diagnosed with terminal colon cancer, and must spend days at a time undergoing painful chemotherapy. **His love of life** has been an inspiration to me.*

Bargain word practice

1. *Eleanor mourned her cat for several weeks.*
2. *David scrutinized his test results.*
3. *The girls in the car babbled for hours.*
4. *The coach harangued us about our lack of effort in the first half.*

Toning down practice

1. *Follow your doctor's instructions.*
2. *Ordinary people hate liars, but the nobility love them.*

Lesson 8—Practice your essay writing skills

1. Practice Essays

PRACTICE ESSAY 1
Time—25 minutes

Directions for Writing the Essay

Plan and write an essay that answers the following question. Do NOT write on another topic. An essay on another topic will receive a score of 0.

Two readers will grade your essay based on how well you develop your point of view, organize and explain your ideas, use specific and relevant examples to support your thesis, and use clear and effective language. How well you write is much more important than how much you write, but to cover the topic adequately you should plan to write several paragraphs.

Your essay must be written only on the lines provided on your answer sheet. You will have enough space if you write on every line, avoid wide margins, and keep your handwriting to a reasonable size. Your essay will be read by people who are not familiar with your handwriting, so write legibly.

You may use this sheet for notes and outlining, but these will not be graded as part of your essay.

Consider carefully the issue discussed in the following quotation; then write an essay that answers the question posed in the assignment.

> Some causes are forced upon us by circumstance. When our survival or the survival of our loved ones is at stake, we often have no choice but to fight. A more noble cause, however, is the survival or the freedom of others, when our own survival and freedom are assured.

Assignment: **How should one decide when a cause is worth fighting for?** Write an essay in which you answer this question and explain your answer with reasoning and examples from literature, the arts, history, politics, science and technology, current events, or your experience or observation.

Abraham Lincoln, FDR,

Write your essay on your answer sheet.

SECTION

1

Essay

Time: 25 minutes
Start: _____

Stop: _____

Write your essay for Section 1 in the space below and on the next page. Do not write outside the box.

PRACTICE ESSAY 2
Time—25 minutes

Directions for Writing the Essay

Plan and write an essay that answers the following question. Do NOT write on another topic. An essay on another topic will receive a score of 0.

Two readers will grade your essay based on how well you develop your point of view, organize and explain your ideas, use specific and relevant examples to support your thesis, and use clear and effective language. How well you write is much more important than how much you write, but to cover the topic adequately you should plan to write several paragraphs.

Your essay must be written only on the lines provided on your answer sheet. You will have enough space if you write on every line, avoid wide margins, and keep your handwriting to a reasonable size. Your essay will be read by people who are not familiar with your handwriting, so write legibly.

You may use this sheet for notes and outlining, but these will not be graded as part of your essay.

Consider carefully the issue discussed in the following quotation; then write an essay that answers the question posed in the assignment.

> The greatest disservice we do to our children is making them believe that the purpose of education is to get them into college or get them a job. Perhaps we dare not proclaim the real purpose of education because we fear that we are falling miserably short of serving that purpose—to create happy and competent human beings.

Assignment: **What is the primary purpose of education?** Write an essay in which you answer this question and explain your answer with reasoning and examples from literature, the arts, history, politics, science and technology, current events, or your experience or observation.

Write your essay on your answer sheet.

SECTION

1

Essay

Write your essay for Section 1 in the space below and on the next page. Do not write outside the box.

PRACTICE ESSAY 3
Time—25 minutes

Plan and write an essay that answers the following question. Do NOT write on another topic. An essay on another topic will receive a score of 0.

Two readers will grade your essay based on how well you develop your point of view, organize and explain your ideas, use specific and relevant examples to support your thesis, and use clear and effective language. How well you write is much more important than how much you write, but to cover the topic adequately you should plan to write several paragraphs.

Your essay must be written only on the lines provided on your answer sheet. You will have enough space if you write on every line, avoid wide margins, and keep your handwriting to a reasonable size. Your essay will be read by people who are not familiar with your handwriting, so write legibly.

You may use this sheet for notes and outlining, but these will not be graded as part of your essay.

Consider carefully the issue discussed in the following quotation; then write an essay that answers the question posed in the assignment.

> Ours is the most over-protective society that humanity has ever known. We regulate every aspect of our children's lives, strapping them into life so that they cannot be hurt by sudden jolts. But this prevents them from learning how to manage themselves, and places fear above freedom and achievement.

Assignment: **To what extent should our loved ones be protected from potential harm?** Write an essay in which you answer this question and explain your answer with reasoning and examples from literature, the arts, history, politics, science and technology, current events, or your experience or observation.

Write your essay on your answer sheet.

SECTION

1

Essay

Time: 25 minutes   Start: _____

Stop: _____

Write your essay for Section 1 in the space below and on the next page. Do not write outside the box.

_____
_____
_____
_____
_____
_____
_____
_____
_____
_____
_____
_____
_____
_____
_____
_____
_____
_____
_____
_____
_____
_____
_____
_____

PRACTICE ESSAY 4
Time—25 minutes

Directions for Writing the Essay

Plan and write an essay that answers the following question. Do NOT write on another topic. An essay on another topic will receive a score of 0.

Two readers will grade your essay based on how well you develop your point of view, organize and explain your ideas, use specific and relevant examples to support your thesis, and use clear and effective language. How well you write is much more important than how much you write, but to cover the topic adequately you should plan to write several paragraphs.

Your essay must be written only on the lines provided on your answer sheet. You will have enough space if you write on every line, avoid wide margins, and keep your handwriting to a reasonable size. Your essay will be read by people who are not familiar with your handwriting, so write legibly.

You may use this sheet for notes and outlining, but these will not be graded as part of your essay.

Consider carefully the issue discussed in the following quotation; then write an essay that answers the question posed in the assignment.

> We often think that it is better to solve problems on our own than to depend on others. Of course, dependence can be taken to extremes, but interdependence is also part of human nature. The tacit understandings that develop from giving and receiving help are essential to our emotional survival.

Assignment: **To what extent should one depend on others to help solve one's own problems?** Write an essay in which you answer this question and explain your answer with reasoning and examples from literature, the arts, history, politics, science and technology, current events, or your experience or observation.

Write your essay on your answer sheet.

SECTION

I

Essay

Time: 25 minutes Start: _____

Stop: _____

Write your essay for Section 1 in the space below and on the next page. Do not write outside the box.

_____

_____

_____

_____

_____

_____

_____

_____

_____

_____

_____

_____

_____

_____

_____

_____

_____

_____

_____

_____

_____

_____

_____

_____

_____

PRACTICE ESSAY 5
Time—25 minutes

Directions for Writing the Essay

Plan and write an essay that answers the following question. Do NOT write on another topic. An essay on another topic will receive a score of 0.

Two readers will grade your essay based on how well you develop your point of view, organize and explain your ideas, use specific and relevant examples to support your thesis, and use clear and effective language. How well you write is much more important than how much you write, but to cover the topic adequately you should plan to write several paragraphs.

Your essay must be written only on the lines provided on your answer sheet. You will have enough space if you write on every line, avoid wide margins, and keep your handwriting to a reasonable size. Your essay will be read by people who are not familiar with your handwriting, so write legibly.

You may use this sheet for notes and outlining, but these will not be graded as part of your essay.

Consider carefully the issue discussed in the following quotation; then write an essay that answers the question posed in the assignment.

> Perhaps the most dangerous word in popular discourse is "decency." It is a buzz-word used by those who want to control our lives and restrict our freedoms. These people believe that all humans are idiots who are incapable of managing their own thoughts or raising their own children. They believe that expunging every dirty word and thought from our lives somehow makes us better people, when in fact it makes us less human.

Assignment: **Are there any important limits to the principle of free speech in a democratic society?** Write an essay in which you answer this question and explain your answer with reasoning and examples from literature, the arts, history, politics, science and technology, current events, or your experience or observation.

Write your essay on your answer sheet.

SECTION

1

Essay

Time: 25 minutes

Start: _____

Stop: _____

Write your essay for Section 1 in the space below and on the next page. Do not write outside the box.

_____

_____

_____

_____

_____

_____

_____

_____

_____

_____

_____

_____

_____

_____

_____

_____

_____

_____

_____

_____

_____

_____

2. Sample graded essays

Practice Essay 1

> **Assignment:** How should one decide when a cause is worth fighting for?

The following passage received the highest possible score of 12. (Each grader gave it a score of 6.) This *outstanding* essay develops a clear and interesting point of view with appropriate examples. It demonstrates outstanding critical thinking and mastery of the standards of writing and organization.

More than two hundred years ago, Immanuel Kant formulated his "Categorical Imperative," as a means of creating an objective and rational theory of morality. His Categorical Imperative states that any act must be motivated by a principle which one would will to become universal, that is, applicable to all moral agents, or else it is irrational. In other words, if you do intentionally something that you wouldn't want everyone else to do, too, then you are immoral and irrational. This principle is an excellent basis for determining what causes are worth fighting for. We should fight for those causes that do not just benefit us individually, but that would benefit us even if they were applied universally throughout the world.

For instance, fighting to fool a jury into believing that you did not drive while intoxicated, while knowing full well that you did, is not a moral cause. If everyone did this, we would have people driving drunk with impunity, threatening our loved ones with their immoral and dangerous behavior. On a larger scale, the militaristic policies of the United States in the last four years are immoral not only because they lead directly to the killing of innocent people, but because if every country held such policies, the world would end violently. Trying to solve all of our problems through force rather than reason and persuasion leads to a world of terror and violence.

One excellent example of a man who well chose a cause to fight for is Atticus Finch in To Kill a Mockingbird. He had very little to gain on a personal level by defending Tom Robinson, a black man accused of raping a white woman. Many in town believed that it was immoral for a man to defend someone accused of such a terrible crime, let alone a black man. But these people would scarcely have wanted to be treated the same way if they were accused, so their cause violates the categorical imperative, and is therefore immoral. Atticus, on the other hand, chose to treat the accused man as he would want to be treated under those circumstances. He represents true justice, blind to race and social status.

Many people choose their causes based on what would help them or their group. Gun advocates think only of what they would do if they were attacked, and not how terrible a world full of guns is. Religious fundamentalists think that only those who share their beliefs are worthwhile, and that unbelievers have lower status. Viewing such "causes" from the attitude of the categorical imperative shows how grossly immoral they really are. If everyone were allowed to have deadly weapons, and everyone were justified in killing those who challenged their beliefs, the world would descend into violence. We see this at its worst when militarily powerful governments are controlled by religious fundamentalists. Such governments invariably claim that they are killing others in the name of great principles, like democracy or freedom or religious purity, but reason shows us that the true "causes" for which these governments kill are in fact immoral.

Reader's comments   **6 points out of 6**

Point of view. The thesis that Kant's Categorical Imperative provides a basis for determining what causes are worth fighting for is thoughtful and intelligent. The author states this thesis clearly, explaining a complicated concept with straightforward language and good examples, and maintains this point of view consistently throughout the essay.

Reasoning. The author analyzes the issues of violence and justice with keen insight. He demonstrates how each example either violates or complies with the Categorical Imperative, and uses this reasoning to draw conclusions about the moral behavior of individuals as well as societies.

Support. The examples of the drunk driver, Atticus Finch, militaristic governments and the gun control issue are very appropriate and are marshalled effectively to support the author's thesis.

Organization. The essay is well organized, with a clear introduction, development and conclusion. The conclusion effectively examines an alternative viewpoint and refutes it, establishing a strong point of view on morality and society.

Use of language. The author's word choice is effective, if not superior. Although the sentences are consistently on the long side, they are written clearly and with syntactic variation.

Practice Essay 2

Assignment: **What is the primary purpose of education?**

The following passage received the highest possible score of 12. (Each grader gave it a score of 6.) This *outstanding* essay develops a clear and interesting point of view with appropriate examples. It demonstrates outstanding critical thinking and mastery of the standards of writing and organization.

From one-room schoolhouses to village huts to technologically advanced college classrooms, education assumes many forms and functions. Yet uniting every kind of learning is a common promise that fuels both teachers and students and generates the widespread belief that education is one of society's most important pillars. The primary purpose of education is to create opportunity: the opportunity to teach values, learn skills, and accumulate new knowledge.

Education offers unlimited opportunities to teachers because it opens the door to younger generations, thus allowing educators to influence the present and the future. For example, in the novel "A Northern Light," a small-town school teacher named Ms. Wilcox uses her position to inspire the children of the community. She teaches the main character Mattie to cultivate her writing talent and to abandon prevailing social prejudices. Through her interaction with students, Ms. Wilcox alters the mindset of the whole town, creating new avenues of respect and peace between racial and class groups and encouraging all families to embrace their children's gifts. Her ability to teach tolerance, courage, and acceptance illustrates how education offers teachers a way to change important aspects of society.

Clearly one of the primary purposes of education is to teach students the skills necessary for survival and success. It gives people the opportunity to discover their talents and to learn how best to use them. Without schooling, how would Albert Einstein have discovered his aptitude for logic and math? If Phyllis Wheatley, taught by her masters to read and write, had been kept illiterate like most slaves in the eighteenth century, how could she have cultivated and eventually made public her poetic talent? Education gives students the opportunity to discover and use their unique abilities and teaches them how to support themselves and their societies.

Education also allows generations of students to build on the work of earlier thinkers, thus permitting society to move on to new discoveries. It is hardly a coincidence that students of masters also go on to become innovators. Degas, a painter who greatly admired the French artists Ingres and Delacroix, studied their methods to expand his skills, eventually going on to break artistic ground as an early Impressionist. Plato, a student of Socrates, built upon the teachings of his master in introducing his own philosophical ideas. Education gives new minds access to old knowledge and thus ensures the constant forward progression of discovery.

Although the opportunity offered by education seems entirely beneficial, one cannot forget that education's power can be wielded to do harm as well. Just as it can teach acceptance, education can propagate hatred and violence. For example, schools in Nazi Germany helped spread the intolerance that lead to horrific crimes against Jews. Therefore, it is as vital to recognize education's dangers as it is to take advantage of its benefits as a powerful influence on the present and future.

Reader's comments   **6 points out of 6**

Point of view. The thesis that the primary purpose of education is creating opportunity through learning values, skills and knowledge is thoughtful and well-reasoned. The author maintains a meaningful perspective on this topic throughout the essay.

Reasoning. The author analyzes the purpose of education carefully and insightfully. The acknowledgement of the dangers of education in the conclusion serves to round out a well-reasoned analysis. The only lapse in the author's train of thought is in the first paragraph where the concept of "uniting every kind of learning" is not adequately explained.

Support. The examples of Ms. Wilcox as a teacher of values, of Albert Einstein and Phyllis Wheatley as those who acquired important skills, and of Degas and Plato as those who built upon the knowledge of their teachers, are exceptional choices.

Organization. The essay is well organized, with a clear introduction, development and conclusion. The conclusion provides a caveat without compromising the thesis.

Use of language. The author demonstrates a strong vocabulary as well as an expert grasp of syntax and sentence variation.

Practice Essay 3

> **Assignment:**   To what extent should our loved ones be protected from potential harm?

The following passage received the highest possible score of 12 (Each grader gave it a score of 6.) **This** *outstanding* **essay develops a clear and interesting point of view with appropriate examples. It demonstrates outstanding critical thinking and mastery of the standards of writing and organization.**

I recently saw The Human Comedy, a 60 year-old movie based on the William Saroyan novel. In the opening scene, a young child playing in his yard suddenly hears a train whistle. He runs through town as fast as he can until he reaches the train tracks. Like so many modern viewers, I regarded the train whistle ominously. That kid's going to kill himself! I thought. But wait, I've read the book—there's no splatter! Then I realized how different my world was from that of 60 years ago. We are perhaps more afraid of getting hurt, or having our loved ones get hurt, than ever before. The kid was fine—he just wanted to wave to the train as it passed. Today, our overprotective parents would never let us run out of the yard, let alone come anywhere near railroad tracks! We're buckled in, insured, and monitored like never before. We're on color-coded alert for terrorist threats. But this focus on safety has made us a more anxious and less competent society.

Parents place their toddlers in little protective scooters so that they can almost never fall and hit themselves. What these parents don't realize is that they are also preventing their children from developing coordination and balance, precisely the skills they will need to stay out of danger as they grow. In an ironic twist, overprotection endangers child welfare. We learn by making mistakes, not being protected from them.

As we grow, this overprotection takes new forms. Before I was twelve years old, I never rode my bicycle around my neighborhood without an adult with me, not to mention my helmet and knee pads. During the summer of seventh grade, however, I read "Kidnapped" by Robert Louis Stevenson. It is a story of a boy named David Balfour, perhaps no older than I whose father dies and who, as he seeks his father's inheritance, is essentially sold into slavery by his uncle Ebenezer. Through cunning and fortitude, David eventually returns to take revenge on his Uncle and reclaim his estate. Okay, so my condition was not exactly comparable to David's slavery. But, I thought, who is better off, one who is free to live a life of danger by his own wiles, or a kid forced to bike around his block in a helmet and report home every hour?

I hope in the years ahead that I will be willing to take risks even though I have been conditioned for sixteen years against it. Maybe I can take a trip on my own, preferably not shanghaied by an evil sea captain and forced to avoid pursuers across an entire country by foot, but at least one on which I must live by my own wits. Perhaps I can learn the ways of the world and conquer it on my own terms, but not if I am protected from ever getting hurt in it. Perhaps soon, also, our country will learn to shake itself of its fear of terrorism and its delusion that a great country must seal itself off from all threats. As Franklin Roosevelt said, "The only thing we have to fear is fear itself."

Reader's comments   **6 points out of 6**

Point of view. The thesis that the "focus on safety has made us a more anxious and less competent society" is well-articulated and interesting, It is supported consistently throughout the essay.

Reasoning. The author examines the issue of protection, or overprotection, with several well-considered and very effective examples, particularly young parents, the *Human Comedy,* and *Kidnapped*. In each case, the author makes a clear and logical connection between the example and his thesis. The extension of the thesis in the final paragraph is poignant and effective.

Support. The examples of David Balfour, the author himself, and young modern parents, are appropriate and effective.

Organization. The essay is well organized, with a clear introduction, development and conclusion. The conclusion provides insight into the author's personal hopes for himself and his country in keeping with his theme of overprotection.

Use of language. The author consistently uses strong and effective vocabulary. The contrast between the author himself and David Balfour are very humorous and serve the author's purpose well. The author adopts a casual tone to good effect without becoming careless or flippant.

Practice Essay 4

Assignment: To what extent should one depend on others to help solve one's own problems?

The following passage received the highest possible score of 12. (Each grader gave it a score of 6.) This *outstanding* essay develops a clear and interesting point of view with appropriate examples. It demonstrates outstanding critical thinking and mastery of the standards of writing and organization.

Human beings are social animals, endowed with brains that are not designed for us to live alone. We have the innate ability to cooperate, and we learn to do it instinctively at a very young age. The myth of the "self-made millionaire" is not one to which we should aspire. Far more important to today's society are those who can play well with others, and who learn to give and receive help freely. This is where true power and happiness comes from.

Many people believe that human beings are naturally competitive, and that nothing is truly worthwhile unless we earn it ourselves, often at the expense of others. I had an interesting conversation with my friend Yuri, who came to the United States from Russia when he was fifteen years old. He was surprised to hear me talking negatively about some acquaintances of mine who helped each other to cheat on a math test. Yuri said that, in Russia, that was standard practice, and that it wasn't really frowned upon. What they did frown upon was the unwillingness to help one's friends.

I thought about this conversation for a long time, particularly about how it demonstrated very keenly the difference between the socialist mindset and the capitalist mindset. Even though Russia has been essentially free of communism for over a decade, old cultural habits are hard to break. I wondered whether it was truly better for our society to be so highly competitive, to pit students against each other for grades, rather than encouraging them to work together to acquire knowledge. I came to the conclusion that some kind of compromise was possible, a meeting of East and West. Cooperation was no good unless the students learned something. Otherwise, it was pointless cheating. But competition also can often get in the way of learning. If we stop viewing learning as a zero-sum game, perhaps our educational system can begin to compete with the more enlightened schools of Europe and Asia.

American individualism is a wonderful thing, embodied by the adventurous explorers of the frontier, the brazen Industrialists of the gilded age, and American artists, scientists and thinkers. But a country becomes great not by defeating other countries in competitions, but by working together with them to build a more peaceful and prosperous world. Is it harmful to us if other countries can make better cars, or provide certain services, than we can? Basic principles of economics state that they do not; that both parties can gain from doing what they do best and then freely trading with each other.

It's not healthy to think that all of your problems are yours alone, and that it's a sign of weakness to ask for help. On the contrary, the strongest people, and the strongest nations, are those that understand the reality that they can't do everything themselves, and know how to seek help when they need it.

Reader's comments   **6 points out of 6**

Point of view. The thesis that "true power and happiness comes from…giv[ing] and receiv[ing] help freely" is intriguing and well considered. The author maintains her point of view on this thesis consistently throughout the essay.

Reasoning. The author analyzes the issue of mutual dependence versus competition with perspicuity. The author demonstrates the connection between each example and the issue of interdependence. The author's discussion of the socialist mindset versus the capitalist mindset was astute and informative.

Support. Although the author did not use any literary or historical examples, the brief discussion of human instinct, the discussion of the author's friend Yuri, and the discussion of education provide more than adequate support for the author's thesis.

Organization. The essay is well organized, with a clear introduction, development and conclusion. The conclusion does not do much more than repeat the thesis, but with a more substantial, poignant and resonant scope.

Use of language. The author uses very effective vocabulary, without descending into cliche. The effectual use of such words as "brazen," "mindset," "aspire," and "keenly," are notable. The author effectively varies sentence length and structure throughout the essay.

Practice Essay 5

Assignment: Are there any important limits to the principle of free speech in a democratic society?

The following passage received a very good score of 10. (Both readers gave it a 5.) This *effective* essay develops a point of view with appropriate examples. It demonstrates strong critical thinking, coherence, and appropriate vocabulary.

Beyond such basic duties as representing and protecting the people, the extent to which freedom should be extended to citizens in a democracy is hardly an uncontroversial matter. How much to limit speech, for example, is an unsettled question in many free societies. This liberty allows citizens a way of preserving themselves, their ideas, and their convictions from government encroachment. Yet when it threatens the safety and well-being of others, many believe that it must be restricted. Therefore, citizens and their elected leaders must determine when the freedom of speech guaranteed by the first amendment to the Constitution endangers the general health of the nation. When a democracy reaches this point, it must check liberties like free expression.

There are times when a democracy must stray from some promises in order to keep other, more important ones. Freedom of speech, for instance, has been limited to preserve the essential safety of the nation. During World War I, the American government passed the Espionage Act, a portion of which contained severe penalties for distributing military information, spreading false documents, and engaging in other forms of expression that were harmful to the war effort. This case shows the importance of preserving a safe balance between a free society's dedication to free speech and its promise of protection for its citizens. As valuable as freedom of information can be in peace time, it can threaten the welfare of millions of people in times of war. The right to tell a terrorist the security code for entering a nuclear facility, for instance, is not one that our country should protect.

Free speech should also be restricted when society itself calls for it. For instance, many free citizens believe that children must be protected from harmful aspects of adult free speech. Spurred by this general consensus, the governments of free states have passed laws restricting the language and content of the media. For instance, the United States' FCC (Federal Communications Commission) places strict limits on the foul language that one can use in publicly-accessed media like radio stations, television, and newspapers. When society agrees that a group of its citizens deserve protection from certain content, freedom of speech can be limited.

Though free speech can be reined in for society's good, no free state should use the quest for utopia to justify unnecessary restriction. Conflict and dissent are inevitable side effects of allowing people to express their contending ideas, and people understand that with the good of free expression comes the side effect of a heterogeneous, conflict-ridden society. Therefore, only when the absolute welfare and basic interests of all people—not just one small group—are threatened is the limitation of free speech warranted.

Reader's comments　　　　　**5 points out of 6**

Point of view. The author presents a consistent and well-reasoned point of view centered on the thesis that "when…freedom of speech…endangers the general health of the nation…citizens and their leaders…must check liberties like free expression."

Reasoning. The author provides cogent and consistent reasoning for her arguments. The discussions of the Espionage Act and the FCC are effective. There are some weaknesses with the reasoning however, such as the failure to acknowledge the wide and vehement disagreement about whether such things as "foul language" are an affront to the "absolute welfare and basic interests of all people."

Support. The examples of the Espionage Act, contemporary terrorism and the FCC are appropriate and effective. However, the author's argument would have been bolstered with explanations of what "the quest for utopia" or "unnecessary restriction" refer to.

Organization. The essay is well organized, with a clear introduction, development and conclusion. The conclusion qualifies the author's thesis in an appropriate way, acknowledging that there are limits to restrictions on free speech.

Use of language. The author demonstrates a good grasp of language. She varies the length and structure of her sentences, and uses effective phrases such as "government encroachment," "spurred by this general consensus" and "heterogeneous, conflict-ridden society."

Part III
The Multiple-Choice Questions

Lesson 9—Improving sentences

Lesson 10—Identifying sentence errors

Lesson 11—Improving paragraphs

Lesson 9—Improving sentences

1. How to attack Improving Sentences questions

The SAT Writing will include about 25 Improving Sentences questions. These ask you to determine whether an under-lined portion of a sentence contains one or more errors in grammar, wordiness, or awkwardness and, if so, to choose the best correction. If it contains no error, you are to choose (A), which leaves the sentence as it is.

The children <u>couldn't hardly believe their eyes</u>.

(A) couldn't hardly believe their eyes
(B) would not hardly believe their eyes
(C) could hardly believe their eyes
(D) couldn't nearly believe their eyes
(E) could hardly believe his or her eyes

The original sentence contains just one error, a double negative, *couldn't hardly*. The correct choice should fix this mistake without introducing any other problems. Choices (C) and (E) both fix the double negative, but choice (E) introduces a new problem—*his or her* does not agree in number with the antecedent *children*. Therefore the correct answer is (C).

Improving Sentences questions require you to *fix* grammatical mistakes rather than merely *find* them. Therefore, the best way to attack these questions is to look actively for errors, and then think about how to correct them before checking the choices.

The College Hill Method for attacking Improving Sentences questions:

1. Read the *entire* sentence naturally and let your ear tell you if anything sounds wrong.

2. If the underlined portion contains an obvious error, try to identify the error and how to fix it. The error must violate one of the rules of grammar discussed in Lessons 13–23. Then eliminate choice (A) as well as any other choices that repeat the same error.

3. If the underlined portion does *not* contain an error, be inclined to choose (A), but test any choices that are *shorter* than (A) to see if they convey the idea as clearly as the original. If you find a more concise option that is just as clear and logical as the original, choose the more concise option.

4. Reread the sentence with your choice, and make sure that the sentence works as a whole and that it does not contain any other errors. Remember that a sentence may have more than one mistake!

2. Be careful

Make sure that any error is a legitimate error in grammar or usage, and not just a matter of personal preference. In other words, don't assume that an underlined portion contains an error just because you might have phrased it differently. Try to identify the error as a violation of one of the grammatical rules discussed in Lessons 13–23.

The captains were given awards despite the team's loss, <u>for they had sacrificed a great deal for the sake of the team</u>.

(A) for they had sacrificed a great deal for the sake of the team
(B) in the sense of sacrificing a great deal for the sake of the team
(C) but had sacrificed a great deal for the sake of the team
(D) their sacrifice for the sake of the team being the reason for them
(E) nevertheless, they sacrificed a great deal for the sake of the team

The original sentence may sound a bit odd to your ear, so you may be inclined to assume that the sentence contains an error. But it should be just as obvious that no other choice is much clearer or more logical. In fact, the original sentence is best. The original sentence uses the word *for*, which is usually used as a preposition, as a conjunction similar to *because* or *since*.

> There are often several ways to fix a mistake, so be flexible.

The coaches weren't very interested in winning games during <u>spring training, they considered it</u> as an opportunity to experiment with different permutations of players.

(A) spring training, they considered it
(B) spring training; but they considered it
(C) spring training, but
(D) spring training as they were in using it
(E) spring training they were in using it

You might notice that the original sentence is a "run-on" (see Lesson 23). It joins two related independent clauses with only a comma. Usually, run-ons can be fixed by replacing the comma with a semicolon, colon, or conjunction. So you might go through the choices and eliminate those that also don't contain a semicolon, colon, or conjunction, leaving you with (B) and (C). But these don't work. Choice (B) incorrectly combines the semicolon and the conjunction, and choice (C) is illogical. Choice (D) is the correct answer because it is the only one that logically completes the *as* comparison.

3. All else being equal, shorter is better

If you read a lot of good prose, then when a sentence sounds okay to you, it probably is. In these situations, you should be inclined to choose (A). But some writing problems are hard to identify. For instance, some needlessly wordy phrases don't sound so terrible at first. Even if a sentence sounds okay, always read any choices that are *shorter* than the original. If a choice says the same thing in fewer words, it's probably better.

> The best sentences convey ideas clearly and concisely. Avoid wordiness.

Several reviewers suggested that the article was not only frequently inaccurate, <u>but additionally it was needlessly obtuse and, ultimately, it was insubstantial</u>.

(A) but additionally it was needlessly obtuse and, ultimately, it was insubstantial
(B) but it was also needlessly obtuse and it was ultimately also insubstantial
(C) but they also commented on the needless obtuseness and also the ultimate insubstantiality
(D) although it was also needlessly obtuse and ultimately insubstantial
(E) but also needlessly obtuse and ultimately insubstantial

This sentence doesn't contain an obvious grammatical mistake, but it is wordy and awkward. Don't pick (A) immediately just because no mistake jumps out. Notice that (B), (D), and (E) are more concise than the original. The most concise is (E), which is the correct answer.

4. Check for danglers

> Improving Sentences questions often test your ability to fix dangling modifiers (Lesson 17). Make sure you know how to handle them. Just remember a simple rule: any modifying phrase must be as close as possible to the word it modifies.

<u>Chosen from the best players from around the county</u>, the coaches found the recruits to be extraordinarily easy to work with.

(A) Chosen from the best players from around the county
(B) Being chosen from the best players from throughout the county
(C) Having chosen the best players from around the county
(D) Being the best players from throughout the entire county
(E) The best players having been chosen by them from throughout the county

The underlined phrase is a participial phrase based on the participle *chosen*. *Who* was chosen? The *recruits*, not the *coaches*. Since *coaches* is closer to the modifying phrase than *recruits* is, the modifier is misplaced (see Lesson 17). Notice that choice (C) changes the participle from *chosen* to *having chosen* so that it modifies *coaches*, the noun that follows. This choice makes it clear that the coaches *have chosen the best players*.

5. Watch out for extra problems

Remember that the sentence may have more than one problem. Always reread the sentence with your choice to make sure there are no extra problems.

The entire editorial staff wrote <u>diligent for completing</u> the article in time for the midnight deadline.

    (A) diligent for completing
    (B) diligent in order to complete
    (C) diligently for completing
    (D) diligent to complete
    (E) diligently to complete

The most obvious problem is that *diligent*, an adjective, should be changed to *diligently,* an adverb, because it modifies the verb *wrote*.   But don't jump right to choice (C), because the sentence also contains an error in idiom (see Lesson 19). To show purpose, the infinitive *to complete* should be used instead of *for completing*. The best answer is (E).

Improving Sentences practice

Each of the sentences below contains one underlined portion. The portion may contain one or more errors in grammar, usage, construction, precision, diction (choice of words), or idiom. Some of the sentences are correct.

Consider the meaning of the original sentence, and choose the answer that best expresses that meaning. If the original sentence is best, choose (A), because it repeats the original phrasing. Choose the phrasing that creates the clearest, most precise, and most effective sentence.

EXAMPLE:

The children couldn't hardly believe their eyes.

(A) couldn't hardly believe their eyes
(B) would not hardly believe their eyes
(C) could hardly believe their eyes
(D) couldn't nearly believe their eyes
(E) could hardly believe his or her eyes

ANSWER: C

1 Being the oldest team member, we chose Joe to be our captain.

(A) Being the oldest team member, we chose Joe
(B) As the oldest team member, we chose Joe
(C) Since Joe was the oldest team member, we chose him
(D) Because of being the oldest team member, we chose Joe
(E) In being the oldest team member, Joe was chosen by us

2 The dramatic flying buttresses of the cathedral are designed not as decorative elements, but they provide essential support to the structure.

(A) they provide essential support to
(B) as essential supports to
(C) for providing essential support to
(D) they support essentially
(E) as providing essential support to

3 The reason I am late is because my plane was delayed by the weather.

(A) because my plane was delayed
(B) because of my plane being delayed
(C) for my plane's being delayed
(D) that my plane was delayed
(E) the delaying of my plane

4 Although Bowler composed many advertising jingles, he never considered them to be worthy of his musical talents.

(A) he never considered them
(B) never considering them
(C) never having considered them
(D) they were never considered
(E) never being considered

5 Many physicists were skeptical of Heisenberg's theory because they believed that if you could conduct the right experiments to determine them, every characteristic of a particle could be determined theoretically to any degree of accuracy.

(A) if you could conduct the right experiments to determine them, every characteristic of a particle could be determined theoretically
(B) in conducting the right experiments, they could determine theoretically every characteristic of a particle
(C) experiments could theoretically be conducted to determine every characteristic of a particle
(D) experiments, if conducted to determine them, would determine theoretically every characteristic of a particle
(E) if you conduct the right experiments, you could theoretically determine every characteristic of a particle

Answer Key

Improving Sentences practice

1. **C** The original phrase suggests that *we* is the subject of the participle *being*, that is, that *we are the oldest team member*, which is illogical. Choices (B) and (D) commit similar errors. Choice (E) is incorrect because the prepositional phrase is illogical and the passive voice is awkward. The only choice that logically conveys the relationship between the ideas is (C).
    (Lesson 17, Modifier problems)
    (Lesson 23, Awkwardness and coordination)

2. **B** The phrase *not as…but…* suggests a parallel phrasing. Therefore, the underlined phrase should have a similar structure to *as decorative elements*. The most parallel option is (B).
    (Lesson 14, Parallelism)

3. **D** The underlined phrase must represent a *reason*, and so must be a noun phrase. Constructions of the form *the reason is because* are incorrect for this reason. The original phrase is not a noun phrase, but a subordinate clause. Choices (D) and (E) are noun phrases, but choice (D) conveys the idea more clearly.
    (Lesson 15, Comparison problems)

4. **A** The sentence is correct. Because the sentence starts with *although,* the phrase that follows the comma must be an independent clause that contrasts the first clause. The original sentence does this in the active voice to parallel the first clause. Choice (D) provides an independent clause, but it is vague because it does not indicate who *considered.*
    (Lesson 23, Awkwardness and coordination)

5. **C** The underlined phrase must be an independent clause that represents the belief of the skeptical physicists. Since it conveys a general belief, the phrase *you could* in the original sentence is inappropriate. Further, the pronoun *them* does not agree in number with its antecedent *particle.* The only choice that avoids both of these errors is (C).
    (Lesson 16, Pronoun problems)

Lesson 10—Identifying sentence errors

1. How to attack Identifying Sentence Errors questions

Every SAT will include about 18 Identifying Sentence Errors questions, each of which consists of a sentence with four underlined portions. Your job is to determine whether any of these underlined portions contains an error in grammar or usage. If it does, choose the portion that contains the error. If it does not, choose (E), for "no error."

An error in an Identifying Sentence Error question must be correctable by replacing or deleting *only* the underlined section, leaving every other part of the sentence unchanged. Although you only need to locate the error, you should have an idea of how to fix it by replacing or deleting the underlined portion.

The team <u>diligently</u> practiced and <u>prepared</u> several trick plays, but <u>were</u> never given the opportunity
      A   B   C
to use <u>them</u>. <u>No error</u>
   D   E

You might rather say that the team *practiced diligently* than that the team *diligently practiced,* but choosing (A) would be incorrect, because this "correction" would require moving the underlined portion of the sentence to a non-underlined part of the sentence, which is not allowed. (Actually, either phrasing is fine: the adverb *diligently* can come before or after the verb *practiced.*) The sentence does contain a blatant grammatical error, though. The subject of the verb *were*, which is plural, is the noun *team*, which is singular. (At least it is in standard American English. In standard British English, however, collective words like *team* are considered plural, so be careful, Brits—this is an American test!) So choice (C) is the correct response, because the correct verb form is *was*.

The College Hill Method of attacking Identifying Sentence Errors questions:

1. Read the entire sentence normally, ignoring the underlined parts. Just try to understand what the sentence is trying to say and don't analyze too deeply.

2. If any part of the sentence sounds wrong, notice whether the problem can be fixed by changing an underlined portion. Although the question does not require you to correct the error, do your best to identify the error as one of the grammatical errors discussed in Lessons 13–23.

3. If the sentence sounds correct, choose (E).

4. For easier questions, trust your ear. For tougher questions, rely on your knowledge of the formal rules.

2. Make sure it's a legitimate mistake

If an underlined portion sounds wrong, try to make sure that it's a legitimate grammatical mistake, like those discussed in Lessons 13–23. Just because you can say something differently doesn't mean that the original phrasing is wrong.

<u>Had the speeches been</u> any longer, the assembly <u>would have needed to be</u> extended <u>into</u> the next
    A   B   C
<u>class period</u>. <u>No error</u>
  D   E

The first phrase, *Had the speeches been,* may sound strange to your ear. You may prefer to say *If the speeches had been.* However, both phrases are acceptable. The original phrase doesn't violate any rule of grammar. Similarly, instead of *would have needed to be*, you might prefer to say *would have had to be.* But this is merely a matter of preference. The original phrasing is fine too. The correct response to this question is (E), no error. Every grammar or usage error that you are expected to spot and fix is detailed in Lessons 13–23.

3. How to attack tough Identifying Sentence Errors questions

Process of elimination

What if your ear doesn't catch a mistake? In this case, the sentence might be correct, or it might contain a subtle error. First eliminate the underlined portions that are clearly okay. If you can get it down to two choices, make your best guess.

The systematic approach

If you know your grammar rules, you can attack the tougher questions systematically. Identify the parts of speech in the suspicious portion, and check the following questions as necessary.

Check any verbs

- Does the verb agree with its subject in person and number? (see Lesson 13)
- Is the verb in the right tense? (see Lesson 18)
- Does the verb require the subjunctive mood? If so, is it in standard form? (see Lesson 20)
- Are any past participles in the incorrect form? (see Lesson 22)

Check any pronouns

- Does it require an antecedent, and if so, is the antecedent clear? (see Lesson 16)
- Does it agree in number and person with its antecedent? (see Lesson 16)
- Is the pronoun in the proper case, that is, subjective (*I, he, she, we, they*), objective (*me, him, her, us, them*), or possessive (*my, your, his, her, our, their*)? (see Lesson 16)

Check any prepositions

- Is the preposition part of an idiomatic phrase, and if so, is it in the standard form? (see Lesson 19)

Check any modifiers

- Is every modifier near the word it modifies, or is it misplaced or dangling? (see Lesson 17)
- Is every modifier in the correct form? (see Lesson 17)
- Is every modifier logical? (see Lesson 17)

Check any comparisons

- Are the things being compared the same *kind* of thing? (see Lesson 15)
- Are any of the *two vs. many* errors being made? (see Lesson 15)
- Are any of the *countable vs. uncountable* errors being made? (see Lesson 15)
- Are the things being compared in parallel form? (see Lesson 14)

Check any lists

- Are the items in the list in parallel form? (see Lesson 14)

Check any odd-sounding words

- Is an illogical or redundant word being used? (see Lesson 21)

Don't fear perfection

Like any other answer choice, (E), no error, should occur about 20% (or 1/5) of the time. (If it didn't, the test would contain a bias that the "test-tricks" folks would jump all over.) Therefore, don't be afraid to choose (E), no error, when the sentence seems to have no clear problems. If you choose (E) half of the time, though, perhaps you should look more closely for errors.

Identifying Sentence Errors practice

The following sentences may contain errors in grammar, usage, diction (choice of words), or idiom. Some of the sentences are correct. No sentence contains more than one error.

If the sentence contains an error, it is underlined and lettered. The parts that are not underlined are correct.

If there is an error, select the part that must be changed to correct the sentence.

If there is no error, choose (E).

EXAMPLE:

By the time <u>they reached</u> the halfway point
                 A

<u>in the race</u>, most <u>of the runners</u> <u>hadn't hardly</u>
  B   C   D

begun to hit their stride. <u>No error</u>
                        E

ANSWER: D

1 There <u>seemed</u> to be no hope that either Franklin <u>nor</u>
       A   B

his brother <u>would be chosen</u> for the team, since
           C

neither was <u>able to attend</u> practices. <u>No error</u>
          D   E

2 Ever since the town <u>was founded</u> over three
               A

hundred years ago, there <u>was</u> a family-owned
                B

tavern <u>in the center</u> of the town square, but now
      C

it <u>is in danger</u> of demolition. <u>No error</u>
    D   E

3 The college has long endeavored to bolster

<u>their</u> endowment in order <u>to provide</u> financial
A   B

aid <u>to</u> all students <u>in need</u> of assistance.
    C   D

<u>No error</u>
  E

4 The means <u>by which</u> fusion reactors <u>create</u> energy
           A   B

by <u>turning</u> hydrogen into helium is nearly identical
    C

to <u>the sun</u>. <u>No error</u>
   D   E

5 Although most voters <u>claim to have</u> liberal
                A

views on many political issues, <u>but</u> many of
                 B

them <u>tend to vote for</u> socially <u>conservative</u>
    C   D

candidates. <u>No error</u>
      E

6 The most recent <u>plan to ease</u> hostilities <u>between</u> the
        A   B

warring factions addresses the matter of civil rights

but <u>fails to resolve</u> the long-standing <u>dispute over</u>
   C   D

minority representation in the government.

<u>No error</u>
  E

Answer Key

Identifying Sentence Errors practice

1. **B** The use of *either* in this sentence requires the use of *or* rather than *nor*. Don't be mislead by the "negativity" of the phrase *no hope—either* and *or* belong together.
   (Lesson 14, Parallelism)

2. **B** The phrase *ever since the town was founded* conveys a tense extending from the past to the present, that is, the present perfect tense. Therefore the main verb should be changed to *has been*.
   (Lesson 18, Tense and voice problems)

3. **A** The plural pronoun *their* does not agree with its singular antecedent *college*, and should be changed to *its*.
   (Lesson 16, Pronoun problems)

4. **D** The original sentence makes an illogical comparison. The *means by which fusion reactors create energy* should be compared to *the means by which the sun creates energy*, rather than to *the sun* itself.
   (Lesson 15, Comparison problems)

5. **B** The word *but* is redundant, because the word *although* has already established the contrasting relationship between the clauses.
   (Lesson 17, Modifier problems)
   (Lesson 23, Awkwardness and coordination)

6. **E** The sentence is correct.

Lesson 11—Improving paragraphs

1. How to attack Improving Paragraphs questions

The SAT Writing includes about six Improving Paragraphs questions. In this section, you are given a draft of a short essay that needs revision, and are asked questions regarding how to improve the diction, logic, and grammar of the passage.

Although they look somewhat similar, don't confuse Improving Paragraphs questions with Critical Reading questions. Improving Paragraphs passages are much more rudimentary, and the questions are focused on improving the essay. You don't need to read the passage as carefully as you would a Critical Reading passage, but it's often a good idea to get the basic gist of the passage—as long as it doesn't take too long—before looking at the questions.

Isolated Sentences

Some Improving Paragraphs questions ask you to improve a single sentence in the passage. These are like Improving Sentences questions, except that often choice (A) might *not* leave the sentence as is. In other words, there may not be a "no error" choice.

Which of the following is the best way to revise sentence 7 (reproduced below)?

If the students would of known in advance about the shortage, they could have prevented the crisis.

(A) If the students would have known
(B) It being that the students might have known
(C) If the students had known
(D) Being known by the students
(E) If it had been that the students knew

The verb phrase *would of known* uses improper diction for the subjunctive mood. Choice (C) corrects the problem.

Sentences in Context

Some Improving Paragraphs questions ask you to revise particular sentences in terms of the context of the passage. These questions usually begin with the phrase *In context...*

To answer "in context" questions, read the sentences *before* the one mentioned and think about how to link the sentences logically. These questions often focus on transitions, or logical guideposts for a reader. Transition words include *therefore, yet, nonetheless, although,* and *furthermore.*

In context, which of the following is the best version of sentence 12 (reproduced below)?

The racers were shivering as the race began.

(A) (as it is now)
(B) Nevertheless, the racers were shivering
(C) Furthermore, the racers were shivering
(D) Therefore, the racers were shivering
(E) All the while, the racers were shivering

Since the question begins with the phrase *In context*, the correct answer depends on what immediately precedes sentence 12. If the previous sentence were something like *The race organizers had arranged for large, powerful heaters to be placed all around the starting line,* then (B) would provide the most logical transition, because the sentence describes something unexpected. If, however, the previous sentence were *The temperature had plummeted twenty degrees in the hours before the race was to start,* then (D) would make more sense because it shows a cause and effect.

Adding, Arranging, or Removing Sentences

Some Improving Paragraphs questions ask you how adding, rearranging, or removing sentences might improve the unity or logic of the paragraph.

> Which of the following sentences contributes the least to the cohesiveness of the third paragraph?
>
> Which of the following is the most logical order for the sentences in the second paragraph?
>
> Which of the following would be the most suitable sentence to insert after sentence 5?

These questions require you to consider how the sentences fit together in a paragraph. A paragraph may require an extra sentence or phrase to clarify an idea. Also, any sentence that doesn't pertain to the main idea of the paragraph should be removed. A paragraph may also be more logical if the sentences are rearranged.

2. Consider your attack options

On the Improving Paragraphs section, you may attack the questions in one of two ways. You can read the passage quickly and answer the questions in the order they are given—a classic, straightforward approach. Getting the gist of the passage helps most students to answer the questions more efficiently, and it doesn't take too long. However, you may prefer to first answer the Isolated Sentences questions—before even reading the passage—because they don't require you to understand the passage as a whole. This approach gives some students a sense of control over the questions, and helps them to get through the questions more efficiently.

Improving Paragraphs practice

Below is a draft of an essay that needs improvement. Some sentences may contain grammatical errors, and the paragraphs may need to be altered to improve their logic, clarity, and cohesiveness. Read the passage and answer the questions that follow.

(1) Scientists have proposed many theories about the extinction of the dinosaurs. (2) This issue is very interesting because it seems that many dinosaurs were very fierce and meat-eating. (3) Today, when a species becomes extinct, we usually assume that it was because of competition from other species or some human activity. (4) But the dinosaurs had very little competition for food, except among other dinosaurs, and they became extinct well before the rise of *homo sapiens*. (5) A few scientists believe that disease could have played a small role, but this doesn't explain the fact that so many different species were eliminated. (6) The most widely held theories attribute the demise of the dinosaurs to climate changes or some catastrophic geological event, like a meteor impact.

(7) For decades, the consensus among paleontologists has been that a large meteor or comet struck what is now the Yucatan peninsula in Mexico some 65 million years ago. (8) This impact caused the earth's atmosphere to fill with enormous amounts of fine particles, which blocked the sun's rays, producing dramatic shifts in climate.

(9) Evidence for this theory includes a widespread layer of iridium, a rare element that is abundant in meteorites, in rock strata that correspond to the era in which the dinosaurs became extinct. (10) Recent studies have questioned whether the Yucatan impact could have been the one that killed off the dinosaurs. (11) One scientist has published a study suggesting that the Yucatan impact actually occurred 300,000 years before the dinosaurs became extinct. (12) But this does not question the theory that a meteor contributed to the extinction of the dinosaurs, only which meteor.

1 Which sentence contributes the least to the first paragraph?

(A) sentence 2
(B) sentence 3
(C) sentence 4
(D) sentence 5
(E) sentence 6

2 Which of the following is the best revision of the underlined portion of sentence 3 (reproduced below)?

Today, when a species becomes extinct, we usually assume that it was because of competition from other species or some human activity.

(A) say it was because of
(B) attribute the demise to
(C) chalk it up to
(D) assume that it was probably because of
(E) make it due to

3 In context, which of the following is the best way to revise sentence 5?

(A) Change "were" to "have been".
(B) Change the comma to a period and eliminate the rest of the sentence.
(C) Change "many" to "much".
(D) Change "could have" to "would have".
(E) Change "this" to "this theory".

4 Which of the following is the best sentence to insert after sentence 8 to end the second paragraph?

(A) It is now necessary to shift our discussion from the theory to the facts.
(B) However, scientists are not in full agreement about what caused the extinction of the dinosaurs.
(C) These shifts likely killed off the dinosaurs' food supply, causing their demise in a matter of years.
(D) Some dinosaurs were taller than an apartment building, while others were as small as dogs.
(E) Several very instructive documentaries have been made recently about the manner in which the dinosaurs became extinct.

Answer Key

Improving Paragraphs practice

1. **A**   Sentence 2 can be eliminated because it does not contribute to the topic of the paragraph, which is the extinction of the dinosaurs and theories explaining it. The fact that some dinosaurs were *fierce and meat-eating* is not related to any theory of extinction.

2. **B**   In the original sentence, the pronoun *it* does not have a clear antecedent. It refers to the *extinction* or *demise*, but neither of these words is used in the sentence. Choice (B) clarifies the reference.

3. **E**   Sentence 5 is unclear because the pronoun *this* does not have an obvious antecedent. It can be taken to refer to *the fact that some scientists have a particular theory*, to *disease*, or to the *small role*. None of these are logical, though. The pronoun must be referring to the theory itself, and choice (E) is the only one that clarifies this reference.

4. **C**   The second paragraph begins to explain the theory that the dinosaurs became extinct because a meteor impact disrupted the earth's climate. The theory is not explained in much detail, however, and a sentence showing how climate shift killed the dinosaurs would strengthen the explanation. This is what choice (C) does. Choices (B), (D), and (E) stray from the topic of the second paragraph, and choice (A) provides no information whatsoever. It merely provides an awkwardly self-conscious transition that is unnecessary because sentence 9 provides a clear transition from a discussion of a theory to a discussion of evidence.

Part IV
The Fundamental Rules of Grammar for Writing and Editing

Interlude—Keeping perspective

Lesson 12—The parts of speech

Lesson 13—Subject-verb agreement

Lesson 14—Parallelism

Lesson 15—Comparison problems

Lesson 16—Pronoun problems

Lesson 17—Modifier problems

Lesson 18—Tense and voice problems

Lesson 19—Idiom problems

Lesson 20—Mood problems

Lesson 21—Diction problems

Lesson 22—Irregular verbs

Lesson 23—Awkwardness and coordination

Interlude—Keeping perspective

I. Don't Sweat the Small Stuff

Sometimes it may seem as if there are hundreds of grammar rules to memorize. Perhaps a teacher once told you that you should never start a sentence with *Because*. Why? *Because it's a rule.* All irony aside, the SAT Writing will only test your knowledge of about a dozen grammatical rules that form the foundation of clear and logical writing. It won't test you on the silly pet peeves. Therefore, you should know the difference between the standard rules of practice and the arbitrary pet peeves.

2. Don't worry about *who* vs. *whom*

The SAT Writing test will probably not include any *who* vs. *whom* questions. These pronouns differ in *case*, a topic discussed in Lesson 16. You should know how to correct certain mistakes involving pronoun case, such as changing *just between you and I* to *just between you and me*. The distinction between *who* and *whom*, however, is not as clear as the distinction between *I* and *me*. For instance, *me* is always used in situations that call for an **object** to a verb, as in *The man approached me.* Similarly, *whom* is usually preferred in situations that call for an object, but **not always**. For instance, a sentence like *For whom are you voting?* is often excessively formal, even for published prose. Therefore, it is often acceptable to write *Who are you voting for?* even though the pronoun is acting as an object to the verb.

In fact, English pronouns have been evolving away from such "case markers" for centuries. For instance, where English used to have the subjective *thou* and the objective *thee*, it now has just one word to play both roles: *you.* Quite likely, English is evolving away from *whom* in the same way.

3. Don't worry about split infinitives

Split infinitives will not appear on the SAT Writing, so you won't have to spot or correct them. An infinitive is a *to*-phrase, like *to drop,* that represents the basic form of a verb (see Lesson 12). An infinitive is "split" when an adverb is wedged in the middle, as in *The news caused the stock price **to suddenly drop**.* In this case, you should "unsplit" the infinitive: *The news caused the stock price **to drop suddenly**.* The rule against splitting an infinitive, however, is not universal, because some ideas can't be expressed concisely without splitting infinitives. For instance, any unsplitting of the infinitive in the sentence *The company plans **to more than double** its revenue next year* will make the sentence wordier or more awkward. Try it and see.

4. Don't worry about ending a sentence with a preposition

One of the most popular pet peeves among English teachers is the preposition at the end of a sentence, as in *Who are you going with?* The SAT Writing will not include prepositions at the ends of sentences, so you won't need to spot or correct them. You should know, however, the "rule" against them is really just a suggestion, and that clear expression sometimes requires ending sentences with prepositions. We already noted one example above: the sentence *Who are you voting for?* sounds needlessly formal when we try to avoid ending it with a preposition. Winston Churchill once said, after someone had chastised him about this rule, *"That is the type of arrant pedantry up with which I will not put!"* **The best way to understand the "rule" is as a suggestion: avoid ending sentences with a preposition unless you have no better option.**

5. Don't worry about starting a sentence with *And, But,* or *Because*

Another thing that upsets some English teachers is starting a sentence with *And, But,* or *Because*. Because such rules are frequently broken by very good writers, you shouldn't worry about them on the SAT.

> *Next to the groundless notion that it is incorrect to end an English sentence with a preposition, perhaps the most widespread of many false beliefs about the use of our language is the equally groundless notion that it is incorrect to begin one with "but" or "and." As in the case of the superstition about the prepositional ending, no textbook supports it, but apparently about half of our teachers of English go out of their way to handicap their pupils by inculcating it. One cannot help wondering whether those who teach such monstrous doctrine ever read any English themselves.*
>
> —Charles Allen Lloyd, *We Who Speak English, and Our Ignorance of Our Mother Tongue* (1938)

Many eminent writers have flouted this rule.

> *Because of the war the situation in hospitals is, of course, serious.*
>
> —E. B. White, "A Weekend with the Angels," in *The Second Tree from the Corner* (1954)

> *If we view the paragraph as a discursive development of a proposition, we can predict that the topic sentence of the paragraph in question will generate a development based on objectives. And this is exactly what we do find.*
>
> —W. Ross Winterowd, *Rhetoric: A Synthesis* (1968)

> *But it must not be assumed that intelligent thinking can play no part in the formation of the goal and of ethical judgments.*
>
> —Albert Einstein, "Science and Religion" (1939) in *Ideas and Opinions* (1954)

Don't worry about fixing sentences on the SAT that begin with *And, But,* or *Because*. However, **always** fix clauses following a semicolon (;) or colon (:) that begin with *and, but* or *because*. A clause that follows a semicolon or colon must usually be an *independent clause* (see Lesson 12) that supports the previous independent clause. Therefore, starting such a clause with *and* is redundant, because the semicolon or colon already performs the job of a conjunction. Starting such a clause with *but* is illogical, because the semicolon or colon indicates a **supportive** relationship between the clauses, not a contrasting one. Starting such a clause with *because* is ungrammatical, because such a clause is **dependent** rather than **independent.**

6. Don't worry about starting sentences with adverbs like *Hopefully* or *Clearly*

Some English teachers claim that every adverb must modify a particular verb, adjective, or adverb in the sentence, so a sentence like *Obviously, the muddy windshield obscured her vision* is wrong, because the adjective *obviously* doesn't properly modify the verb *obscured*. (How can something *obscure obviously*?) This advice is plainly wrong. The word *Obviously* in this sentence is a **sentence modifier**. It conveys the speaker's attitude toward the statement the sentence makes, rather than modifying a particular word in the sentence. The word *Obviously* here simply means *I consider the following fact to be obvious*. But I think you'd agree it says so in a much more concise and elegant way.

Here is a partial list of some common sentence modifiers:

accordingly	*admittedly*	*arguably*	*consequently*
clearly	*curiously*	*fortunately*	*hopefully*
ironically	*paradoxically*	*regrettably*	*sadly*
strangely	*theoretically*		

7. Don't worry about possessive antecedents

The 2002 PSAT Writing contained the following question:

> Toni Morrison's genius enables <u>her to create</u> novels <u>that arise from</u> and <u>express</u> the injustice
>   A   B   C
> African Americans <u>have endured</u>. <u>No error</u>
>   D   E

The ETS gave an original answer of E, no error. But some teachers argued that the answer should be A, because *her* refers to the possessive *Toni Morrison's*. Possessives such as *Toni Morrison's* are adjectives, not nouns, and some English teachers were taught that pronouns cannot refer to nouns that have been "possessified" into adjectives. The ETS responded, appropriately, that to correct such an "error" would make the sentence sound very awkward—the word *her* would have to be replaced by *Toni Morrison*, which is clearly redundant. To avoid needless wrangling, however, the ETS threw out the question. Although most textbooks agree that there is no such rule against possessive antecedents (the antecedent is the word the pronoun refers to), you can be sure the ETS will try to avoid such "mistakes" on future SATs.

You won't need to worry about the "problem" of possessive antecedents on the SAT. However, you do need to be sure that definite pronouns such as *it, he, she,* or *they* refer to clear and unambiguous antecedents.

8. Don't worry about *that* vs. *which*

Some writers make themselves nuts trying to figure out whether to use *that* or *which* when they write. Thankfully, you won't need to worry about this on the SAT Writing.

However, if you want to know how best to choose between *that* and *which* when you write, here's the rule: *which* is best in **non-restrictive** clauses and *that* is best in **restrictive** clauses. A restrictive clause gives **essential** information about the noun that precedes it, as in *The books **that are on that table** are for sale.* A non-restrictive clause, on the other hand, gives **incidental or non-essential** information about the noun that precedes it, as in *The books, **which have been discounted**, are all best-sellers.* Still too complicated? Here's a simpler rule: *which* almost always follows a comma. If there's no comma, *that* probably works better. Another simple rule: *what* usually works better than *that which*.

Incorrect:	*Second Federal is the only bank in town **which** does not finance mortgages.*
Better:	*Second Federal is the only bank in town **that** does not finance mortgages.*

The clause following *town* is **restrictive**. If it were omitted, the meaning of the sentence would change completely.

Incorrect:	*The corporation approved of the commercial **which** lasted all of 20 seconds.*
Better:	*The corporation approved of the commercial, **which** lasted all of 20 seconds.*

The clause following *commercial* is **non-restrictive**, and so should be separated from the main part of the sentence with a comma. Even if this clause were omitted, the sentence would still make sense.

Awkward:	*We pursue most fervently **that which** we cannot have.*
Better:	*We pursue most fervently **what** we cannot have.*

The two adjacent pronouns in the original sentence serve as the objects of the two clauses, but since they refer to the same thing, we replace them with a single pronoun.

9. Don't worry too much about *bad/badly* and *good/well*

On the SAT Writing, you will sometimes be expected to spot and fix problems with modifiers, such as an adjective being used where an adverb is needed. Don't worry too much about the *bad/badly* or *good/well* issue, though.

Some folks think that you should never say *I feel good,* that you should say *I feel well* instead, because *well* is an adverb modifying the verb *feel.* Likewise, they think you shouldn't say *This tastes bad,* but rather *This tastes badly* because *badly* is an adverb modifying the verb *taste.* Such an analysis is completely wrong. Both *I feel good* and *I feel well* are good, grammatical sentences. In the first sentence, *feel* is a linking verb joining *I* to its adjective *good.* Likewise, in the second sentence, *feel* is a linking verb joining *I* to its adjective *well.* In this sentence, *well* is **not** an adverb (as in *she plays very well*), but an adjective meaning *healthy* (as in *they were sick, but now they are well*). The sentence *This tastes badly,* on the other hand, is illogical. The sentence is describing the *bad taste* of something, not the *bad manner in which something tastes.* The correct phrasing is *This tastes bad.*

10. Don't worry about disappearing *thats*

On some SAT Writing questions, you might notice a "disappearing *that*" as in *I like the sweater you gave me* rather than *I like the sweater **that** you gave me.* You should know that either sentence is fine. The sentence *I like the sweater you gave me* uses ellipsis—the omission of one or more words that are understood implicitly. Since no reader would ever be confused about what *I like the sweater you gave me* means, there's no need for the *that.*

11. Don't worry about disappearing words, as long as they are implied by parallelism

Consider this sentence.

> *The Republicans reacted to the president's speech with sustained applause; the Democrats, studied silence.*

This may sound a bit strange to your ear, and therefore wrong. It may also seem to violate a standard rule of grammar, namely, that phrases following a semicolon must be independent clauses; that is, they should be able to stand alone as sentences. The phrase *the Democrats, studied silence* may not seem like a well-constructed sentence. However, this sentence is perfectly acceptable because it is equivalent to

> *The Republicans reacted to the President's speech with sustained applause; the Democrats [reacted to the President's speech with] studied silence.*

The comma in the original sentence indicates ellipsis, or the deliberate omission of words. These words can be omitted because they are implied by parallelism with the first clause. When good readers read the complete sentence, they get the sense that they are being told something they already know, and so the writer is wasting space and time. A good writer can omit these words and expect that the reader will pull them from the previous clause.

Lesson 12—The parts of speech

1. Words are what words do

Mercifully, the SAT Writing does not test your ability to identify parts of speech. You won't be asked to circle the verbs, the pronouns, or the prepositions in a sentence. Nevertheless, to ace the multiple-choice portion of the SAT Writing, it helps enormously to know your parts of speech. If you know your parts of speech, you can begin to see whether or not they are being used properly. In the following Lessons, we will make liberal use of the parts of speech, because knowing them is the only way to explain why a sentence doesn't work and how to correct it.

Don't try to learn the parts of speech by memorizing lists of words. The *part of speech* of a word is simply *what role it is playing* within a sentence. Prepositions, for example, are not simply words that are on a preposition list, and pronouns are not simply words on a pronoun list. They are words that perform particular roles in a sentence. If you know the role a word or phrase plays in a sentence, then you know its part of speech. Words are what words do within a sentence.

2. Verbs—the sentence drivers

The most important word in every sentence is a **verb**, and every sentence requires one. In fact, a verb is the *only* word that a sentence requires. The shortest sentence in English is just a verb: *Go.* This single word conveys a complete thought: *You should go now.* Without a verb, a sentence can't convey an idea. Therefore, understanding sentences begins with understanding their verbs. Every verb must have a **subject**, that is, a **noun or pronoun** that does the action of the verb. In the sentence *Go*, the implied subject is *you,* since it is understood that the speaker is addressing the listener. Often, a verb also requires an **object**, that is, a **noun or pronoun** that receives the action of the verb. The sentence *Go* has no object, because the sentence is not telling the listener where to go. If the sentence were *Go to the store*, then *store* would be an indirect object of the verb.

A verb is not merely an action word. In fact, many kinds of words convey action. The verb is the word that, when combined with the subject (and perhaps an object), conveys the central idea of the sentence.

Is the word *swimming* a verb? If you have simply learned that a verb is an action word, then you might say yes, *swimming* represents an action, so it must be a verb. Not so fast. Consider these three sentences.

> *I am swimming.*
>
> *I love swimming.*
>
> *I fed the swimming ducks.*

What is the verb in the first sentence? The central idea of the sentence is that *I am doing something*; therefore the verb is *am swimming.* (Yes, a verb is often a phrase.) The word *swimming* is part of the verb phrase, and so it is called a verb **participle.**

What is the verb in the second sentence? The central idea of the sentence is that *I love something*; therefore the verb is *love.* The word *swimming* represents the thing that I love, so it is the **object** of the verb *love*, and is therefore a **noun**. Words that come from verbs ending in *-ing* but are used as nouns are called **gerunds**.

What is the verb in the third sentence? The central idea of the sentence is that *I fed something*; therefore the verb is *fed,* and its object is *ducks.* The word *swimming* in this case modifies the noun *ducks*, and therefore is an **adjective.**

3. Nouns

Although you probably learned that nouns are words that represent *people, places,* and *things,* it's important to know that they can also represent *states of being, emotions, qualities, quantities, events,* and *activities.* But, as we just discussed, looking up a word in a list does not identify it as well as determining its role in the sentence. So what do nouns *do* in a sentence?

A noun is a word that represents what *does* the action of a verb or what *receives* the action of a verb. It also is what complements a preposition.

> *The party planners did a lot of negotiating because they really wanted to get the best prices.*

Okay, so where are the nouns in this sentence? Take a minute and circle them before reading on.

It turns out it's not so easy. The nouns are *planners, lot, negotiating, to get,* and *prices.* You get partial credit if you circled *they,* because although it is a **pronoun** (which we will discuss next), it plays the same role as a noun in the sentence. Did you circle *party*? Although *party* is usually used as a noun, this sentence uses it as an **adjective**. It describes the *planners.* You might also have missed *negotiating* and *to get* because they look like verbs. But remember, what matters is not how the words look, but how they are used. The central idea of the sentence is that *the planners did something.* What was the *something?* A *lot.* Therefore *lot* is the **object** of the verb, so it is a noun. A lot *of what? Negotiating.* So *negotiating* is the object of the **preposition** *of.* (As we just discussed, *-ing* words that are used as nouns are called **gerunds.**) There is a second idea in the sentence, also—*they wanted something.* What did they want? *To get something.* Therefore *to get* is the object of the verb *wanted,* so it is a noun. Phrases that represent the basic form of a verb, like *to eat, to think,* and *to be,* are called **infinitives.** Although infinitives come from verbs, they usually play the role of **nouns** in sentences, just as gerunds do. So your sentence should look something like this:

> *The party planners did a lot of negotiating because they really wanted to get the best prices.*
>   *n.*   *n.*   *n.*   *pron.*   *n.*   *n.*

4. Clauses

A phrase with a subject and verb that conveys a complete thought is called a clause. If the clause could stand alone as a sentence, it is called an *independent clause.* If it cannot, it is called a *subordinate* or *dependent clause.*

> *The pipes froze because the furnace broke.*

This sentence consists of two clauses—*the pipes froze* and *because the furnace broke.* Notice that each phrase contains a subject and verb and conveys a thought. The first clause could be a sentence, but the second could not. The first is an independent clause, but the conjunction *because* makes the second a subordinate clause.

5. Pronouns

A pronoun is a word that takes the place of a specified noun, or refers to an unspecified thing. Pronouns that refer to specific nouns (like *it, she,* and *they*) are called *definite,* and nouns that refer to unspecified things (like *anyone, neither,* or *something*) are called *indefinite.*

Pronouns are usually pretty easy to spot. The most common are *he, she, you, we, they,* and *it,* but they also include *that, which, those, them, anyone, anything, someone, something, why, where, when, how,* and *what.*

6. Prepositions

> **A preposition is any word that can complete one of these two sentences:**
> *The squirrel ran _____ the tree.*
> *Democracy is government _____ the people.*
> **A preposition indicates *relative position* or *direction* with regard to a noun. Therefore, every preposition is always followed by a noun phrase.**

Two of the most common prepositions are *to* and *for*, as in *I ran to the park* and *The package was for me*. But *to* and *for* are not always used as prepositions. As we just said, prepositions must be followed by noun phrases, because they indicate a position or direction relative to a noun. Consider these two sentences:

> *I like to dance.*

> *The meeting was postponed, for it was getting late.*

In these sentences, neither *to* nor *for* is a preposition, because neither is followed by a noun phrase. In the first sentence, *to* is followed by the verb *dance*. In the second sentence, *for* is followed by the clause *it was getting late*. In the first sentence, *to* is used as part of an **infinitive**, which, as we just discussed, is a noun phrase. In the second sentence, *for* is used as a **conjunction**, much like *because* or *since*.

7. Prepositional phrases

> A prepositional phrase is a preposition and the noun phrase that follows it. Every prepositional phrase is a modifying phrase, serving to modify some noun, verb, adjective, or adverb in the sentence.

Examples of prepositional phrases include *in the mood, to the store,* and *with my friend*. In the sentence *Eleanor was not in the mood*, the prepositional phrase *in the mood* modifies the proper noun *Eleanor*, and so it is an **adjective phrase**. In the sentence *I ran to the store*, the prepositional phrase *to the store* modifies the verb *ran*, and so it is an **adverbial phrase**.

8. Modifiers

> A modifier is any word or phrase that helps describe *another* word or phrase. An *adjective* or *adjective phrase* modifies a noun. An *adverb* or *adverb phrase* modifies a verb, adjective, or adverb.

> *The party planners did a lot of negotiating because they really wanted to get the best prices.*

What are the modifiers in this sentence? Take a minute to circle them before reading on.

The modifiers are *party, of negotiating, really,* and *best*. The word *party* tells us what kind of *planners* they are, so it modifies a noun and is therefore an **adjective**. The phrase *of negotiating* modifies the noun *lot*, so it is an **adjective phrase**. The word *really* modifies the verb *wanted*, so it is an **adverb**. The word *best* modifies the noun *prices*, so it is an **adjective.** So your sentence should look something like this:

> *The (party) planners did a lot (of negotiating) because they (really) wanted to get the (best) prices.*
>   adj.   adj.   adv.   adj.

9. Participles

A participle is an adjective that is derived from a verb. There are two kinds of participles—*present* participles like *breaking* and *seeing*, and *past* participles like *broken* and *seen*. Participles, like verbs, have noun *subjects*.

When joined by **helping verbs**, participles can form **verb phrases**, as in *Jane <u>was whistling</u>* or *I <u>have seen</u> that movie*. When they are used without helping verbs, however, they are adjectives.

> *Taking no chances, Greta arrived an hour early for the test.*

This sentence begins with a modifying phrase, *taking no chances*. Since it is not preceded by a helping verb, it is not part of a verb phrase. (The verb in this sentence is *arrived*.) But like a verb, it has a subject, *Greta*, because it suggests that *Greta took no chances*. The relationship between a participle and the noun it modifies is very similar to the relationship between a verb and its subject.

Lesson 13—Subject-verb agreement

1. Subject-verb agreement

One of the most common grammatical mistakes tested on the SAT Writing is **subject-verb disagreement**.

> *The children is playing in the park.*

Here, the verb *is* does not agree in number with its subject *children*. *Children* is plural, but *is* is singular. The verb should be changed to *are*.

Catching subject-verb disagreement is easier when the verb immediately follows the subject. SAT Writing questions, however, aren't usually so easy. They will include more complicated sentences in which the verb doesn't immediately follow the subject.

> You should be able to pick out the subject and verb of each clause in a sentence, and determine whether or not they agree. It helps to know the tricky ways that sentences can hide subject-verb disagreement.

2. Inverted sentences

> In most clauses, the subject comes *before* the verb. Sometimes, however, a clause is inverted—its subject comes *after* the verb. Sentences that start with *There is* or *There are,* for instance, are inverted. To check subject-verb agreement in these sentences, it helps to uninvert them.

> *There is many flies in the barn.*

This sentence is inverted. The verb *is* comes before its subject *flies*. The word *There* serves as a **dummy subject**, holding the place for the real subject, *flies*. Since *there* can be either plural or singular, you can't tell that the sentence has a problem after reading just the first two words. To see the problem more clearly, uninvert the sentence. Simply rearrange the words, and eliminate the dummy subject, so that the subject comes before the verb.

> *Many flies is in the barn.*

The sentence is now right side up. The verb *is* immediately follows the subject *flies*, and you have eliminated the dummy subject. Now the mistake is even more obvious. The verb should be changed to *are*.

3. Intervening words

> Sometimes a subject and verb are separated by a bunch of other words. You need to be able to ignore the intervening words and focus just on the subject and verb.

> *The columnist, like so many other experts, were convinced that the new program would fail.*

If you read this sentence quickly, it may not sound wrong because the verb *were convinced,* which is plural, immediately follows the noun *experts*, which is also plural. But *experts* is not the subject of the verb. It is part of a modifying phrase between commas. This kind of modifying phrase is called an **interrupter**. **Every good sentence must remain grammatical even when its interrupters are removed.** In other words, an interrupter can never contain the main subject and verb of the sentence. Remove the interrupter and look again.

> *The columnist were convinced that the new program would fail.*

Now the mistake is easier to spot. The verb should be *was convinced*.

4. Tricky subjects

Sometimes it's hard to tell whether a subject is singular or plural. Here are some rules to help.

The word *and* combines two nouns into a plural subject, as in *Jane and Bob are sick.* Any nouns within interrupters, however, are not included in the subject, as in *Jane, as well as Bob, is sick.*

The words *neither* and *either* are singular when they stand alone as subjects.

> Neither *is* very expensive.   Either *is* sufficient.

They are also singular when they are part of a *neither of* or *either of* phrase.

> Neither of the boys *is* ready to take the test.

However, the phrases *neither A nor B* and *either A or B* have the same number as the noun in *B*.

> Either Ben or his brothers *have taken* the car.

People often confuse the numbers of the following words, so here's a list to keep them straight.

Singular	Plural	Correct sentence
phenomenon	*phenomena*	*Phenomena* like that *are* surprisingly common.
medium	*media*	The *media have ignored* this story completely.
datum	*data*	The *data* on my computer *have been* corrupted.
criterion	*criteria*	Such a *criterion has* yet to be met.

Subject-verb agreement practice

Next to each noun or noun phrase, write "S" if it is singular and "P" if it is plural.

1. *Neither rain nor snow* _____
2. *A crowd of rowdy fans* _____
3. *Media* _____
4. *Criterion* _____
5. *One or two* _____
6. *Everything* _____
7. *Either of the candidates* _____
8. *Phenomena* _____

Circle the subject in each sentence, and choose the correct verb.

9. *The flock of geese (was/were) startled by the shotgun blast.*

10. *The data on my computer (was/were) completely erased when the power failed.*

11. *Neither of the twins (is/are) allergic to penicillin.*

12. *Much of what I hear in those lectures (go/goes) in one ear and out the other.*

13. *Amy, along with Jamie and Jen, (is/are) applying to Mount Holyoke.*

14. *Amid the lilies and wildflowers (were/was) one solitary rose.*

15. *Either David or his brothers (is/are) in charge of bringing the drinks.*

16. *There (is/are) hardly even a speck of dirt left on the carpet.*

17. *"Stop right there!" (shout/shouts) the Bailey Brothers, who are standing in front of me.*

18. There (were/was) at least a hundred people in the room.

19. There (is/are), in my opinion, far too many smokers in this restaurant.

20. Over that hill (is/are) thousands of bison.

21. Never before (have/has) there been such voices heard on the public airwaves.

Label each verb in the following sentences with a "V" and each subject with an "S." If any verbs are incorrect, cross them out and write the correct form in the blank.

22. Every player on both the Falcons and the Rockets were at the party after the game. _____

23. There has been a theater and a toy store in the mall ever since it opened. _____

24. Either Eric or his brother is hosting the party this year. _____

25. The proceeds from the sale of every auctioned item goes to charity. _____

26. There is more than three years remaining on her contract. _____

27. Neither of the girls were frightened by the wild animals that scurried incessantly past their tent. _____

28. The technology behind high definition television, DVDs, and CDs have transformed nearly every aspect of the home entertainment industry. _____

29. Every player on both teams were concerned about the goalie's injury. _____

30. The company's sponsorship of charitable foundations and mentorship programs have garnered many commendations from philanthropic organizations. _____

31. Neither the children nor their parents utters a word when Mrs. Denny tells her stories. _____

32. How important is your strength training and your diet to your daily regimen? _____

5. Trimming Sentences

Spotting subject-verb disagreement is easier when you ignore the non-essential parts of a sentence. At College Hill Coaching, we call this process "trimming," and we teach it as an essential writing tool. It does more than just help you to spot subject-verb disagreement. Trimming isolates the most important part of each sentence, the subject-predicate "core," so that you can check whether your writing is clear and effective.

How to trim a sentence

Let's examine a sentence and see how trimming helps you to improve it.

> *My chief concern with this budget, which I have not voiced until today, are the drastic cuts in school funds.*

Step 1: Cross out all non-essential prepositional phrases.

Remember that a **prepositional phrase** is a phrase that starts with a preposition and includes the noun or noun phrase that follows, like *from sea to shining sea, in the beginning,* and *with hat in hand.*

> *My chief concern ~~with this budget~~, which I have not voiced ~~until today~~, are the drastic cuts ~~in school funds~~.*

Step 2: Cross out all interrupting phrases.

An **interrupting phrase** is a modifying phrase, usually separated from the main sentence by commas, that interrupts the flow of the sentence. In this case, the interrupter is the phrase between the commas.

> *My chief concern ~~with this budget, which I have not voiced until today~~, are the drastic cuts ~~in school funds~~.*

Step 3: Cross out any other non-essential modifiers and modifying phrases.

Remember that modifiers are **adjectives** and **adverbs**, as well as modifying phrases like **participial phrases** (see Lesson 12). (Most modifiers are not essential to the basic meaning of a sentence, but some are, such as *smart* in the sentence *Martha is smart.* In this case, *smart* is the **predicate adjective**, and therefore essential to the sentence.) In our sentence, the non-essential modifiers are *chief* and *drastic.*

> *My ~~chief~~ concern ~~with this budget, which I have not voiced until today~~, are the ~~drastic~~ cuts ~~in school funds~~.*

What remains is the core of the sentence: *My concern are the cuts.* The most obvious problem here is the subject-verb disagreement—*concern* is singular, but *are* is plural. To make it more grammatical, you may want to simply change the verb: *My concern is the cuts.* But this isn't a great sentence either. The *concern* is singular, but the *cuts* are plural, so equating them seems illogical. Furthermore, the verb *is* is very weak, and doesn't convey much meaning. Trimming the sentence shows us that the core of the sentence is weak. It should be reworded with a stronger verb.

> *Although I have not said so until today, I object to the drastic cuts in school funds that are proposed in this budget.*

Trimming sentences practice

Trim each of the following sentences and correct any verb problems.

1. *The team of advisors, arriving ahead of schedule, were met at the airport by the Assistant Prime Minister.*

2. *The flock of birds that darted over the lake were suddenly an opalescent silver.*

3. *Carmen, along with her three sisters, are unlikely to be swayed by arguments supporting David's position.*

4. *Juggling the demands of both school and my social agenda often seem too much to bear.*

5. *Others on the committee, like the chairman Amanda Sanders, is concerned about the lack of attention given to school safety.*

6. *One in every three Americans agree strongly with the statement: "Anyone who would run for political office is not worth voting for."*

7. *The fact that humans have committed so many atrocities have forced some historians to adopt a cynical perspective on human nature.*

Trim each sentence; then revise it to make it clearer and more forceful, changing the subject and verb, if necessary.

8. *Nearly inevitably, advancements, or those being popularly regarded as such, have to do with modifications, not overhaul.*

   Trimmed: _____

   Revised: _____

   _____

9. *The development of the new country's governmental system was affected in a negative regard by the lack of cohesiveness of the revolutionary army.*

   Trimmed: _____

   Revised: _____

   _____

6. Tips for improving your essay

When writing your essay, pay close attention to the subject-verb pair in each sentence. Trim your sentences mentally to make sure that the subject and verb agree and convey your idea clearly and forcefully. You may not be able to do this for every sentence, but do it at least for important sentences like thesis statements.

> *The lack of economic programs and no big country being ready to join it symbolized the problems the League of Nations had in getting established.*

Trim the sentence and check it for agreement and strength.

> *The lack and no country being ready to join it symbolized the problems.*

Yikes! That does *not* convey a clear and forceful idea. Revise it using a stronger subject-verb-object.

> *The League of Nations never established itself because it lacked viable economic programs and the support of the larger countries.*

Try to avoid "dummy" subjects, because they usually produce weak sentences.

> *There is a lot of concern among the teachers about extending the school day.*

This sentence is weak because of the dummy subject and weak verb—*There is*. The logical subject of the sentence is *the teachers*.

> *The teachers are very concerned about extending the school day.*

7. Tips for the multiple-choice questions

If a verb is underlined on a multiple-choice question, trim the sentence to check that it agrees with its subject. The ability to trim a sentence is one of the most useful editing skills, so perfect your trimming skills with the exercises on the preceding pages.

> The thrill of exploring undersea caves and <u>swimming</u> with fish and dolphins <u>were</u> beyond <u>what</u>
>   A   B   C
> Alicia <u>had even dreamed</u>. <u>No error</u>
>   D   E

Most students will not spot a problem with this sentence right away. If you trim away the prepositional phrase *of exploring undersea caves and swimming with fish and dolphins*, the error is easier to catch: *The thrill were beyond what Alicia had even dreamed.* Clearly, the verb does not agree with its subject and (B) should be changed to *was*.

Also, make sure that you can tell when a sentence is inverted, and can uninvert it to check subject-verb agreement.

> There <u>is</u> no more <u>than</u> twelve but certainly more than five rabbits currently <u>occupying</u> Farmer
>   A   B   C
> Bradley's hutch, and they all <u>must be fed</u> every day. <u>No error</u>
>   D   E

The dummy subject *there* indicates that this sentence is inverted. If we omit the dummy subject and uninvert the sentence, it reads *No more than twelve but certainly more than five rabbits is currently occupying Farmer Bradley's hutch, and they all must be fed every day.* The verb should clearly be changed to *are*, so the correct answer is (A).

Answer Key

Subject-verb agreement practice

1. S
2. S
3. P
4. S
5. P
6. S
7. S
8. P

9. *was* (the subject is *flock*)

10. *were* (the subject is *data*)

11. *is* (the subject is *neither*)

12. *goes* (the subject is *much*)

13. *is* (the subject is *Amy*)

14. *was* (the subject is *rose*)

15. *are* (the subject is *brothers*)

16. *is* (the subject is *speck*)

17. *shout* (the subject is *Bailey Brothers*)

18. *are* (the subject is *people*)

19. *are* (the subject is *smokers*)

20. *are* (the subject is *thousands*)

21. *have* (the subject is *voices*)

22. S-*every*, V-*were* (change to *was*)

23. S-*a theater and a toy store;* V-*has been* (change to *have been*)

24. S-*either Eric or his brother*, V-*is* (no change)

25. S-*proceeds*, V-*goes* (change to *go*)

26. S-*years*, V-*is* (change to *are*)

27. S-*neither*, V-*were* (change to *was*)

28. S-*technology*, V-*have transformed* (change to *has transformed*)

29. S-*player*, V-*were* (change to *was*)

30. S-*sponsorship*, V-*have garnered* (change to *has garnered*)

31. S-*Neither the children nor their parents*, V-*utters* (change to *utter*); S-*Mrs. Denny*, V-*tells* (no change)

32. S-*your strength training and your diet*, V-*is* (change to *are*)

Trimming sentences practice

1. *The team were* (change to *was*) *met.*

2. *The flock were* (change to *was*) *silver.*

3. *Carmen are* (change to *is*) *unlikely to be swayed.*

4. *Juggling the demands seem* (change to *seems*) *too much to bear.*

5. *Others is* (change to *are*) *concerned.*

6. *One agree* (change to *agrees*) *with the statement: "Anyone who would run for political office is not worth voting for."*

7. *The fact have forced* (change to *has forced*) *some historians to adopt a cynical perspective.*

8. Trimmed: *Advancements have to do with modification.*
   The verb *(have to do with)* is weak, vague, and inactive, and the subject *(advancements)* and object *(modification)* are abstract and vague. To improve the sentence, think about the *intended* meaning of the sentence, and use stronger and less abstract terms. Here's a good revision: *Typically, societies progress by making small modifications to their institutions, not by overhauling them completely.*

9. Trimmed: *The development was affected.*
   The verb *(was affected)* is weak, passive, and vague. Here's a good revision: *The incohesiveness of the revolutionary army hindered the development of the new government.*

Lesson 14—Parallelism

1. The law of parallelism

> Whenever a sentence contains a *list* or *comparison*, the items in that list or comparison should be parallel; that is, they should have the same grammatical form. This rule is called the *law of parallelism*.

> *Gina hated <u>to take</u> charge, <u>draw</u> attention to herself, and <u>she hated seeming</u> like a know-it-all.*

This sentence lists three things that Gina hated, but those things are given different grammatical forms. The underlined phrases are not parallel. The sentence sounds much better if the three items are phrased as gerunds.

> *Gina hated <u>taking</u> charge, <u>drawing</u> attention to herself, and <u>seeming</u> like a know-it-all.*

The underlined words all have the same form, so the sentence reads more smoothly. Comparisons should be parallel also.

> *Believe it or not, I like to read more than I like going to parties.*

This sentence compares two things: *to read* and *going to parties*. The first phrase is an infinitive, but the second contains a gerund. The sentence reads more smoothly if the items have the same form.

> *Believe it or not, I like to read more than I like to go to parties.*

> *Believe it or not, I like reading more than I like going to parties.*

2. Infinitives and gerunds

Using the law of parallelism often involves choosing between infinitives and gerunds (see Lesson 12). Remember that infinitives are noun phrases like *to run, to see,* and *to think*, and that gerunds are nouns like *running, seeing,* and *thinking*.

> *I like pizza.*   *I like to swim.*   *I like swimming.*

These sentences all have the same basic structure. In the first sentence, *pizza* is the object of the verb *like*. In the next two sentences, *to swim* (an infinitive) and *swimming* (a gerund) play the same role. Therefore, they must also be nouns. Gerunds and infinitives are often interchangeable. For instance, saying *I like to swim* is very much like saying *I like swimming*. But the sentences aren't identical. If you are unable to swim, but enjoy watching swim meets, then *I like swimming* conveys your sentiment but not *I like to swim*.

Although infinitives and gerunds are often interchangeable, here are some simple rules to help you to choose between them in certain situations.

> The gerund is usually better for indicating a general class of activity, while the infinitive is often better for indicating a specific activity in which someone actively participates.

> *<u>Kayaking</u> is a healthful sport, but can sometimes be dangerous.*

> *Curtis and Dan want <u>to kayak</u> this afternoon.*

The first sentence discusses a *general* activity, but the second discusses a *specific* activity.

> The infinitive often indicates *purpose* more strongly than does the gerund.

> *Maia went to the store to buy groceries.*

Notice that the gerund *buying* could not logically replace the infinitive *to buy*, because Maia had a *purpose* in going to the store, and this purpose is conveyed by an infinitive and not by a gerund.

3. Parallel constructions

The English language contains many **parallel constructions**, which are the common ways of phrasing comparisons.

A is like B	*A more than B*	*prefer A to B*
neither A nor B	*either A or B*	*both A and B*
the more A, the less B	*the better A, the better B*	*not only A but also B*
not A but B	*less A than B*	*more A than B*

When you use any of these parallel constructions, you must make sure of two things: that you use the correct phrasing, and that *A* and *B* are parallel. To improve your use of parallelism, practice underlining the *A*'s and *B*'s when you see any of these parallel constructions, and making sure that they have the same form.

We should be concerned *more <u>about saving the planet</u> than <u>about making higher profits</u>*.

$\qquad\qquad\qquad\qquad\qquad\qquad$ A $\qquad\qquad\qquad\qquad\qquad\qquad$ B

Parallelism practice

In each of the sentences below, circle the words or phrases that are parallel, and then write the *form* of those words or phrases (adjectives, prepositional phrases, gerunds, infinitives, nouns, etc.) in the blank.

1. *You can register for the test by mail, by phone, or on the Web.* _____

2. *Having good study practices is even more important than working hard.* _____

3. *The more you get to know her, the more you will like her.* _____

4. *The produce is not only exceptionally fresh, but also reasonably priced.* _____

5. *The show is less a concert than it is a three hour nightmare.* _____

Complete each of the sentences below with the appropriate word or phrase—infinitive or gerund—using the given verb.

6. *(Exercise) _____ is essential, but so is (eat) _____ intelligently.*

7. *The purpose of this trip is (show) _____ you what life was like in the 18th century.*

8. *I have always loved (dance) _____ although my condition has always prevented me from doing it myself.*

9. *Is it better (study) _____ a little each night, or a lot the night before?*

10. *The director called a meeting (discuss) _____ the coordination of the marketing phase.*

Correct any infinitive/gerund problems in the sentences below.

11. *The defendant was unwilling to give up his right of having his lawyer present at all questioning.*

12. *I would not dream to try out for the team until I have learned to throw a football.*

13. *Within the next three weeks, we plan having all of the work on the roof completed.*

Fix the parallelism errors in the following sentences.

14. *I like working with Miss Bennett because she is very supportive and has a lot of knowledge.*

15. *I can't decide whether I should give Maria the tickets or Caitlyn.*

4. Tip for improving your essay

Good writers use parallel phrasing to emphasize points and clarify the relationships between ideas. Fluent use of parallelism is one mark of a competent writer.

> *The government had long taken a laissez-faire position, but now the shift is toward a more protectionist stance.*

The change in phrasing in the second clause suggests, to most readers, an entirely unrelated idea. But the ideas in the two clauses are closely related, and so a parallel phrasing clarifies the relationship.

> *The government had long taken a laissez-faire position, but now it is taking a more protectionist stance.*

5. Tip for the multiple-choice questions

Pay attention to underlined words or phrases that are part of a list or comparison, particularly if one part of the list is *not* underlined. The underlined portion may need to be changed to maintain parallelism. Although parallelism problems show up occasionally in Identifying Sentence Errors questions, they are more common in Improving Sentences questions.

> My father is not one to raise his voice <u>and also he does not like to</u> lose his composure.
>
> (A) and also he does not like to
> (B) or
> (C) nor
> (D) and not
> (E) nor does he like to

The portion of the sentence that follows the underlined portion, *lose his composure*, is already parallel to *raise his voice*. The underlined portion of the original sentence destroys the parallelism. Choice (B) does the best job of restoring it. Choice (C) is incorrect because *nor* should not be used without *neither*.

Answer Key

Parallelism practice

1. *by mail; by phone; on the web*
   prepositional phrases

2. *having; working*
   gerunds

3. *you get to know her; you will like her*
   independent clauses

4. *exceptionally fresh; reasonably priced*
   adverb-adjective phrases

5. *concert; three-hour nightmare*
   nouns

6. *<u>Exercising</u> is essential but so is <u>eating</u> intelligently.*
   The sentence discusses general activities, so gerunds are more appropriate.

7. *T<u>he purpose of this trip is <u>to show</u> you what life was like in the 18th century.*</u> The infinitive shows purpose more effectively than does the gerund.

8. *I have always loved <u>dancing</u> although my condition has always prevented me from doing it myself.* Since the speaker cannot dance, the infinitive is inappropriate.

9. *Is it better <u>to study</u> a little each night, or a lot the night before?* The infinitive shows a clearer link between the action and a particular subject.

10. *The director called a meeting <u>to discuss</u> the coordination of the marketing phase.* The infinitive shows purpose more effectively than does the gerund.

11. *The defendant was unwilling to give up his right <u>to have</u> his lawyer present at all questioning.*

12. *I would not dream <u>of trying</u> out for the team until I have learned to throw a football.*

13. *Within the next three weeks, we plan <u>to have</u> all of the work on the roof completed.*

14. *I like working with Miss Bennett because she is very supportive and <u>knowledgeable</u>.*

15. *I can't decide whether I should give <u>the tickets to Maria or to Caitlyn.</u>*

Lesson 15—Comparison problems

1. Illogical comparisons

> Pay close attention to comparisons in sentences. They should be both parallel and logical. Things being compared in a sentence must be in the same category. For instance, comparing *apples* to *apples* is much more logical than comparing *apples* to *the increase in the price of apples due to an unforeseen climatological disaster.*

> *Her chances of passing that test aren't much better than the lottery.*

The comparison here is illogical: *chances* are not in the same category as *lottery*, so the comparison doesn't make sense. The sentence should compare *chances* to *chances*.

> *Her chances of getting an A aren't much better than <u>her chances of winning</u> the lottery.*

> Nothing can be different from itself. Any sentence that suggests otherwise must be revised.

> *Elisa has sung in more concerts than any singer in her school.*

This sentence suggests that Elisa is a singer who goes to school. So *any singer in her school* includes Elisa herself. Of course, she could not have sung in more concerts than herself, so the comparison is illogical.

> *Elisa has sung in more concerts than any <u>other</u> singer in her school.*

2. Check for countability: *fewer/less, number/amount,* and *many/much*

> When do you use *less* and when do you use *fewer*? Use *fewer* (or *number* or *many*) only when comparing countable things like *cars, dollars,* and *popsicles.* Use *less* (or *amount* or *much)* when comparing uncountable or continuous quantities like *traffic, money,* and *food.*

> *The team owners were concerned about the increasing amount of rowdy fans, so they raised ticket prices and ever since there have been a lot less fans at the games.*

Since *fans* can be counted and don't come in fractional parts, it is incorrect to use *amount* and *less.*

> *The team owners were concerned about the increasing <u>number</u> of rowdy fans, so they raised ticket prices and ever since there have been a lot <u>fewer</u> fans at the games.*

The situation is trickier when the quantity is both countable *and* continuous. For instance, units like *miles, pounds,* and *gallons* are countable, but, unlike rowdy fans, they can come in fractional parts, such as *1.23 miles.* So should you say *less miles* or *fewer miles*? Fortunately, the SAT avoids such tricky cases. In such situations in your own writing, however, consider whether you want to emphasize the **countability** of the quantity (in which case you should use *fewer, number,* or *many*) or the **continuity** of the quantity (in which case you should use *less, amount,* or *much*).

3. Check the number: *more/most, between/among,* and *-er/-est*

> When do you use *more* and when do you use *most*? Use *more* (or *between* or an *-er* adjective) whenever comparing exactly two things. Use *most* (or *among* or an *-est* adjective) when comparing more than two things.

> *The two superpowers seemed to be in a constant battle to see who was the strongest.*

Since there are only two superpowers, the superlative *strongest* is incorrect.

> *The two superpowers seemed to be in a constant battle to see who was the <u>stronger</u>.*

The same rule applies to the choice between *more* and *most.*

> *Of the dozens of students in the club, Deborah was the more popular.*

Since there are more than two students, the comparative *more* is incorrect.

> *Of the dozens of students in the club, Deborah was the <u>most</u> popular.*

4. Number shift

> Items being compared or equated should, whenever possible, have the same number—either both plural or both singular.

> *They were both hoping to be a winner.*

The word *both* is plural and suggests a pair, but *each* is singular and suggests an individual.

> *They were both hoping to be <u>winners</u>.*

> *They were <u>each</u> hoping to be a winner.*

> *The sailors' main point of reference was the two lighthouse beacons.*

In this case, it is easier and more logical to change the number of the first part.

> *The sailors' main <u>points</u> of reference <u>were</u> the two lighthouse beacons.*

Comparison practice

In each sentence below, underline any items that are being compared or equated. If the comparison is illogical or contains some other error, correct the sentence.

1. *The critics' guild praised the show, saying that it was consistently more intelligent and provocative than anything on the air.*

2. *Team unity and commitment to practice were regarded by the players as the key to their success.*

3. *Mathematics lessons in Japanese classrooms, unlike American classrooms, are often focused on solving a single complex problem rather than many simplistic problems.*

4. *The electric-combustion engines of the new hybrid cars burn much more cleanly and efficiently than conventional cars.*

5. *To the critics of the time, the surrealists were regarded as being as inscrutable, if not more so, than the dadaists.*

6. *I prefer a lot of modern poetry to Shakespeare.*

7. *Her suitcase would not close because she had packed too much of her towels into it.*

8. *The year-end bonus was equally divided between Parker, Herriot, and me.*

9. *Many students wanted to be a lifeguard at the club.*

10. *The toughest thing about her class is you have to do tons of homework every night.*

5. Tip for improving your essay

Good persuasive writers frequently make comparisons, particularly when arguing for the merits of one position over another. When making such a comparison, always be sure that your comparison is logical and well-phrased so that the reader can understand your point.

> *The belief that profits are paramount stands in stark contrast to environmentally and socially conscious companies like Ben & Jerry's ice cream.*

This comparison isn't logical. It contrasts a *belief* with a *company*.

> *The belief that profits are paramount stands in stark contrast <u>to the belief among companies like Ben & Jerry's that a business can be environmentally and socially conscious</u>.*

6. Tip for the multiple-choice questions

The SAT Writing multiple-choice section will likely include between one and three comparison errors. The most common error is the illogical comparison, and the next most common is the number shift. Always pay special attention to an underlined portion that is part of a comparison.

> The modernist theory of art that was <u>embraced</u> by painters <u>such as</u> Kandinsky and Picasso <u>differed</u>
>   A   B   C
> starkly from <u>impressionists</u> such as Claude Monet. <u>No error</u>
>   D   E

This sentence indicates that something *differed starkly from* something else. What is being compared to what? The first part of the sentence establishes that one *theory of art* is being compared to another *theory of art*. Yet the sentence suggests that the *modernist theory* is being compared to *impressionists*. This is illogical. Choice (D) should be changed to *the impressionist theory embraced by painters*.

Answer Key

Comparison practice

1. This is an illogical comparison. The sentence compares *the show* to *anything on the air,* which includes the show itself. Logically, *the show* can only be better than *anything <u>else</u> on the air.*

2. This contains a number shift. The sentence equates *team unity and commitment*, which is plural, with *the key*, which is singular. The word *key* should be replaced with *keys*.

3. This is an illogical comparison. The sentence compares *mathematics lessons* to *American classrooms.* Instead, it should compare *the lessons in Japanese classrooms* to *the lessons in American classrooms.*

4. This is an illogical comparison. The sentence compares *electric-combustion engines* to *conventional cars.* Instead, it should compare *electric-combustion engines* to *the engines in conventional cars.*

5. This comparison is logical but not grammatically correct. The sentence should make sense even when the interrupter *if not more so* is removed. The comparison should read *the surrealists were regarded as being as inscrutable as the dadaists, if not more so.*

6. This is an illogical comparison. It should read *I prefer a lot of modern poetry to <u>the poetry of Shakespeare</u>.*

7. This contains a *many/more* error. It should read *Her suitcase would not close because she had packed too <u>many</u> of her towels into it.*

8. *The year-end bonus was equally divided <u>among</u> Parker, Jim, and me.*

9. *Many students wanted to be <u>lifeguards</u> at the club.*

10. *The toughest thing about her class is <u>having</u> to do tons of homework every night.*

Lesson 16—Pronoun problems

1. Pronoun-antecedent agreement

Recall from Lesson 12 that a pronoun is a word such as *it, he, she, what,* or *that* that substitutes for a noun. Pronouns that refer to a specific thing—like *it, you, she,* and *I*—are **definite**. Pronouns that do not refer to a specific thing—like *anyone, neither,* and *those*—are **indefinite**.

Every definite pronoun must have a clear antecedent with which it agrees in *number* and *kind.* It must point to a noun, called the *antecedent*, in the sentence. If the antecedent is singular, the pronoun must be singular also. If the antecedent is personal, the pronoun must be personal also.

> *The policy of the bank is to maintain the confidentiality of their clients.*

This sentence contains the definite pronoun *their*, which is plural. What does *their* refer to? It must refer to *bank*, because the clients are the bank's clients. But *bank* is singular, so the pronoun does not agree with its antecedent.

> *The policy of the bank is to maintain the confidentiality of <u>its</u> clients.*

> *David was the one that first spotted the error.*

This sentence uses an impersonal pronoun, *that,* to refer to a person, *David.* This is a disagreement in **kind**.

> *David was the one <u>who</u> first spotted the error.*

An interrogative pronoun like *what, where, when, why, who, which,* or *how* must agree in kind with its antecedent. Use *what* only to refer to a thing, *where* to refer to a place, *when* to refer to a time, *why* to refer to a reason, *who* to refer to a person, and *how* to refer to an explanation.

> *A filibuster is where senators extend a debate in order to delay or prevent a vote.*

Even if you don't know what a *filibuster* is, the sentence makes clear that it isn't a *place*, but rather a procedure. Therefore it is not a *where* but a *which*.

> *A filibuster is <u>a procedure by which</u> senators extend a debate in order to delay or prevent a vote.*

A pronoun in a modifying phrase usually takes the closest preceding noun as its antecedent.

> *The actors will design their own sets, who are participating in the workshop.*

The modifying phrase *who* are the *actors*, not the *sets*. Move the modifying phrase over.

> *The actors <u>who are participating in the workshop</u> will design their own sets.*

2. Missing or ambiguous antecedents

The antecedent of any definite pronoun must be clear. Avoid using a definite pronoun if the antecedent is missing or ambiguous.

> *At the meeting, they discussed the need to raise taxes to meet the rising costs of the sewer project.*

Who are *they* in this sentence? The sentence should be revised to eliminate the pronoun or specify its antecedent.

> *<u>One topic introduced at the meeting was</u> the need to raise taxes to meet the rising costs of the sewer project.*

> *Roger told Mike that he was going to start the next game.*

This sentence contains the definite pronoun *he.* Whom does it refer to, Roger or Mike? The sentence could make sense either way, so the antecedent is ambiguous. The simplest way to fix the problem is to eliminate the pronoun.

> *Roger told Mike that <u>Mike</u> would start the game.*

3. Pronoun consistency

Be consistent with any pronouns that refer to the same antecedent.

Even when one is dieting, you should always try to get enough vitamins.

The inconsistent pronouns make the writer sound indecisive. Make up your mind!

Even when you are dieting, you should always try to get enough vitamins.

Pronoun agreement practice

Circle all pronouns, and make any necessary corrections.

1. *There are many times in a game where a player can lose focus.*

2. *If a student wants to memorize the meaning of a word, you should begin by understanding the concept it represents.*

3. *Caroline passed the phone to Julia, but she couldn't bring herself to speak.*

4. *Not wanting to be the one that slowed the team down, David dropped out of the race.*

5. *Brown University is committed to assisting their students by providing him or her with any necessary financial aid.*

6. *The media ignored the reports because it didn't consider them newsworthy.*

7. *No one that has been through the first week of boot camp ever believes that they will make it through the entire six weeks.*

8. *Although you shouldn't read carelessly, one doesn't need to read slowly, either.*

9. *Neither Glen nor Don thought that their team would lose the championship.*

10. *Students sometimes aren't ready to handle the extra work when his or her courses become more demanding.*

11. *The anthology is filled with stories where love goes unrequited.*

12. *Everyone is expected to do their share.*

13. *The museum received so many donations that they actually had to return over a million dollars to the benefactors.*

14. *The judges usually give the trophy to the skater that makes the fewest mistakes.*

15. *I like movies where the bad guy gets punished in the end.*

16. *Each swimmer will have a lane to themselves.*

17. *Who was the player that hit the home run?*

4. Pronoun case

The case of a pronoun indicates its role within the sentence. English uses four common cases. Subjective pronouns like *I, you, he, she, we, they,* and *who* are usually subjects of verbs. Objective pronouns like *me, you, him, her, them,* and *whom* are usually objects of verbs or prepositions. Possessive pronouns like *my, mine, her, hers, their, theirs,* and *whose* indicate attribution or ownership. Reflexive pronouns like *myself, yourself, himself, herself,* and *themselves* usually show that the object of a verb is the same as the subject.

5. Subjective pronouns

Any pronoun that serves as the subject of a verb must take the subjective case.

> *Jenna and me were the only two at the meeting.*

The subject of this sentence is the plural *Jenna and me,* but *me* is in the wrong case. It's easier to see the mistake if you imagine the pronoun acting alone in the subject. You would not say *Me was at the meeting;* you would say *I was at the meeting.*

> *Jenna and I were the only two at the meeting.*

Even if the verb is only *implied*, its subject must still take the subjective case.

> *My brother is taller than me.*

You can say things like this in conversation, but not in formal writing. The sentence suggests an implied verb. It is really saying that *My brother is taller than I am.* The verb *am* is understood by parallelism. Even if you omit the verb, the pronoun must keep the subjective case.

> *My brother is taller than I.*

Any pronoun that is equated with the subject in a predicate nominative takes the subjective case.

> *The winner of the prize was her.*

The subject of the sentence, *winner,* is linked to the pronoun *her* by a **linking verb**, *was.* Since the pronoun is equated with the subject, the pronoun should take the subjective case.

> *The winner of the prize was she.*

6. Objective pronouns

Any pronoun that is the object of a verb or preposition must take the objective case.

> *My father raised my brother and I all by himself.*

The object of the verb *raised* is *my brother and I,* but *I* is in the wrong case. Again, you can catch the error more easily by imagining the pronoun acting alone. You would not say *My father raised I;* you would say *My father raised me.*

> *My father raised my brother and me all by himself.*

> *This should be a great opportunity for you and she.*

The indirect object in this sentence is *you and she.* Indirect objects are often objects of prepositions. In this case *for you and she* is a prepositional phrase. All objects of prepositions must be in the objective case.

> *This should be a great opportunity for you and her.*

7. Possessive pronouns

Don't use the objective case for a pronoun that is not an object. Analyze the objects of verbs logically to determine which case to use.

> *Mrs. Brown appreciated him taking such an interest in literature.*

What is the object of the verb *appreciated*? In other words, what did Mrs. Brown appreciate? Since the pronoun *him* is in the objective case, the sentence suggests that Mrs. Brown appreciated *him*. But that isn't what the sentence really means. Mrs. Brown actually appreciated the *interest* he took in literature. To avoid this confusion, put the pronoun in the possessive case.

> *Mrs. Brown appreciated <u>his</u> taking such an interest in literature.*

8. Reflexive pronouns

Use reflexive pronouns to show that the object of a verb is the same as its subject, or to emphasize a noun or pronoun.

For instance, when you use the reflexive pronoun *myself* in a sentence like *I pinched myself to make sure I wasn't dreaming*, you are indicating that you *did* the pinching and you also *received* the pinching. Also, when you use the reflexive pronoun *himself* in a sentence like *She was standing next to Usher himself*, you are emphasizing *Usher*.

> *My opponent did not prepare his case as diligently as myself.*

Since this sentence does not indicate that the person who performed the action also received it, and since the pronoun *myself* is not used to emphasize an adjacent noun, the pronoun should not take the reflexive case.

> *My opponent did not prepare his case as diligently as <u>I did</u>.*

Pronoun case practice

Circle the correct pronoun in each sentence.

1. *The climb was much easier for them than it was for Jeff and (I/me/myself).*

2. *The other contestants did not seem as confident as (he/him/himself).*

3. *(Us/We) detectives are always careful to follow every lead.*

4. *Every student should make (his or her/their) own study plan.*

5. *They never seem to listen to the opinions of (us/we) students.*

6. *Jim gave control of the project to Fiona and (me/myself/I).*

7. *The university presented the honor to David and (he/him).*

8. *Justine and (me/I) have always been closest friends.*

9. *There is no point in (our/us) delaying the tests any longer.*

10. *It seems quite clear that you and (I/me) will have to work together to solve this problem.*

11. *It might be hard for (him and me/he and I) to agree.*

12. *(We/Us) and the other members debated the issue for over two hours.*

13. *The owners of the club offered my wife and (me/I) a free bottle of wine with dinner.*

14. *No other runner on the team could outrun (myself/me).*

15. *The teachers were getting tired of (him/his) constantly falling asleep in class.*

16. *The ballpark always held a special attraction for Dave and (I/me).*

9. Tip for improving your essay

When writing, use pronouns carefully, particularly when they refer to ideas mentioned in previous sentences. Make sure that your references—your *antecedents*—are clear to your reader.

Remember that the essay readers grade you on *logic* and *clarity*. In order to develop a logical train of thought, you must connect your ideas clearly.

> *Journalists often believe that their job is simply to get the facts, and not to question the motivations, analyses, or logic of those politicians who want to develop policy on the basis of popularity. That kind of thinking is dangerous.*

What does the word *that* in the second sentence refer to? The sentence discusses two kinds of thinking: that of the *journalists* and that of the *politicians,* so the reader isn't sure who the writer is criticizing. A good writer always clarifies such references.

> *Journalists often believe that their job is simply to get the facts, and not to question the motivations, analyses, or logic of those politicians who want to develop policy on the basis of popularity. <u>Such uncritical journalism</u> is dangerous.*

10. Tip for the multiple-choice questions

On the multiple-choice SAT Writing questions, make sure that any underlined definite pronoun refers clearly and unambiguously to a noun in the sentence, that it agrees with that noun in number and kind, and that all pronouns referring to the same antecedent are consistent. Also, examine the relationship between the pronoun and the verbs to make sure that the pronoun is in the correct case.

> My school <u>has</u> very strict rules <u>regarding student behavior</u> inside and outside the classroom,
>   A   B
> but <u>they</u> don't have any kind <u>of dress code</u>. <u>No error</u>
>   C   D   E

The only underlined pronoun in this sentence is *they*. What does it refer to? Perhaps you imagine that it refers to the faculty and administrators in the school, but they are not mentioned in the sentence. The only possible antecedent in the sentence is the singular noun *school*. Therefore, the pronoun has the wrong number and should be changed to *it*. The correct answer is (C).

Answer Key

Pronoun agreement practice

1. pronouns: *there, where. There are many times in a game <u>when</u> a player can lose focus.*

2. pronouns: *you, it. If a student wants to memorize the meaning of a word, <u>he or she</u> should begin by understanding the concept it represents.*

3. pronouns: *she, herself. Caroline passed the phone to Julia, but <u>Julia</u> couldn't bring herself to speak.*

4. pronouns: *one, that. Not wanting to be the one <u>who</u> slowed the team down, David dropped out of the race.*

5. pronouns: *their, him, her. Brown University is committed to assisting <u>its</u> students by providing <u>them</u> with any necessary financial aid.*

6. pronouns: *it, them. The media ignored the reports because <u>they</u> didn't considered <u>those reports</u> newsworthy.*

7. pronouns: *no one, that, that, they, it. No one <u>who</u> has been through the first week of boot camp ever believes that <u>he or she</u> will make it through the entire six weeks.*

8. pronouns: *you, one. Although you shouldn't read carelessly, <u>you don't</u> need to read slowly, either.*

9. pronouns: *neither, that, their. Neither Glen nor Don thought that <u>his</u> team would lose the championship.*

10. pronouns: *his, her. Students sometimes aren't ready to handle the extra work when <u>their</u> courses become more demanding.*

11. pronoun: *where. The anthology is filled with stories <u>in which</u> love goes unrequited.*

12. pronouns: *everyone, their. Everyone is expected to do <u>his or her</u> share.*

13. pronoun: *they. The museum received so many donations that <u>it</u> actually had to return over a million dollars to the benefactors.*

14. pronoun: *that. They usually give the trophy to the skater <u>who</u> makes the fewest mistakes.*

15. pronouns: *I, where. I like movies <u>in which</u> the bad guy gets punished in the end.*

16. pronoun: *themselves. Each swimmer will have a lane to <u>herself (or himself)</u>.*

17. pronouns: *who, that. Who was the player <u>who</u> hit the home run?*

Pronoun case practice

1. *The climb was much easier for them than it was for Jeff and <u>me</u>.*

2. *The other contestants did not seem as confident as <u>he</u> (was).*

3. *<u>We</u> detectives are always careful to follow every lead.*

4. *Every student should make <u>his or her</u> own study plan.*

5. *They never seem to listen to the opinions of <u>us</u> students as they should.*

6. *Jim gave control of the project to Fiona and <u>me</u>.*

7. *The university presented the honor to David and <u>him</u>.*

8. *Justine and <u>I</u> have always been closest friends.*

9. *There is no point in <u>our</u> delaying the tests any longer.*

10. *It seems quite clear that you and <u>I</u> will have to work together to solve this problem.*

11. *It might be hard for <u>him and me</u> to agree.*

12. *<u>We</u> and the other members debated the issue for over two hours.*

13. *The owners of the club offered my wife and <u>me</u> a free bottle of wine with dinner.*

14. *No other runner on the team could outrun <u>me</u>.*

15. *The teachers were growing tired of <u>his</u> constantly falling asleep in class.*

16. *The ballpark always held a special attraction to Dave and <u>me</u>.*

Lesson 17—Modifier problems

1. Dangling and misplaced participles

Present participles are words like *colliding*, *writing*, and *fighting* when they are used in verb phrases like *was fighting* or as adjectives as in *the fighting fish*. Past participles are words like *collided*, *written*, and *fought* when they are used in verb phrases like *had written* or as adjectives as in *the written language*.

A participial phrase is a modifying phrase that includes a participle but not its subject. It is usually separated from the main part of the sentence by one or more commas. Every participial phrase should be near its subject.

> *<u>Eating ravenously</u>, the vultures remained on the carcass until it was picked clean.*

> *The runners, <u>exhausted from the final sprint</u>, stumbled through the finish line.*

Notice that each participial phrase does not contain the subject of the participle. The subject of *eating* in the first participial phrase is *vultures*, and the subject of *exhausted* in the second participial phrase is *runners*. These participial phrases work because, although the subjects do not appear in the participial phrases themselves, their subjects are nearby. If the subject doesn't show up in a timely fashion, the participle is said to **dangle.**

> *After having studied all night, the professor postponed the test until Friday.*

There is something wrong with this sentence. The participial phrase, *having studied all night*, lacks a subject. *Who* has studied all night? Certainly *the professor* didn't have to study, but the sentence doesn't indicate who did. Therefore, the participle dangles.

There are two general ways to fix a dangling participle. You can modify the main part of the sentence to include the subject of the participle, or you can turn the participial phrase into a clause, complete with a subject.

> *After having studied all night, <u>I</u> learned that the professor had postponed the test until Friday.*

> *After <u>I had studied</u> all night, the professor postponed the test until Friday.*

The first sentence has modified the main clause, but this changes the emphasis of the sentence. The second sentence has turned the participial phrase into a dependent clause, incorporating the subject *I*.

Sometimes the subject of a participle is in the sentence, but not close by. In these situations, the participial phrase is *misplaced*. You can fix the problem by moving the participial phrase so that its subject is clear, or by turning the participial phrase into a clause.

> *Bob found his watch walking to the bathroom.*

It sounds as if the *watch* was *walking to the bathroom*. Of course, that's absurd. You can fix the problem by just moving the phrase, or by turning it into a dependent clause.

> *<u>Walking to the bathroom</u>, Bob found his watch.*

> *Bob found his watch <u>as he was walking to the bathroom</u>.*

> *It was difficult for William to hear the announcements waiting for the train.*

Were the *announcements* waiting for the train? Of course not. Here are two good fixes.

> *While waiting for the train, William found it difficult to hear the announcements.*

> *William found it difficult to hear the announcements while he was waiting for the train.*

Dangling and misplaced participles practice

Circle the participle in each sentence; then circle its subject and draw an arrow between the participle and its subject. Then rewrite the sentence to fix any problems with the participle.

1. *Looking at your essay, it seems to me that you need to use more specific examples.*

2. *Turning the corner, the stadium came into my view.*

3. *Although exhausted after the night's work, Martha's creative instincts compelled her to keep writing.*

4. *Without waiting for an answer, David's eagerness got the better of him and he rushed out the door.*

5. *Thinking her friends were right behind her, it was frightening for Alison to discover that they were gone.*

6. *Although angered by the irrationality of his opponent, Senator Sanchez's plan was to address each point calmly.*

7. *Watching from the bridge, the fireworks bloomed spectacularly over the water.*

8. *Exhausted from the day's climbing, the looming storm forced the hikers to pitch an early camp.*

9. *Having studied for hours, it was very disappointing that I did so poorly on the exam.*

10. *Without being aware of it, termites can infest your home if you don't take the proper precautions.*

11. *Before getting the job at the bank, no one thought I could hold such a responsible position.*

12. *Lacking any real sailing skills, David's concern was mainly with keeping the ship afloat.*

2. Other misplaced modifiers

> Any modifier or modifying phrase can be misplaced. Modifiers must obey the Rule of Proximity—every modifier or modifying phrase should be as close as possible to the word or phrase that it modifies.

Misplaced prepositional phrases

A **prepositional phrase**, as we discussed in Lesson 12, is a preposition and the noun phrase that follows. Prepositional phrases can be adjectival, meaning they modify nouns, or adverbial, meaning they modify verbs, adjectives, or adverbs.

> *The dog <u>in the car</u> was barking.*   *David walked <u>into the pole</u>.*

In the first sentence, the prepositional phrase *in the car* modifies the noun *dog*, so it is an adjective phrase. In the second sentence, the prepositional phrase *into the pole* modifies the verb *walked*, so it is an adverbial phrase.

> *In an emergency, I am amazed at how calm Juanita can be.*

This sentence suggests that I am only *amazed* in an emergency. What it really means, however, is that Juanita *is calm* in an emergency. To clarify, move the prepositional phrase *in an emergency* closer to the verb it modifies.

> *I am amazed at how calm Juanita can be <u>in an emergency</u>.*

Misplaced appositives

An **appositive** is a noun phrase that explains an adjacent noun, and is often set off by a comma or commas.

> *Franklin, <u>the only one of us who owned a car</u>, agreed to drive us all to the game.*

The underlined noun phrase is an appositive explaining who *Franklin* is. Like any modifier, an appositive can be misplaced.

> *A splendid example of Synthetic Cubism, Picasso painted* Three Musicians *in the summer of 1924.*

The phrase *a splendid example of Synthetic Cubism* is a misplaced appositive. *Picasso* is not an example of Synthetic Cubism; the painting is. Here are two acceptable fixes.

> *A splendid example of Synthetic Cubism,* Three Musicians *was painted by Picasso in the summer of 1924.*

> *Picasso painted* Three Musicians, *a splendid example of Synthetic Cubism, in the summer of 1924.*

Misplaced infinitives

As we discussed in Lesson 12, **infinitives** are phrases like *to run, to think,* and *to believe* that are often used as nouns. However, they are also sometimes used as modifiers, and so can be misplaced.

> *We have many more math problems <u>to do</u>.*   *We are working <u>to earn</u> money for the trip.*

In the first sentence, the infinitive *to do* modifies the noun *problems*, so it is an adjective phrase. In the second sentence, the infinitive *to earn* modifies the verb *are working*, so it is an adverbial phrase.

> *To get our attention, we saw Mr. Genovese take out a giant boa constrictor.*

The infinitive *to get* logically modifies the verb *take*. It answers the question, *why did he take it out?* But it is incorrectly placed closer to a different verb, *saw*. Here are two good fixes.

> *To get our attention, Mr. Genovese took out a giant boa constrictor.*

> *We saw Mr. Genovese take out a giant boa constrictor to get our attention.*

Misplaced modifiers practice

In each of the following sentences, underline and label all participial phrases (PART), prepositional phrases (PREP), appositives (APP), and infinitive phrases (INF), and rewrite any sentence to fix any misplaced modifiers.

1. *Without so much as a blink, the gleaming sword was unsheathed by the warrior.*

2. *To maintain good health, physicians suggest that both vigorous exercise and good eating habits are required.*

3. *We found my lost earring walking through the parking lot.*

4. *Having run for over four hours, the finish line was still 10 miles ahead of her.*

5. *Even with a sprained ankle, the coach forced Adam back into the game.*

6. *To find a good restaurant, there are many good online guides to help you.*

7. *In search of a good calculator, not a single store in the mall could help me.*

8. *A dutiful wife and mother, we were surprised to hear Carol complaining about domestic life.*

9. *To get a good jump out of the starting blocks, most sprinters say that good body positioning is essential.*

10. *Among the most sought-after collectibles on the market, we found the antique toys at a garage sale.*

3. Confusing adjectives and adverbs

Don't use an adjective to do the job of an adverb. Adjectives like *green, generous,* and *gargantuan* modify nouns. Adverbs like *gently, globally,* and *grossly* modify verbs, adjectives, or other adverbs.

> *I was impressed by how cogent his argument was presented.*

The modifer *cogent* is intended to answer the question *how* was it *presented?* Therefore it modifies a verb, and so should take the adverbial form *cogently.*

> *I was impressed by how <u>cogently</u> his argument was presented.*

Some modifiers can be used as either adjectives or adverbs. For instance, *fast* and *well* can be used either way. In the phrase *the fast car,* the word *fast* is used as an adjective modifying the noun *car.* But in the clause *he ran fast,* it is an adverb modifying the verb *ran.* In the clause *I haven't been well lately,* the word *well* is an adjective meaning *healthy* modifying the pronoun *I.* But in the clause *she sings very well,* it is an adverb modifying the verb *sings.*

> *I couldn't write fast enough to finish the essay on time.   I feel pretty good.*

Although some people don't like how the words *fast* and *good* are used in these sentences, these usages are both fine. In the first sentence, the word *fast* is an adverb meaning *quickly* modifying the verb *write.* In the second sentence, the word *good* is an adjective modifying the pronoun *I* and joined to it by a linking verb *feel.* It is also fine to say *I feel well,* but only because *well* in this case is also an adjective meaning *healthy.*

4. Comparative adjectives and adverbs

Use the proper form when using comparative modifiers. Comparative adjectives come in one of two forms. For instance, *fast* becomes the comparative *faster* by adding *-er,* but *adorable* becomes the comparative *more adorable* by adding *more.* (*Adorabler* just doesn't sound right, does it?) Comparative adverbs almost always include *more* as in *more rapidly,* but some irregular adverbs can take *-er,* as in *she runs faster than her brother.*

> *The briefcase feels more light than it did this morning.*

The phrase *more light* is in the incorrect comparative form.

> *The briefcase feels <u>lighter</u> than it did this morning.*

> *Please try to hold the baby gentler next time.*

The word *gentler* is a comparative adjective, not a comparative adverb. Most comparative adverbs use *more.*

> *Please try to hold the baby <u>more gently</u> next time.*

Some modifiers are absolute modifiers, and so should never take the comparative form. For instance, one thing cannot logically be *more unique* than another thing, because *unique* means *one of a kind,* which indicates an absolute quality. Nothing can be *somewhat* unique; it either *is* unique or it *isn't* unique.

> *The loss was made more inevitable by the injury to our starting pitcher.*

The concept of inevitability doesn't come in degrees. Something is either *inevitable* or it's not. There is no in-between, so the phrase *more inevitable* is illogical.

> *The loss was made inevitable by the injury to our starting pitcher.*

5. Redundancy

The SAT Writing may ask you to eliminate redundancy in sentences. A redundancy is an unnecessary repetition of an idea. To check whether a word or phrase is redundant, reread the sentence without that word or phrase. If the meaning of the sentence remains unchanged, then the word or phrase is redundant.

With only seconds remaining to go in the game, Michael sped quickly down the court.

Since *remaining* means roughly the same as *to go*, we don't need to say both. Also, to *speed* means to *move quickly*, so *sped quickly* is redundant. Eliminate the redundancies.

With only seconds remaining in the game, Michael sped down the court.

More modifier practice

1. Cross out any redundant words or phrases in the paragraph below. (Hint: There are at least 10 redundancies.)

When we refer back to past history, we can see that whenever a new innovation is introduced for the first time, people rarely accept the whole entire concept, at least not right away. If and when something threatens the ways of the past, people don't easily accept this new concept. Although not everyone necessarily needs to maintain the status quo, consistency and predictability make people feel comfortable. Even when technology comes up with a way to do things better, people often continue on with their older, less efficient ways. For instance, it's not uncommon for people to use e-mail while at the same time continuing to correspond through "snail mail." If they would quickly pause for a moment, they would see that they can communicate more effectively through the Internet—and save some trees!

Correct any modifier problems in the sentences below.

2. *The latest political commercials make their points stronger than previous ones.*
3. *My shirt smelled quite foully after rugby practice.*
4. *We never usually get to go to such elegant restaurants.*
5. *Although both of my parents are level-headed, my father is the most patient.*
6. *The third graders weren't hardly interested in going to the museum after school.*
7. *I can sing in front of a crowd easier than I can give a speech.*
8. *In many areas of the country, wind energy can be converted to electricity even more efficient than can fossil energy.*
9. *I felt surprisingly good after Saturday's 10-mile run.*
10. *The microscopic size of the fracture made it more impossible to detect, even with special instruments.*
11. *These measures won't barely address the state's deficit.*
12. *The teacher never told us about the test until the day before.*
13. *Students never usually bother to examine the veracity of the "facts" they are supposed to memorize in history class.*

6. Tip for improving your essay

The Elements of Style, a classic guide to writing by William Strunk and E. B. White, encourages writers to "write with nouns and verbs." In other words, do not rely excessively on adjectives and adverbs to convey your ideas. Many writers feel that modifiers make their writing more colorful or lively. This is true only in moderation. In fact, poor writers tend to rely too much on modifiers.

> *Although well into her eighties, Kiera had quick, intelligent eyes that were as shimmering as sunlight on a pond on a bright summer's day, and as revealing and lively as a boisterous, impetuous child.*

This sentence is overloaded with adjectives. The author can characterize Kiera much more effectively with nouns and verbs.

> *Although well into her eighties, Kiera had eyes that shimmered and revealed the soul of a child.*

7. Tip for the multiple-choice questions

On the Improving Questions section, look out for dangling and misplaced modifiers. The most common is the dangling participle, which is likely to show up two or three times on the SAT Writing.

> Having lived abroad for several decades, <u>we learned a lot from our professor</u> about foreign perceptions of the United States.
>
> (A) we could learn a lot from our professor
> (B) we would have learned a lot from our professor
> (C) our professor could teach us a lot
> (D) our professor teaching us a lot
> (E) we were taught a lot by our professor

The participle *having* dangles because its subject, *professor*, is too far away. The correct response should bring the subject closer to the participle and avoid other grammatical problems. The best choice is (C).

Answer Key

Dangling and misplaced participles practice

Each sentence below represents only one possible revision. There may be other correct answers.

1. The participle *looking* is not close to its subject. *As I look at your essay, it seems to me that you need to use more specific examples.*

2. The participle *turning* dangles. *As I turned the corner, the stadium came into view.*

3. The participle *exhausted* dangles. *Although Martha was exhausted after the night's work, her creative instincts compelled her to keep writing.*

4. The participle *waiting* dangles. *David's eagerness got the better of him and, without waiting for an answer, he rushed out the door.*

5. The participle *thinking* is not close to its subject. *Thinking her friends were right behind her, Alison was frightened to discover that they were gone.*

6. The participle *angered* dangles. *Although angered by the irrationality of her opponent, Senator Sanchez planned to address each point calmly.*

7. The participle *watching* dangles. *As we watched from the bridge, the fireworks bloomed spectacularly over the water.*

8. The participle *exhausted* is not close to its subject. *The looming storm forced the hikers, exhausted from the day's climbing, to pitch an early camp.*

9. The participle *having* is not close to its subject. *Having studied for hours, I was very disappointed to have done so poorly on the exam.*

10. The participle *being* dangles. *Without your being aware of it, termites can infest your home if you don't take the proper precautions.*

11. The participle *getting* is not close to its subject. *Before I got the job at the bank, no one thought I could hold such a responsible position.*

12. The participle *lacking* dangles. *Lacking any real sailing skills, David was mainly concerned with keeping the ship afloat.*

Misplaced modifiers practice

Each of these answers provides only one possible correction. On some sentences, other corrections are possible.

1. *Without so much as a blink (PREP), the gleaming sword was unsheathed by the warrior (PREP).*
   Correction: *Without so much as a blink, the warrior unsheathed the gleaming sword.*

2. *To maintain good health (INF), physicians suggest that both vigorous exercise and good eating habits are required.*
   Correction: *Physicians suggest that both vigorous exercise and good eating habits are required to maintain good health.*

3. *We found my lost earring walking through the parking lot (PART containing a PREP).*
   Correction: *Walking through the parking lot, we found my lost earring.*

4. *Having run for over four hours (PART containing a PREP), the finish line was still 10 miles ahead of her (PREP).*
   Correction: *Although she had run for over four hours, the finish line was still 10 miles ahead of her.*

5. *Even with a sprained ankle (PREP), the coach forced Adam back into the game (PREP).*
   Correction: *Even through Adam had a sprained ankle, the coach forced him back into the game.*

6. *To find a good restaurant (INF), there are many good on-line guides to help you (INF).*
   Correction: *There are many good online guides to help you find a good restaurant.*

7. *In search of a good calculator (PREP), not a single store in the mall (PREP) could help me.*
   Correction: *Not a single store in the mall could help me find a good calculator.*

8. *A dutiful wife and mother (APP), we were surprised to hear Carol complaining about domestic life (PREP).*
   Correction: *We were surprised to hear Carol, a dutiful wife and mother, complaining about domestic life.*

9. *To get a good jump (INF) out of the starting blocks (PREP), most sprinters say that good body positioning is essential.*
   Correction: *Most sprinters say that good body*

positioning is required for getting a good jump out of the starting blocks.

10. <u>*Among the most sought-after collectibles*</u> *(PREP)* <u>*on the market*</u> *(PREP), we found the antique toys* <u>*at a garage sale*</u> *(PREP).*
    Correction: *We found the antique toys, which are among the most sought-after collectibles on the market, at a garage sale.*

More modifier practice

1. *When we refer* ~~back~~ *to* ~~past~~ *history, we can see that whenever* ~~a new~~ <u>*an*</u> *innovation is introduced* ~~for the first time~~*, people rarely accept the* ~~whole~~ *entire concept, at least not right away.* ~~If~~ ~~and~~ *when something threatens the ways of the past, people don't part easily with their old ways. Although not everyone* ~~necessarily~~ *needs to maintain the status quo, consistency and predictability make people feel comfortable. Even when technology comes up with a way to do things better, people often continue* ~~on~~ *with their older, less efficient ways. For instance, it's not uncommon for people to use e-mail while* ~~at the same time~~ *continuing to correspond via "snail mail." If they would* ~~quickly~~ *pause for a moment, they would see that they can communicate more effectively through the Internet—and save some trees!*

2. *The latest political commercials make their points* <u>*more strongly*</u> *than previous ones.* (Use an adverb, not an adjective.)

3. *My shirt smelled quite* <u>*foul*</u> *after rugby practice.* (The modifier is an adjective describing the noun *shirt*. The verb *smelled* acts as a linking verb.)

4. *We* <u>*rarely*</u> *get to go to such elegant restaurants.* (The use of *never* is illogical, since it occasionally happens.)

5. *Although both of my parents are level-headed, my father is the* <u>*more*</u> *patient.* (Use *more* when comparing two things.)

6. *The third graders* <u>*were hardly*</u> *interested in going to the museum after school.* (The phrase *weren't hardly* is a double negative.)

7. *I can sing in front of a crowd* <u>*more easily*</u> *than I can give a speech.* (Use an adverb, not an adjective.)

8. *In many areas of the country, wind energy can be converted to electricity even* <u>*more efficiently*</u> *than fossil energy.* (Use an adverb, not an adjective.)

9. *I felt surprisingly good after Saturday's 10-mile run.* (This is fine. You don't have to say *I felt well* unless you mean that you are simply not sick.)

10. *The microscopic size of the fracture made it* <u>*impossible*</u> *to detect, even with special instruments.* (*Impossible* is an absolute adjective.)

11. *These measures* <u>*won't*</u> *address the state's deficit.* (The phrase *won't barely* is a double negative.)

12. *The teacher* <u>*didn't tell*</u> *us about the test until the day before.* (The use of *never* is illogical, since it eventually happened.)

13. *Students* <u>*rarely*</u> *bother to examine the veracity of the "facts" they are supposed to memorize in history class.* (*Never usually* is illogical.)

Lesson 18—Tense and voice problems

1. Tricky tenses

The tense of a verb must logically indicate the time and extent of an action or state of being. It must coordinate with the other time references in the sentence.

> *Since the early 20th century, the United States was the world's wealthiest nation.*

The phrase *since the early 20th century* indicates a condition that has lasted from the distant past to the present. However, the verb in this sentence, *was*, is in the **past tense**. To indicate a condition that extends from the past to the present, you must use the **present perfect tense**.

> *Since the early 20th century, the United States <u>has been</u> the world's wealthiest nation.*

Fortunately, most of us can spot and correct most tense problems, so we won't dicuss every single English verb tense in detail. We will discuss just the trickiest situations.

2. The perfect tenses

The perfect tenses are usually used to indicate that an event or state of being is completed before some other point in time. (The word *perfect* in this case means *completed*, not *flawless*.) In English, the perfect tenses always use the helping verb *to have* together with a past participle, as in *has eaten, have begun,* and *will have swum*. Perfect tenses are relative tenses; that is, they show a relationship between actions or states of being.

The past perfect tense, which uses the helping verb *had*, indicates that an event was completed *before* another point in the past. You can think of it as the "before the past" tense.

> *By the time we arrived at the reception, Glen had already given the toast.*

This sentence contains two verbs: *arrived* and *had given*. The first is in the simple past tense, and the second is in the past perfect tense. This suggests that the second event mentioned, the giving of the toast, was completed before the first event mentioned, the arrival at the reception. It may help to visualize the events on a timeline.

```
        past perfect        past        now
   <────────┼───────────────┼───────────┼──────────────► time
        had given        arrived
```

When a sentence contains two past tense verbs, check whether one event was completed before the other. If so, the earlier event should be in the past *perfect* tense.

> *We ate the entire pie by the time Ellen realized it was missing.*

This sentence contains two verbs in the past tense: *ate* and *realized*. The sentence suggests, however, that the eating of the pie was completed before Ellen realized it was missing. Therefore you need the past perfect tense to indicate the proper sequence.

> *We had eaten the entire pie by the time Ellen realized it was missing.*

The present perfect tense, which uses the helping verb *has* or *have*, indicates that an event or condition either extends from the past to the present or *possibly* extends from the past to the present or beyond. You can think of it as the "past plus present or future" tense.

> *She has been very nice to me.*
> *We have taken only two tests this semester.*

The first sentence contains the present perfect verb *has been*. This indicates that something was true in both the past *and* the present—she *was* nice to me and she *still is* nice to me. The present perfect tense here combines past and present. In the second sentence, the present perfect verb *have taken* indicates that we took the tests in the past, but *also* that we might take more in the future.

If a single event or condition starts and finishes in the past, it is best described with the past tense. If an event or condition extends from the past to the present, it is best described with the present perfect tense.

In the short time since her sixteenth birthday, she became a best-selling artist.

The phrase *since her sixteenth birthday* suggests a condition that is still true in the present. Therefore, the present perfect tense works better than the past tense.

In the short time since her sixteenth birthday, she <u>has become</u> a best-selling artist.

The future perfect tense indicates an event or condition that will have been completed before some time in the future.

By Friday, we will have completed the entire project.

The verb *will have completed* suggests that the project will be complete before some future point in time—*Friday.*

Present participles can be perfect also. A participle must be in the perfect form, using the helping verb *having,* whenever it indicates an action or condition completed before the event or condition expressed in the main part of the sentence.

Walking all night, we were desperate to find rest at dawn.

The sentence indicates that the *walking* occurred at night, but the main idea of the sentence, that *we were desperate,* happened at dawn. Therefore, the walking was *completed* by dawn, and should be expressed with the present perfect participle.

<u>Having walked</u> all night, we were desperate to find rest at dawn.

3. Verbs expressing ideas or works of art

A verb indicating a theory, artistic work, or a non-historic fact is usually given the present tense, to indicate that these ideas and works are still available.

The ancient Greek philosopher Zeno believed that all motion was an illusion.

This sentence contains two verbs, *believed* and *was.* Since Zeno isn't around to believe things anymore, the first verb must be in the past tense. But Zeno's theory is still available to us. We can still wonder whether motion *is* an illusion or *is not* an illusion. Therefore, the second verb should be in the present tense.

The ancient Greek philosopher Zeno believed that all motion <u>is</u> an illusion.

In Macbeth, *Shakespeare portrayed the madness that accompanies the pursuit of power.*

Although Shakespeare wrote *Macbeth* centuries ago and is long dead, the play is still available to us, so you should use the present tense to indicate its life today.

In Macbeth, *Shakespeare <u>portrays</u> the madness that accompanies the pursuit of power.*

Verb tense practice

Circle the correct verb.

1. Glen *(came/has come)* to work exhausted this morning because he *(stayed/had stayed)* up all last night.

2. Already, and without *(spending/having spent)* so much as an hour on research, Dale *(wrote/has written)* the first draft of her essay.

3. *(Developing/Having developed)* the first compressed-air automobile, he *(hoped/had hoped)* to reveal it to the world at the exposition.

Fix any tense problems in the following sentences.

4. *Right after school, we had gone to Mario's for a pizza and a few Cokes.*

5. *Finding no evidence against the accused, the detective had to release him.*

6. *When I got home, I wrote an essay about the baseball game that I saw that afternoon.*

7. *By the time the committee had adjourned, it voted on all four key proposals.*

8. *In the evening, we ate a nice meal with the same group of people we skied with that afternoon.*

9. *By the time I am done with finals, I will write four major papers.*

10. *It surprised us to learn that Venus was almost the same size as Earth.*

11. *Over the last three years, real estate values increased by over twenty percent.*

12. *Buyers often worry too much about finding a good mortgage rate and will forget to scrutinize the terms of the contract.*

13. *By the time we arrived at the tent where the reception would be held, the caterers set up all the chairs.*

4. The passive voice

The passive voice is a way of phrasing an idea to emphasize the *object* of an action rather than the *subject* of an action.

For instance, the sentence *Ellen rode the roller coaster* is in the active voice, but *The roller coaster was ridden by Ellen* is in the passive voice. In the active voice, the subject of the verb is the subject of the action: *Ellen* is the one who *rode*. In the passive voice, the subject of the verb is the *object* of the action: the *roller coaster* is what *received* the riding.

In general, active voice verbs are preferable to passive voice verbs because they are more concise and clear. The passive voice should only be used to indicate that the subject of an action is unknown, or to emphasize deliberately the object of an action.

> *The necklace was mysteriously returned.*

This sentence clearly indicates that the action was a mystery, so the passive voice is required to indicate that the subject of the action is unknown.

> *Having known Jose for years, we were astonished to hear that he had been arrested.*

This sentence clearly emphasizes the idea that Jose was the *object* of the arrest, so the last clause, *he had been arrested* is properly in the passive voice. Placing this in the active voice would change the emphasis inappropriately.

5. Tip for improving your essay

As we discussed in Lessons 7 and 13, the effectiveness of a sentence often depends on its verbs. Your verbs should be clear, forceful, and logical. Use strong, active verbs, and minimize the use of *to be* and passive verbs.

6. Tips for the multiple-choice questions

When a verb is underlined on a multiple-choice question, check that it agrees not only with its subject, but also with any other verbs in the sentence. If a sentence has more than one verb, their tenses must be related logically. Verbs showing actions or states of being with the same time and extent must have the same tense. If one is completed before another, it must take a perfect tense.

> The harvest was hardly <u>sufficient</u> to meet the needs of the villagers <u>because</u> the rain <u>was</u> meager
>   A   B   C
> <u>throughout</u> the growing season. <u>No error</u>
>   D   E

The only verb underlined in this sentence is *was*, a verb in the past tense. It agrees with its subject *rain*, but it does not coordinate with the other verb in the sentence. Since the growing season is an extended period before the harvest, it is "perfect" relative to the harvest. Therefore the second verb should be changed to the perfect *had been*.

When deciding between two good-sounding choices on Improving Sentences questions, check the voice and precision of the verbs. Active and precise verbs are generally preferable to passive and wordy verbs.

Answer Key

Verb tense practice

1. *came; had stayed*

2. *having spent; has written*

3. *having developed; hoped*

4. *Right after school, we <u>went</u> to Mario's for a pizza and a few Cokes.* Since there is only one event being discussed, there is no need for the past perfect tense.

5. *<u>Having found</u> no evidence against the accused, the detective had to release him.* The search for evidence was completed before the *release*.

6. *When I got home, I wrote an essay on the baseball game that I <u>had seen</u> that afternoon.* The *seeing* was completed before the *writing*.

7. *By the time the committee <u>adjourned</u>, it <u>had voted</u> on all four key proposals.* The *voting* was completed before the *adjournment*.

8. *In the evening, we ate a nice meal with the same group of people we <u>had skied</u> with that afternoon.* The *skiing* was completed before the *eating*.

9. *By the time I am done with finals, I <u>will have written</u> four major papers.* The *writing* will be completed before the finals.

10. *It surprised us to learn that Venus <u>is</u> almost the same size as Earth.* This fact is true even now.

11. *Over the last several years, real estate values <u>have increased</u> by over twenty percent.* The *increase* occurred from the past to the present.

12. *Buyers often worry too much about finding a good mortgage rate and <u>forget</u> to scrutinize the terms of the contract.* Tense consistency requires the present tense.

13. *By the time we arrived at the tent where the reception would be held, the caterers <u>had set</u> up all the chairs.* The *setting up* was completed before we arrived.

Lesson 19—Idiom problems

1. What is an idiom?

An idiom is a phrase, like *pass the buck, pull your leg,* or *get your feet wet,* that convention has given a meaning independent of the literal meaning of the individual words. An idiom only works with precisely the right phrasing. For instance, being *concerned about* something is different from being *concerned with* something. Similarly, you can say that a building is *on fire,* but people will look at you funny if you say the building is *with fire.* In an idiom, a tiny change can make a big difference.

2. Watch your prepositions

On the SAT Writing, idiom errors will usually be "wrong preposition" errors. Remember that prepositions are words like *to, from, of, for, by, in, before, with, beyond,* and *up* that show relative position or direction. Certain idioms require specific prepositions. For instance, English idiom requires us to say that we are *arguing with* a person, but *arguing against* an idea.

> *We were no longer satisfied at the level of service we were receiving.*

This sentence contains two idioms: *satisfied with* and *level of service.* Are the prepositions correct? The *of* in *level of service* is correct, but the *at* in *satisfied at* is not. The correct idiom is *satisfied with.*

> *We were no longer satisfied <u>with</u> the level of service we were receiving.*

3. Tip for improving your essay

When we speak, we often insert extra prepositions to make our language sound less formal. In an essay, however, these prepositions are usually redundant and therefore unnecessary. Your writing will sound more polished if you eliminate any unnecessary prepositions. Notice that in phrases like the following the preposition is unnecessary.

> *The pole did not extend ~~out~~ far enough.*
> *Ever since I was injured, it hurts to climb ~~up~~ the stairs.*
> *Although clearly angry, the students were not yet ready to fight ~~against~~ the ruling.*
> *We were unsuccessful in our attempt to extract ~~out~~ the chemical from the venom.*
> *The illness can make one dizzy and prone to falling ~~down~~.*
> *If you don't hurry, you'll miss ~~out on~~ all the fun!*
> *There were plenty of volunteers to help ~~out~~ with the race.*
> *Before we prepare the steaks, we should fry ~~up~~ some peppers.*
> *Her speed and strength helped her to dominate ~~over~~ her opponents.*

4. Tip for the multiple-choice questions

When a preposition is underlined in an Identifying Sentence Errors or Improving Sentences question, think about whether it is part of an idiom. If it is, make sure that it is the correct preposition for that idiom.

> Although many students <u>had professed</u> not to be interested <u>about the Civil War</u>, many were
>   A   B
> <u>inspired by</u> Ken Burns' documentary <u>to read further</u> on the subject.   <u>No error</u>
>   C   D   E

There are two prepositions underlined in this sentence: *about* and *by.* Notice that the word *to* in (D) is part of an infinitive, and therefore is not a preposition. The second idiom, *inspired by,* is correct, but the first, *interested about,* is not. It should be changed to *interested in,* so the correct answer is (B).

Idiom practice

Choose the correct preposition or phrase (if any) to complete each of the following sentences. If no word or phrase is required, circle the dash (–).

1. *I prefer spaghetti (to/over/more than/–) linguine.*

2. *We all agreed (on/with/about/–) the decision to go skiing rather than hiking.*

3. *The defendant would not agree (to/on/with/about) the plea bargain.*

4. *We found dozens of old photographs hidden (in/–) between the pages.*

5. *Good study habits are necessary (to/for/in/–) academic success.*

6. *The new house color is not very different (from/than/to/–) the old one.*

7. *His girlfriend was angry (with/at/–) him for not calling sooner.*

8. *They were both angry (about/at/with) the boys' behavior.*

9. *We will make sure that your contract complies (with/to/–) the laws of your state.*

Consider the idiom in each sentence and fill in the correct preposition, if one is required.

10. *The interview provided insight _____ what great directors think about.*

11. *We were very angry _____ him for ignoring our phone calls.*

12. *We all agreed _____ the color scheme for the wedding.*

13. *Her tests include questions that seem very different _____ those that we see in the homework.*

14. *My mother preferred my singing _____ my practicing guitar.*

15. *When she arrived on campus, she felt truly independent _____ her parents for the first time.*

16. *We were very angry _____ the exorbitant price of gasoline at the corner gas station.*

17. *It was hard not to agree _____ her offer of a free movie ticket.*

18. *I arrived at the meeting too late to raise my objection _____ the proposal.*

19. *If we don't act soon, we may miss _____ the opportunity to lock in the lowest rates.*

Answer Key

Idiom practice

1. *I prefer spaghetti <u>to</u> linguine.*

2. *We all agreed <u>on</u> the decision to go skiing rather than hiking.* (You *agree on* mutual decisions or plans.)

3. *The defendant would not agree <u>to</u> the plea bargain.* (You *agree to* offers.)

4. *We found dozens of old photographs hidden* (none needed) *between the pages.*

5. *Good study habits are necessary <u>to</u> (or sometimes <u>for</u>) academic success.*

6. *The new house color is not very different <u>from</u> the old one.* (Only use *than* with **comparatives** like *bigger*; *different* is not a comparative.)

7. *His girlfriend was angry <u>with</u> him for not calling sooner.* (You get *angry with* people.)

8. *They were both angry <u>about</u> the boys' behavior.* (You get *angry about* situations.)

9. *We will make sure that your contract complies <u>with</u> the laws of your state.*

10. *The interview provided insight <u>into</u> what great directors think about.*

11. *We were very angry <u>with</u> him for ignoring our phone calls.*

12. *We all agreed <u>on</u> the color scheme for the wedding.*

13. *Her tests include questions that seem very different <u>from</u> those that we see in the homework.*

14. *My mother preferred my singing <u>to</u> my practicing guitar.*

15. *When she arrived on campus, she felt truly independent <u>of</u> her parents for the first time.*

16. *We were very angry <u>about</u> the exorbitant price of gasoline at the corner gas station.*

17. *It was hard not to agree <u>to</u> her offer of a free movie ticket.*

18. *I arrived at the meeting too late to raise my objection <u>to</u> the proposal.*

19. *If we don't act soon, we may miss* (no preposition required) *the opportunity to lock in the lowest rates.*

Lesson 20—Mood problems

1. The subjunctive mood

The **mood** of a verb indicates the *factuality* or *urgency* of an action or state of being. Every verb in English takes one of three moods.

Verbs in the **indicative mood** indicate something real or factual, as in *you are going*.

Verbs in the **subjunctive mood** indicate something hypothetical, conditional, wishful, suggestive, or counter to fact, as in *I wish you were going*.

Verbs in the **imperative mood** indicate a direct command, as in *Go!*

The only mood that we sometimes get wrong is the subjunctive mood. The SAT Writing might contain a question or two involving verbs in the subjunctive mood, but they are not very common. You should recognize the common situations in which the subjunctive mood must be used, and know how to change the form of the verb accordingly.

A verb that is in the subjunctive mood is usually accompanied by auxiliaries like *would, should, might,* and *may*. When the verb *to be* is in the subjunctive mood, it usually takes the form *were* or *be*.

Hypothetical:	He *would feel* better if only he would eat.
	If I *were* faster, I could play wide receiver.
Wishful:	I wish that he *would not act* so superior.
	I wish I *were* two inches taller.
Suggestive:	She said that we *should practice* harder.
	He asks that we *be* there at six o'clock sharp.
Doubtful:	I truly doubt that she *would ever say* such a thing.
	I think she *might be* in over her head.
Counter to fact:	We thought that she *might win* the election, but she lost by a lot.
	He plays as though he *were* not even injured.

2. Don't overdo it

In English, the subjunctive is a **mood**, not a **tense**. This means that the rules for altering verbs are not as strict as they are with a tense. Sometimes a sentence gives enough clues about the subjunctivity of a verb so that auxiliaries are unnecessary. Other times, the subjunctive form sounds too archaic.

Don't use subjunctive forms if they make the sentence sound awkward or archaic.

If that be so, we may see dramatic changes in the market.

The sentence indicates a condition, so the verb *be* is in subjunctive form. But today this form is considered archaic. It is now standard English to keep the verb in the indicative mood, even though the situation is subjunctive.

If that is so, we may see dramatic changes in the market.

3. Watch your *ifs*

The past subjunctive construction *if…would have* is non-standard. Use the construction *if…had* instead.

If he would have arrived a minute sooner, he would not have missed her.

The first verb is subjunctive, but proper idiom does not include the auxiliary *would*.

If he had arrived a minute sooner, he would not have missed her.

4. Tip for improving your essay

As you write, avoid non-standard subjunctive phrasing like *If I would have studied* or *I wish I went*. (Say *If I had studied* or *I wish I had gone*.) Frankly, mood problems are unlikely to be a big deal to the essay readers, but such egregious errors don't leave a good impression.

5. Tip for the multiple-choice questions

The most common indicator of the subjunctive mood is the word *if*. When you see a clause that follows the word *if*, or a clause that is clearly suggestive or wishful, make sure that the verb is in the subjunctive mood, so long as it doesn't sound terribly awkward.

Subjunctive practice

Circle the correct verb form in each of the following sentences.

1. *If our wide receiver (was/were) a little faster, he would be more open in the secondary.*

2. *As a matter of fact, Theo (was/would have been) only six years old when the Civil War began.*

3. *Denny would be more successful if only he (promoted/would promote) himself.*

4. *The brochure suggested that we (are/be) at the camp first thing in the morning.*

5. *I wish that my horse (were/was) not so lethargic this morning.*

6. *If the goalie (would have/had) lifted his glove even slightly, the puck would have gotten through.*

7. *He acted as though the concert hall (was/were) filled with screaming fans.*

8. *I wish that summer camp (was/were) two weeks longer.*

9. *If the class (would have/had) voted against it, we would not have been given the chance to visit the museum.*

Circle the verb(s) in each sentence. If the verb mood is incorrect, fix it.

10. *We were very doubtful that Jonna will get the part, since she was sick during her audition.*

11. *If I was in Paris, I'd probably spend most of my time in cafés.*

12. *If I would have known that the food was so good here, I would have come sooner.*

13. *The coach demanded that we were in bed by eleven o'clock.*

14. *Yvonne spoke as if she was a medieval serf complaining about her master.*

15. *Gina wished that she would have chosen the red dress instead of the pink one.*

16. *The professor spoke to us as if he was a member of the British Parliament.*

17. *I would have wanted to have seen the countryside, but I was sick in bed for the entire vacation.*

18. *Had I found his wallet, I would have returned it to him immediately.*

19. *If only the doctor would have told me to cut back on eating red meat, I would have complied.*

Answer Key

Subjunctive practice

1. *If our wide receiver <u>were</u> a little faster…*(The verb indicates a conditional situation.)

2. *As a matter of fact, Theo <u>was</u> only six years old when the Civil War began.* (The sentence indicates a fact, so the subjunctive mood is inappropriate.)

3. *Denny would be more successful if only he <u>would promote</u> himself.* (The verb indicates a situation that is counter to fact.)

4. *The brochure suggested that we <u>be</u> at the camp first thing in the morning.* (The verb indicates an indirect command.)

5. *I wish that my horse <u>were</u> not so lethargic this morning.* (The verb indicates a wishful situation.)

6. *If the goalie <u>had</u> lifted his glove even slightly, the puck would have gotten through.* (This is proper subjunctive idiom.)

7. *He acted as though the concert hall <u>were</u> filled with screaming fans.* (The verb indicates a situation that is counter to fact.)

8. *I wish that summer camp <u>were</u> two weeks longer.* (The verb indicates a situation that is counter to fact.)

9. *If the class <u>had</u> voted against it, we would not have been given the chance to visit the museum.* (This is proper subjunctive idiom.)

10. *We were very doubtful that Jonna <u>would get</u> the part, since she was sick during her audition.* (This verb expresses a doubtful situation.)

11. *If I <u>were</u> in Paris, I'd probably spend most of my time in cafés.* (This verb expresses a conditional situation.)

12. *If I <u>had</u> known that the food was so good here, I would have come sooner.* (This is proper subjunctive idiom.)

13. *The coach demanded that we <u>be</u> in bed by eleven o'clock.* (This verb expresses a suggestion.)

14. *Yvonne spoke as if she <u>were</u> a medieval serf complaining about her master.* (This verb expresses a situation that is counter to fact.)

15. *Gina wished that she <u>had</u> chosen the red dress instead of the pink one.* (This is proper subjunctive idiom.)

16. *The professor spoke to us as if he <u>were</u> a member of the British Parliament.* (This verb expresses a situation that is counter to fact.)

17. *I <u>wanted to see</u> the countryside, but I was sick in bed for the entire vacation.* (This verb expresses a fact, so the subjunctive mood is incorrect.)

18. *Had I found his wallet, I would have returned it to him immediately.* (The sentence is correct.)

19. *If only the doctor <u>had</u> told me to cut back on eating red meat, I would have complied.* (This is proper subjunctive idiom.)

Lesson 21—Diction problems

1. What is a diction error?

A diction error is a "wrong word" error. For instance, if an employer says *we interviewed perspective candidates* instead of *we interviewed prospective candidates*, she has committed an error in diction. *Perspective* means *point of view*, but *prospective* means *potential*. On the SAT, a diction error will be a word that *almost* sounds right.

2. Common diction errors

accept/except   *accept* (v) = *agree to take* <*accept* an offer>   *except* (prep) = *excluding* <everyone went *except* him>

adapt/adopt/   *adapt* (v) = *make suitable for a particular purpose* (from *apt*, which means *suitable*)
adept   *adopt* (v) = *choose as one's own* <*adopt* a child>   *adept* (adj) = *highly skilled* <an *adept* soccer player>

affect/effect   *affect* (v) = *influence* <it *affected* me deeply>   *effect* (n) = *result or consequence* <it had a good *effect*>

allude/elude/   *allude to* (v) = *make an indirect reference to*   *elude* (v) = *escape from capture* <the suspect *eluded* us>
illusion   *allusion* (n) = *indirect reference* <an *allusion* to Macbeth>   *illusion* (n) = *deception or misconception*

ambivalent/   *ambivalent* (adj) = *having conflicting feelings* <I feel *ambivalent* about going to the party>
ambiguous   *ambiguous* (adj) = *unclear or having more than one interpretation* <the message was *ambiguous*>

compliment/   *compliment* (v) = *to make a praising personal comment* <I *complimented* her on her performance>
complement   *complement* (v) = *to make complete* <the jacket *complemented* the outfit nicely>

cite/site/sight   *cite* (v) = *mention as a source of information* <*cite* an article> or *commend publicly* <*cite* her heroism>
   site (n) = *a place where something occurs*   *sight* (v) = *see at a specific location* <*sight* a new galaxy>

council/   *council* (n) = *a consultative committee* <the executive *council*>   *councilor* (n) = *member of a committee*
counsel   *counsel* (v) = *to give advice* <he *counseled* me well>   *counselor* (n) = *advisor* <guidance *counselor*>

discrete/   *discrete* (adj) = *distinct* <another *discrete* item>
discreet   *discreet* (adj) = *prudently modest* <please conduct yourself *discreetly*>

elicit/illicit   *elicit* (v) = *cause to come forth* <the joke *elicited* laughter>   *illicit* (adj) = *illegal* <*illicit* behavior>

eminent/   *eminent* (adj) = *prominently distinguished* <an *eminent* historian>
imminent   *imminent* (adj) = *about to occur* <*imminent* doom>

phase/faze   *phase* (n) = *stage in a process* <third *phase* of the project>   *phase out* (v) = *eliminate in stages*
   faze (v) = *disturb someone's composure* <I was a bit *fazed* by the interruption>

flaunt/flout   *flaunt* (v) = *show something off* <*flaunt* your talents>   *flout* (v) = *show contempt for* <*flout* the rules>

gambit/gamut   *gambit* (n) = *careful strategy or opening move*   *gamut* (n) = *complete range* <run the *gamut*>

imply/infer   *imply* (v) = *suggest or hint at* <she *implied* that she was bored by staring upward>
   infer (v) = *conclude from evidence* <I *infer* from your yawn that you are bored>

its/it's,   Apostrophes can show possession (as in *David's bike*) or indicate missing letters in a contraction
their/they're,   (as in *can't* as a contraction of *cannot*). In each of the word pairs listed here, the words with
whose/who's,   apostrophes are **contractions,** and those without apostrophes are **possessives.**
your/you're   *it's* = *it is* or *it has*   *they're* = *they are*   *you're* = *you are*   *who's* = *who is*

morale/moral   *morale* (mor-AL) (n) = *shared enthusiasm for and dedication to a goal* <the team's *morale* was very high>
   moral (MOR-al) (n) = *lesson or principle about good behavior* <the story had a good *moral*>

precede/   *precede* (v) = *come before* (*pre-* before) <the ceremony *preceded* the game>
proceed/   *proceed* (v) = *go on, usually after a pause* (*pro-* forward) <it was hard to *proceed* after the interruption>
proceeds   *proceeds* (n) = *funds received from a charity drive* <*proceeds* from the raffle>

principal/   *principal* (n) = *head of a school* <*principal* Skinner> or *the initial investment in an account*
principle   *principle* (n) = *guiding rule* <the company is guided by sound business *principles*>

reticent/   *reticent* (adj) = *reserved or reluctant to talk*   (The phrase *reticent to speak* is redundant.)
reluctant   *reluctant* (adj) = *resistant by disposition or mood*

Diction practice

Correct any diction errors in the following sentences.

1. *Even the most trivial news seems to effect the stock price immediately.*

2. *David felt ambiguous about testifying against his partner.*

3. *The moral of the troops was at an all-time low during the Christmas season.*

4. *That scarf really compliments your outfit.*

5. *I tried to stay awake for the lecture, but I was so disinterested that I dozed off before the professor was finished.*

6. *The article mentioned the low voter turnout in order to infer that the senator may not have been elected by a true majority.*

7. *Although the police initially had many solid leads, the suspect alluded them for several months.*

8. *It may be years before we understand how pollution from the new power plant might effect the regional environment.*

9. *The new online store's musical offerings run the gambit from arias to zydeco.*

10. *Heather was the principle author of the study that was recently published in a prominent scientific magazine.*

11. *All of the invited guests accept Anthony arrived promptly.*

12. *For nearly the entire semester, I felt so inhabited that I never so much as razed my hand in class.*

13. *Try as they might, the hikers could not find the anecdote to the snake venom.*

14. *The acid solution was so potent that we had to delude it with water before we could use it safely.*

15. *The symbols on the cave walls are ambivalent; scientists have been debating their meaning for decades.*

16. *Despite a minor setback with the caterers, the Breedens managed to give an eloquent party.*

17. *As someone committed to fairness in education, she could not accept the iniquity of the admissions policy.*

18. *Although most of the manuscripts were signed by their authors, some were written unanimously.*

19. *It was hard for the comic to illicit even the slightest laugh from the crowd.*

20. *We needed to adopt the old engine to fit the new go-cart.*

21. *The imminent congresswoman was reelected easily.*

22. *She thought she should be discrete about her previous relationship with the defendant.*

23. *The counsel will decide how to finance the new city park.*

24. *Rather than cooperating with the rest of the team, Richard always tries to flaunt the rules.*

25. *His knowledge of sports runs the gambit from table tennis to arena football.*

26. *The jury should not imply guilt from the defendant's refusal to answer these questions.*

27. *We are amazed at how adapt a juggler Carl was.*

28. *Rather than eliminate the department all at once, they decided to faze it out gradually.*

29. *Barking dogs can often signal eminent danger.*

30. *After our vacation, we decided to precede with the plan.*

31. *I was trying to infer that I didn't enjoy the movie.*

32. *I always felt reticent to talk in class.*

33. *Deanne's concentration was not even phased by the fire alarm.*

34. *The police officer was sighted for her efforts in the hostage rescue.*

3.Tip for improving your essay

When you write, diction is important. Your choice of words often conveys your level of authority on and sensitivity to your subject. The essay readers on the SAT specifically assess the strength or weakness of your diction when grading your essay, so think carefully about your choice of words. Choose the most effective word for your purpose. For instance, saying *I worked really hard* leaves the impression that you don't have a strong vocabulary. Saying *I worked diligently* leaves a better impression without seeming overbearing. Saying *I worked assiduously* or *I worked sedulously* might seem overbearing and pedantic, depending on the context. Using effective diction does not simply mean showing off every big word you know; it means using *clear* and *appropriate* vocabulary.

4.Tip for the multiple-choice questions

If an underlined word on an SAT Writing question sounds a bit odd, it might be a diction error. On the SAT, diction errors will always be "near misses." That is, they sound *similar* to the right word, but are illogical in context.

<u>Fortunately</u>, the effects of the storm were <u>negligent</u>, because the townspeople <u>had been warned</u> well in
   A   B   C
advance, and had taken all necessary <u>precautions</u>. <u>No error</u>
                                      D   E

The word *negligent* means *lax* or *neglectful.* Only people can be *negligent,* not storms or their effects, so its use in this context is illogical. Choice (B) should be changed to *negligible*, which means *insignificant.*

Answer Key

Diction practice

1. Even the most trivial news seems to <u>affect</u> the stock price immediately.

2. David felt <u>ambivalent</u> about testifying against his partner.

3. The <u>morale</u> of the troops was at an all-time low during the Christmas season.

4. That scarf really <u>complements</u> your outfit.

5. I tried to stay awake for the lecture, but I was so <u>uninterested</u>… (*Disinterested* means *impartial*.)

6. The article mentioned the low voter turnout in order to <u>imply</u>…

7. Although the police initially had many solid leads, the suspect <u>eluded</u> them for several months.

8. It may be years before we understand how pollution from the new power plant might <u>affect</u> the regional environment.

9. The new online store's musical offerings run the <u>gamut</u> from arias to zydeco.

10. Heather was the <u>principal</u> author of the study…

11. All of the invited guests <u>except</u> Anthony arrived promptly.

12. For nearly the entire semester, I felt so <u>inhibited</u> that I never so much as <u>raised</u> my hand in class.

13. Try as they might, the hikers could not find the <u>antidote</u>…

14. The acid solution was so potent that we had to <u>dilute</u> it with water before we could use it safely.

15. The symbols on the cave walls are <u>ambiguous</u>; scientists have been debating their meaning for decades.

16. Despite the setbacks with the caterers, the Breedens managed to give a splendidly <u>elegant</u> party. (*Eloquent* means *well-spoken*.)

17. As someone committed to fairness in education, she could not accept the <u>inequity</u>… (*Iniquity* is sin.)

18. Although most of the manuscripts were signed by their authors, some were written <u>anonymously</u>.

19. It was hard for the comic to <u>elicit</u> even the slightest laugh from the crowd.

20. We needed to <u>adapt</u> the old engine to fit the new go-cart.

21. The <u>eminent</u> congresswoman was reelected easily.

22. She thought it wise to be <u>discreet</u> about her previous relationship with the defendant.

23. The <u>council</u> will decide how to finance the new city park.

24. Rather than cooperating with the rest of the team, Richard is always trying to <u>flout</u> the rules.

25. His knowledge of sports runs the <u>gamut</u> from table tennis to arena football.

26. The jury should not <u>infer</u> guilt from the defendant's refusal to answer these questions.

27. We are amazed at how <u>adept</u> a juggler Carl was.

28. Rather than eliminate the department all at once, they decided to <u>phase</u> it out gradually.

29. Dogs barking can often signal <u>imminent</u> danger.

30. After our vacation, we decided to <u>proceed</u> with the plan.

31. I was trying to <u>imply</u> that I should be considered for the new position.

32. I always felt <u>reluctant</u> to talk in class.

33. Deanne's concentration was not even <u>fazed</u> by the fire alarm.

34. The police officer was <u>cited</u> for her efforts in the hostage rescue.

Lesson 22—Irregular verbs

1. Past participles

Don't use the *past tense* form of a verb where the *past participle* is called for. For instance, don't say *I have spoke* when you mean *I have spoken*.

The perfect tenses and some modifying phrases require the **past participle** of the verb, not the **past tense** form of the verb. For some verbs, like *to golf*, both forms look the same. We may say *I golfed* as well as *I have golfed*. But for many **irregular verbs**, the past participle differs from the past tense form. Make sure you know the **irregular past participle** forms of the following common verbs. It may help to put these on flash cards.

2. Common irregular verbs

Infinitive	Past tense	Past participle
to arise	arose	arisen
to awake	awoke	awoken
to beat	beat	beaten
to begin	began	begun
to blow	blew	blown
to break	broke	broken
to burst	burst	burst
to cast	cast	cast
to come	came	come
to creep	crept	crept
to do	did	done
to draw	drew	drawn
to drink	drank	drunk
to drive	drove	driven
to forsake	forsook	forsaken
to get	got	got, gotten
to go	went	gone
to hurt	hurt	hurt
to kneel	kneeled, knelt	knelt
to know	knew	known
to lay (to put or place)	laid	laid
to lie (to recline)	lay	lain
to ride	rode	ridden
to run	ran	run
to speak	spoke	spoken
to shrink	shrank, shrunk	shrunk, shrunken
to sink	sank	sunk
to speak	spoke	spoken
to spring	sprang	sprung
to take	took	taken
to tear	tore	torn
to write	wrote	written

Past participle practice

Complete the following sentences with the correct form of the verb:

1. *We might have _____ (to ride) the bus as far as Los Angeles if we had had enough money.*

2. *Those issues have not yet _____ (to arise) in this discussion.*

3. *In the last two years, the Patriots have _____ (to beat) the Jets four times.*

4. *Peter told me that I should not have _____ (to drink) the water.*

5. *We should have _____ (to go) to the mall.*

6. *I could not have _____ (to get) such good grades this quarter if I had not changed my study habits.*

7. *The Donnellys have _____ (to run) their corner store for over twenty years.*

8. *Before last night, they had not even _____ (to speak) about the incident.*

9. *I can't believe you put my wool sweater in the dryer and _____ (to shrink) it.*

10. *His batting average has really _____ (to sink) ever since his injury.*

11. *I wish that she had not _____ (to speak) for so long.*

12. *It seems as if the flowers have _____ (to spring) out of the ground overnight.*

13. *We should have _____ (to take) that shortcut to work.*

Circle the past participle(s) or past tense verb(s) in each sentence, and make any necessary corrections.

14. *Elisha could never have went to the state finals if I had not convinced her to join the team in the first place.*

15. *In retrospect, it seems I might have took too much time on the essay portion of the test.*

16. *While we played video games, Danny lay on the couch all afternoon.*

17. *Most people find it amazing to consider that, millions of years ago, life sprung from a primordial swamp.*

18. *Carl would have tore his uniform if he had not stopped his slide at the last second.*

19. *The generals forsook their own troops to surrender and save their own lives.*

20. *When the temperature sunk below zero, the pipes bursted like water balloons.*

21. *The assets of the company were froze as soon as it declared bankruptcy.*

22. *When the cook rung the bell for dinner, the whole camp raced up the hill.*

23. *George needed his friends more than ever, but they had forsook him.*

24. *We sung just about every song we knew, then we went to bed.*

25. *The senator could have spoke a lot longer, but she yielded the floor to her colleague.*

3. Tip for improving your essay

Mistaking the past tense form for the past participle form is a type of diction error. As we discussed in Lesson 21, diction errors make your writing seem unpolished. If you are inclined to say things like *we had spoke* instead of *we had spoken*, use the list of irregular verbs in this lesson to make flash cards with the infinitive form on one side and the past participle form on the other, and study them.

4. Tip for the multiple-choice questions

As we discussed in Lesson 18, any perfect-tense verbs, like *had eaten*, must relate logically to the other verbs in the sentence. You should also make sure that, whenever a perfect tense is called for, the correct past participle form is used. Also, do not use the past participle when the past tense is called for.

In last week's concert, <u>which</u> was attended by many parents and teachers, we <u>sung</u> every song that

             A   B

we <u>had been taught</u> since the beginning <u>of the year</u>. <u>No error</u>

      C   D   E

Two verbs are underlined in this sentence: *sung* and *had been taught*. Since the teaching occurred over an extended time in the past and was completed before the concert began, it is properly in the past perfect tense, and the past participle *taught* is in the correct form. The verb *sung*, however, is in the incorrect form. The past tense of *to sing* is *sang*, and the past participle is *sung*. In this context, the past tense is called for, so choice (B) should be changed to *sang*.

Answer Key

Past participle practice

1. *We might have <u>ridden</u> the bus…*

2. *Those issues have not yet <u>arisen</u> in this discussion.*

3. *In the last two yearsm the Patriots have <u>beaten</u>…*

4. *Peter told me that I should not have <u>drunk</u> the water.*

5. *We should have <u>gone</u> to the mall.*

6. *I could not have <u>gotten</u> such good grades…*

7. *The Donnellys have <u>run</u> their corner store…*

8. *Before last night, they had not even <u>spoken</u> about…*

9. *I can't believe you put my wool sweater in the dryer and <u>shrank</u> it.*

10. *His batting average has really <u>sunk</u> ever since his injury.*

11. *I wish she had not <u>spoken</u> for so long.*

12. *It seems as if the flowers have <u>sprung</u> out of…*

13. *We should have <u>taken</u> that shortcut to work.*

14. *Elisha could never have <u>gone</u> to the state finals…*

15. *In retrospect, it seems I might have <u>taken</u> too much…*

16. *While we played video games, Danny lay on the couch all afternoon.* (The sentence is correct. *Lay* is the past tense of *to lie*.)

17. *Most people find it amazing that, millions of years ago, life <u>sprang</u> from a primordial swamp.*

18. *Carl would have <u>torn</u> his uniform if he had not stopped his slide at the last second.*

19. *The generals forsook their own troops to surrender and save their own lives.* (The sentence is correct. *Forsook* is the past tense of *to forsake*.)

20. *When the temperature <u>sank</u> below zero, the pipes <u>burst</u> like water balloons.*

21. *The assets of the company were <u>frozen</u> as soon as it declared bankruptcy.*

22. *When the cook <u>rang</u> the bell for dinner, the whole camp raced up the hill.*

23. *George needed his friends more than ever, but they had <u>forsaken</u> him.*

24. *We <u>sang</u> just about every song we knew…*

25. *The senator could have <u>spoken</u> a lot longer…*

Lesson 23—Awkwardness and coordination

1. Coordinating ideas

If a sentence contains more than one idea, those ideas must coordinate logically with one other. The main idea must be conveyed with an *independent* clause, but related ideas may be conveyed with independent clauses, subordinate clauses, or modifying phrases.

> *In addition to being a best-selling author, Frances Brown is a native New Yorker and she has written a new book; this new book is likely to cause quite a stir.*

This sentence contains many ideas, but they are poorly coordinated. It contains three independent clauses: *Frances Brown is a native New Yorker, she has written a new book,* and *this new book is likely to cause quite a stir.* Which of these conveys the main idea? The first idea seems trivial compared to the other two. The second and the third are intriguing, but are so closely related that they perhaps belong in the same clause. A good revision would likely combine the last two ideas into the main clause of the sentence, and relegate the other to a modifying phrase with the other less-important idea that she is *a best-selling author.*

> *Frances Brown, a native New Yorker and already a best-selling author, has written a new book that is likely to cause quite a stir.*

2. Run-on sentences

A *run-on* sentence or a *comma splice* is a sentence that uses only a comma to join two independent clauses. To combine two independent clauses, you must use a colon (:), a semicolon (;), or a coordinating conjunction like *but, or, yet, for,* and *nor,* or *so.* (You can remember all of those coordinating conjunctions with the mnemonic BOY-FANS.)

> *I took several science courses last year, my favorite was neuroscience.*

This sentence contains two independent clauses that are joined only by a comma, so the sentence is a run-on. There are many ways to correct this problem. How you fix it depends on what you want to emphasize. For instance, if you want to emphasize both clauses equally, a conjunction or semicolon will work.

> *I took several science courses last year, but my favorite was neuroscience.*

> *I took several science courses last year; my favorite was neuroscience.*

These sentences have slightly different emphases, but are both grammatically correct.

> *The ride was far more harrowing than we expected, several times the car nearly skidded off the mountain.*

This sentence is a run-on because it uses only a comma to join two independent clauses. Since the second clause seems to explain the first, a colon works well.

> *The ride was far more harrowing than we expected: several times the car nearly skidded off the mountain.*

If there is a clear logical relationship between the ideas, consider using subordinating conjunctions like *because, whereas, although,* or *if* to relate the two ideas.

> *Although I enjoy playing golf, I can't stand to watch it on television.*

147

This phrasing emphasizes the second clause as the main idea, which contrasts with the first clause. Since the first sentence is not independent, it can be joined to the main clause with a comma.

> If one idea in a sentence is clearly less important than the main idea, relegate the secondary idea to a modifying phrase.

> *Glenda sang with passion and conviction; she performed for an audience of several thousand.*

This phrasing suggests that the two ideas are closely related and equally important. The first idea, however, seems more significant, so a rephrasing seems in order.

> *Performing for an audience of several thousand, Glenda sang with passion and conviction.*

This turns the second clause into a modifying participial phrase, and coordinates the ideas more effectively.

3. Using colons and semicolons

> Either the colon (:) or the semicolon (;) can be used to combine two independent clauses into a single sentence. The colon usually introduces an *example* or *explanation*. When using a colon or semicolon to splice clauses, the clauses must be *independent* and must not begin with a conjunction.

> *The test was unbelievably difficult; and hardly anyone finished it on time.*

This sentence uses a semicolon, but the second clause begins with the conjunction *and*. You may use a semicolon *or* a conjunction to join two clauses, but not both. You can fix the mistake by simply removing the conjunction.

> *The test was unbelievably difficult; hardly anyone finished it on time.*

You can also combine the two ideas into a single clause, since they are so closely related.

> *The test was so difficult that hardly anyone finished it on time.*

4. Tips for improving your essay

> Make sure that your compound or complex sentences always emphasize the appropriate ideas and relate the ideas logically. You should know how to relegate a minor idea to a modifying phrase, or to emphasize an important idea by elevating it to a clause.

5. Tips for the multiple-choice questions

> On the multiple-choice questions, watch out for comma splices and misused colons or semicolons. Don't join two sentences with only a comma. If a colon or semicolon is underlined, check that both clauses—the one that precedes and the one that follows—are independent.

> We could not help being <u>late, we were</u> delayed by the storm.
>
> (A) late, we were
> (B) late, but we were
> (C) late; having been
> (D) late; we were
> (E) late; because we were

The original sentence is a comma splice. Choice (B) doesn't work because the clauses do not contrast each other, so the conjunction *but* is illogical. Choices (C) and (E) don't work because in both cases the phrase that follows the semicolon is not an independent clause. Choice (D) works best, simply linking the original clauses with a semicolon.

Coordination practice

Write a single sentence that logically and concisely coordinates the given clauses.

1. *Helen Schaffer's latest movie has received widespread critical acclaim. She directed the movie. It is the third movie that she has directed. She is the daughter of famous screenwriter George Schaffer. Her latest movie is a comedy entitled* The Return.

2. *Scientists have made an important discovery. The scientists who made the discovery are from universities and research institutions from all over the world. The discovery concerns a region of the brain called the prefrontal cortex. The scientists have discovered that this region governs impulse control in humans. Studying this region of the brain can help scientists learn more about criminal behavior.*

Make any necessary corrections to the following sentences so that the clauses coordinate logically and concisely.

3. *Electric cars may not be as environmentally sound as they seem, but the electricity they use actually comes from fossil fuels; that electricity is produced in power plants that often burn coal or other fossil fuels.*

4. *Regular exercise is good for your muscles and heart, but it is good for your brain too by keeping it well oxygenated and helping it to work more efficiently, which is surprising.*

5. *We are motivated by our principles; our principles change all the time, though: our experiences and our priorities evolve as we grow.*

Answer Key

Coordination practice

Each sentence below represents one of many possible correct answers.

1. *Director Helen Schaffer, daughter of famous screen-writer George Schaffer, has received widespread critical acclaim for her third movie, a comedy entitled* The Return.

2. *An international team of scientists believes that studying a region of the human brain called the prefrontal cortex, which they have found to govern impulse control, will help them to learn more about criminal behavior.*

3. *Although electric cars may seem environmentally sound, the electricity they use actually comes from power plants that often burn coal or other fossil fuels.*

4. *Regular exercise is good not only for your muscles and heart, but for your brain as well; it helps your brain work more efficiently by keeping it well oxygenated.*

5. *Although we are motivated by our principles, these principles change all the time because our experiences cause our priorities to evolve.*

Part V
Three Practice Tests

Last Name: _____ First Name:_____

Date: _____ Testing Location: _____

Administering the Test

- **Remove these answer sheets** from the book and use them to record your answers to this test.
- This test, which consists only of the Writing portions of the SAT, will require **1 hour** to complete. Take this test in one sitting.
- Use a stopwatch to time yourself on each section. The time limit for each section is written clearly at the beginning of each section.
- Each multiple-choice response must **completely fill the oval. Erase all stray marks completely**, or they may be interpreted as responses.
- **You must stop ALL work on a section when time is called.**
- If you finish a section before the time has elapsed, check your work on that section. **You may NOT move on to the next section until time is called.**

Scoring the Test

- Your scaled score is based 70% on the multiple-choice section and 30% on the essay.
- On the multiple-choice section, you will receive one point toward your raw score for every correct answer.
- You will receive no points toward your raw score for an omitted question.
- For each wrong answer on a multiple-choice question, your raw score will be reduced by 1/4 point.

Time: 25 minutes Start: _____

Stop: _____

Write your essay for Section 1 in the space below and on the next page. Do not write outside the box.

_____
_____
_____
_____
_____
_____
_____
_____
_____
_____
_____
_____
_____
_____
_____
_____
_____
_____
_____
_____
_____
_____
_____
_____

SECTION 2

25 minutes
35 questions

1. Ⓐ Ⓑ Ⓒ Ⓓ Ⓔ
2. Ⓐ Ⓑ Ⓒ Ⓓ Ⓔ
3. Ⓐ Ⓑ Ⓒ Ⓓ Ⓔ
4. Ⓐ Ⓑ Ⓒ Ⓓ Ⓔ
5. Ⓐ Ⓑ Ⓒ Ⓓ Ⓔ
6. Ⓐ Ⓑ Ⓒ Ⓓ Ⓔ
7. Ⓐ Ⓑ Ⓒ Ⓓ Ⓔ
8. Ⓐ Ⓑ Ⓒ Ⓓ Ⓔ
9. Ⓐ Ⓑ Ⓒ Ⓓ Ⓔ
10. Ⓐ Ⓑ Ⓒ Ⓓ Ⓔ
11. Ⓐ Ⓑ Ⓒ Ⓓ Ⓔ
12. Ⓐ Ⓑ Ⓒ Ⓓ Ⓔ
13. Ⓐ Ⓑ Ⓒ Ⓓ Ⓔ
14. Ⓐ Ⓑ Ⓒ Ⓓ Ⓔ
15. Ⓐ Ⓑ Ⓒ Ⓓ Ⓔ
16. Ⓐ Ⓑ Ⓒ Ⓓ Ⓔ
17. Ⓐ Ⓑ Ⓒ Ⓓ Ⓔ
18. Ⓐ Ⓑ Ⓒ Ⓓ Ⓔ
19. Ⓐ Ⓑ Ⓒ Ⓓ Ⓔ
20. Ⓐ Ⓑ Ⓒ Ⓓ Ⓔ
21. Ⓐ Ⓑ Ⓒ Ⓓ Ⓔ
22. Ⓐ Ⓑ Ⓒ Ⓓ Ⓔ
23. Ⓐ Ⓑ Ⓒ Ⓓ Ⓔ
24. Ⓐ Ⓑ Ⓒ Ⓓ Ⓔ
25. Ⓐ Ⓑ Ⓒ Ⓓ Ⓔ
26. Ⓐ Ⓑ Ⓒ Ⓓ Ⓔ
27. Ⓐ Ⓑ Ⓒ Ⓓ Ⓔ
28. Ⓐ Ⓑ Ⓒ Ⓓ Ⓔ
29. Ⓐ Ⓑ Ⓒ Ⓓ Ⓔ
30. Ⓐ Ⓑ Ⓒ Ⓓ Ⓔ
31. Ⓐ Ⓑ Ⓒ Ⓓ Ⓔ
32. Ⓐ Ⓑ Ⓒ Ⓓ Ⓔ
33. Ⓐ Ⓑ Ⓒ Ⓓ Ⓔ
34. Ⓐ Ⓑ Ⓒ Ⓓ Ⓔ
35. Ⓐ Ⓑ Ⓒ Ⓓ Ⓔ

Time: 25 minutes

Start: _____

Stop: _____

SECTION 3

10 minutes
14 questions

1. Ⓐ Ⓑ Ⓒ Ⓓ Ⓔ
2. Ⓐ Ⓑ Ⓒ Ⓓ Ⓔ
3. Ⓐ Ⓑ Ⓒ Ⓓ Ⓔ
4. Ⓐ Ⓑ Ⓒ Ⓓ Ⓔ
5. Ⓐ Ⓑ Ⓒ Ⓓ Ⓔ
6. Ⓐ Ⓑ Ⓒ Ⓓ Ⓔ
7. Ⓐ Ⓑ Ⓒ Ⓓ Ⓔ
8. Ⓐ Ⓑ Ⓒ Ⓓ Ⓔ
9. Ⓐ Ⓑ Ⓒ Ⓓ Ⓔ
10. Ⓐ Ⓑ Ⓒ Ⓓ Ⓔ
11. Ⓐ Ⓑ Ⓒ Ⓓ Ⓔ
12. Ⓐ Ⓑ Ⓒ Ⓓ Ⓔ
13. Ⓐ Ⓑ Ⓒ Ⓓ Ⓔ
14. Ⓐ Ⓑ Ⓒ Ⓓ Ⓔ

Time: 10 minutes

Start: _____

Stop: _____

ESSAY
Time—25 minutes

Directions for Writing the Essay

Plan and write an essay that answers the question below. Do NOT write on another topic. An essay on another topic will receive a score of 0.

Two readers will grade your essay based on how well you develop your point of view, organize and explain your ideas, use specific and relevant examples to support your thesis, and use clear and effective language. How well you write is much more important than how much you write, but to cover the topic adequately you should plan to write several paragraphs.

Your essay must be written only on the lines provided on your answer sheet. You will have enough space if you write on every line, avoid wide margins, and keep your handwriting to a reasonable size. Your essay will be read by people who are not familiar with your handwriting, so write legibly.

You may use this sheet for notes and outlining, but these will not be graded as part of your essay.

Consider carefully the issue discussed in the following quotation; then write an essay that answers the question posed in the assignment.

> Our society deems a person mature by statute. One can drive an automobile at age sixteen, help select a president at eighteen, and drink alcohol at twenty-one. Is this the most effective way to distribute privileges? Perhaps we should ask our young people to pass a test of maturity before we give them a license, a vote, or a beer.

Assignment: **What is the most important test of maturity?** Write an essay in which you answer this question and explain your answer with examples and reasoning from literature, the arts, history, politics, science and technology, current events, or your experience or observation.

Write your essay on your answer sheet.

SECTION 2
Time—25 Minutes
35 Questions

1 The attention that the media have given to the topic of health care is far less than the war.

(A) the war
(B) the war's attention
(C) the attention they have given to the war
(D) that in the war
(E) that compared to the war's attention

2 Students too often become preoccupied with grades, they therefore forget to examine their knowledge critically.

(A) grades, they therefore forget
(B) grades in therefore forgetting
(C) grades; forgetting
(D) grades, and so forget
(E) grades; so they forget

3 We knew that Professor Ferril-Smith was a published author, but we did not know that she was also a distinguished speaker and that she had won several prizes.

(A) a distinguished speaker and that she had won several prizes
(B) distinguished as a speaker and also won several prizes
(C) a distinguished speaker and she had also won several prizes
(D) distinguished as a speaker and winning several prizes
(E) a distinguished speaker and the winner of several prizes

4 Although Liman has used grand cinematographic methods in previous films, a more intimate camera technique has been employed by him in his most recent works.

(A) a more intimate camera technique has been employed by him
(B) employing a more intimate camera technique
(C) he had been employing a more intimate camera technique
(D) his employment of a more intimate camera technique was used
(E) he has employed a more intimate camera technique

5 When presenting a verbal argument, only one point should be articulated at a time by the lawyer, so as not to confuse the jury.

(A) only one point should be articulated at a time by the lawyer
(B) it is the lawyer who should articulate only one point at a time
(C) the lawyer should articulate only one point at a time
(D) articulating only one point at a time is what the lawyer should do
(E) the lawyer should have articulated only one point at a time

GO ON TO THE NEXT PAGE

158

6 Driving for ten consecutive hours, Diane decided that she should look for a motel in which to spend the night.

(A) Driving for ten consecutive hours
(B) Having driven for ten consecutive hours
(C) Having driven consecutively for ten hours
(D) In driving for ten consecutive hours
(E) Being that she drove for ten consecutive hours

7 Many people believe that evolution could not have produced the complex life forms we see today; others, however, believe that these forms could have arisen no other way.

(A) today; others, however, believe that these forms could have arisen
(B) today; others believing however that these forms could have arisen
(C) today but their arising to others could have occurred
(D) today, others believing that these life forms could have arisen
(E) today, but these forms, to others, could not have arisen

8 Because a shark can detect prey by scent and movement, its eyesight does not have to be as acute as other fish.

(A) other fish
(B) of other fish
(C) other fish do
(D) that of other fish
(E) with other fish

9 Scientists have discovered that individual brain cells in the auditory cortex can be tuned for responding to sound frequencies that are particularly important to a species.

(A) for responding to sound frequencies that are
(B) to respond to sound frequencies that are
(C) to respond at sound frequencies that are
(D) to respond to sound frequencies being
(E) responding to sound frequencies that are

10 Because all physical systems store information, many researchers are studying cells and even stars being potential computers.

(A) stars being potential computers
(B) stars as potential computers
(C) those of stars being potential computers
(D) the potential use of stars as computers
(E) potential computers being stars

11 Drawn by the natural beauty of the wilderness, safety is not always the primary concern of campers and hikers.

(A) safety is not always the primary concern of campers and hikers
(B) campers and hikers not regarding safety as a primary concern
(C) the primary concern of campers and hikers is not always safety
(D) safety is not always the campers' and the hikers' primary concern
(E) campers and hikers do not always regard safety as a primary concern

GO ON TO THE NEXT PAGE

12 Filled with a desire <u>to relive</u> the days of her youth,
           A

<u>Anita returned</u> to the playground where she <u>had took</u>
  B   C

her first steps <u>as a child</u> and had made many friends.
         D

<u>No error</u>
  E

13 <u>Ever since</u> the publication of her fourth book, <u>which</u>
  A   B

was very well-received <u>by the critics</u>, Jonas has
          C

found it <u>more easier</u> and more enjoyable to do
      D

interviews with the media. <u>No error</u>
              E

14 Before midterms, <u>there is</u> usually more than fifty
         A

students <u>in the library</u> at one time, so finding an
      B

isolated place <u>to study</u> can be difficult, <u>if not</u>
        C   D

impossible. <u>No error</u>
       E

15 Our coach probably <u>would have extended</u> our
           A

practice <u>by half an hour</u> if <u>it weren't</u> so hot and
        B   C

<u>humid</u> in the gymnasium. <u>No error</u>
 D   E

16 Most of the people <u>which</u> took part in the survey
         A

<u>indicated that</u> they preferred movies with surprise
    B

endings <u>to those</u> with <u>predictable outcomes</u>.
     C   D

<u>No error</u>
 E

17 Deepa was not <u>persuaded to</u> her brother's argument
         A

that, since <u>he</u> is the <u>older</u> of the two siblings, he
      B   C

<u>should be allowed</u> to choose the evening's
    D

entertainment. <u>No error</u>
         E

GO ON TO THE NEXT PAGE

18 The data <u>from</u> the study, which were gathered over
                A

the course of twenty years, <u>reveals</u> that the radiation
                                    B

from distant stars <u>is actually</u> more varied than was
                            C

<u>previously thought</u>. <u>No error</u>
          D   E

19 Many challenges that were <u>encountered by</u> armies
                                        A

fighting two hundred years ago <u>were</u> very
                                        B

<u>different</u> from <u>modern wars</u>. <u>No error</u>
    C   D   E

20 The medical board of the hospital <u>has chosen</u> to
                                            A

purchase large quantities of several new drugs

<u>because many doctors</u> believe that <u>it</u> can be used to
          B   C

save the lives <u>of critically ill patients</u>. <u>No error</u>
                        D   E

21 For <u>at least</u> the last three billion years, the earth's
        A

molten outer core <u>provided</u> the earth with a
                        B

<u>protective magnetic field</u> that has prevented harmful
          C

rays <u>from penetrating</u> the atmosphere. <u>No error</u>
          D   E

22 Historians <u>have long attributed</u> the poor quality of
                        A

ancient manuscripts to deficiencies <u>in techniques</u> of
                                            B

preservation, and so <u>have invested</u> a great deal of
                            C

money in efforts <u>to halt</u> any further deterioration of
                        D

valuable artifacts. <u>No error</u>
                        E

23 The purpose of the recent series of books <u>are</u> to show
                                                    A

students how <u>to develop</u> reasoning skills <u>that lead</u> to
                    B   C

academic and professional success <u>rather than</u>
                                            D

merely to show them how to get better grades.

<u>No error</u>
    E

24 The news of the faculty vote <u>was</u> particularly
                                        A

upsetting to <u>Amanda and I</u>, because we had
                    B

strongly <u>lobbied</u> the professors t<u>o approve</u>
                C   D

the new contract. <u>No error</u>
                        E

25 Without the help <u>of a customer</u> who
                            A

spoke Italian, I <u>would not have been able</u>
                        B

<u>to communicate</u> with the woman who was
          C

trying <u>to buy the purse</u>. <u>No error</u>
              D   E

GO ON TO THE NEXT PAGE

161

26 Protesting the construction of the new mall <u>was</u>
                                      A

the local environmental action committee and

several dozen <u>concerned</u> citizens <u>who prevented</u>
                  B   C

the bulldozers from <u>moving onto</u> the site.
                          D

<u>No error</u>
  E

27 Although the jurors <u>were clearly moved</u> by the
                      A

testimony of the defendant, they evidently did not

find it <u>credulous</u>, probably because <u>it conflicted</u> with
        B   C

the accounts of <u>several other</u> witnesses.
                  D

<u>No error</u>
  E

28 Our youth group <u>has long been</u> concerned <u>in</u>
                    A   B

raising funds for the children's hospital, particularly

<u>because</u> government funding <u>was suspended</u> several
  C   D

years ago. <u>No error</u>
          E

29 <u>Since many</u> doctors are convinced that the new
   A

drug regimen effectively <u>prevents</u> infection,
                   B

but many others <u>are more cautious</u> and want to wait
                C

until further tests <u>demonstrate</u> that the treatment
                 D

has no appreciable side effects. <u>No error</u>
                        E

Directions for Improving Paragraphs Questions

The following passage is an early draft of an essay that may need revision.

Read the passage and select the best answers for the questions that follow. The questions may ask about the diction, logic, and structure of individual sentences. Other questions may ask you about the relationship among sentences or the cohesiveness of entire paragraphs. You are expected to follow the rules of standard written English.

Questions 30–35 are based on the following passage.

(1) When writing e-mail, it is customary for the writer to ignore such things as punctuation and capitalization. (2) Most people think that this is okay in exchange for the more rapid pace of communication. (3) But there are many aspects of e-mail that can cause grief to people who are not careful.

(4) Misunderstandings can arise because of the sterilized nature of instant communication. (5) In the old days, good letter writers were careful with their language to make their point of view clear. (6) They understood that the reader could not see their facial expressions or hear their tone of voice and so they had to convey mood carefully through words. (7) I guess a lot of people consider the pictographic "emoticons" such as smiley faces to be acceptable substitutes for real facial expressions, but they are in fact quite poor. (8) Does a face with a scowl and a tongue sticking out indicate frustration, playful mockery, or something else? (9) A human face can express thousands of distinct emotions, but few e-mail writers use more than a few emoticons. (10) Another problem with e-mail is that it is so fast that writers don't have much time to ponder their words. (11) Years ago, letter writers would think carefully about how they would phrase something, research any necessary facts, and then write carefully so as to express the right emotion. (12) It wasn't going to get there for a few days at least, so the writer did not have to rush the words. (13) Now we can just click "send" and the message arrives in seconds.

(14) It's a rare pleasure to get a personal e-mail that is carefully written and punctuated. (15) If more people took care to write e-mails like they used to write letters on paper, perhaps we would have fewer misunderstandings.

GO ON TO THE NEXT PAGE

30 In context, which of the following is the best revision of the underlined portion of sentence 2 (reproduced below)?

Most people think that this is okay in exchange for the more rapid pace of communication.

(A) these are fine in the exchange of the more rapid pace of communication
(B) it's not a bad exchange in trade for more rapid communication
(C) such things exchange fairly for something like more rapid communication
(D) such omissions are a fair exchange for more rapid communication
(E) this is not a bad exchange for more rapid communication

31 In context, which of the following should be inserted at the beginning of sentence 4?

(A) Naturally,
(B) Nevertheless,
(C) For example,
(D) In response,
(E) Fortunately,

32 In context, which of the following is the most appropriate way to change sentence 7?

(A) Remove the quotation marks from "emoticons".
(B) Change "such as" to "like".
(C) Change "I guess a lot of" to "Many".
(D) Change "real facial expressions" to "those of real facial expressions".
(E) Eliminate "in fact".

33 Where is the most logical place to begin a new paragraph?

(A) After sentence 5
(B) After sentence 6
(C) After sentence 7
(D) After sentence 8
(E) After sentence 9

34 In context, which of the following is the best revision of the underlined portion of sentence 12 (reproduced below)?

It wasn't going to get there for a few days at least, so the writer did not have to rush the words.

(A) It would not have arrived for at least a few days
(B) For at least a few days, it would not arrive
(C) The letter was not likely to arrive for at least a few days
(D) It was unlikely for the letter to have arrived for a few days at least
(E) Because the letter was not likely to arrive for a few days at least

35 Which of the following is the most appropriate sentence to insert between sentences 14 and 15?

(A) These include commas, colons, and exclamation points.
(B) Some of the worst writing comes from people trying to sell something.
(C) Instant communication has been a great asset to modern economies.
(D) We can't expect everyone to be a great writer.
(E) Such courtesies indicate a consideration for the reader that most modern communication lacks.

 **STOP** You may check your work, on this section only, until time is called.

SECTION 3
Time—10 Minutes
14 Questions

Directions for Improving Sentences Questions

Each of the sentences below contains one underlined portion. The portion may contain one or more errors in grammar, usage, construction, precision, diction (choice of words), or idiom. Some of the sentences are correct.

Consider the meaning of the original sentence, and choose the answer that best expresses that meaning. If the original sentence is best, choose (A), because it repeats the original phrasing. Choose the phrasing that creates the clearest, most precise, and most effective sentence.

EXAMPLE:

The children <u>couldn't hardly believe their eyes</u>.

(A) couldn't hardly believe their eyes
(B) would not hardly believe their eyes
(C) could hardly believe their eyes
(D) couldn't nearly believe their eyes
(E) could hardly believe his or her eyes

ANSWER: C

1 The appeal of the carnival rides <u>were apparent in the faces of the children standing</u> in line for tickets.

(A) were apparent in the faces of the children standing
(B) were apparent in the faces of the children that were standing
(C) was apparent in the faces of the children that stood
(D) was apparent in the faces of the children standing
(E) was apparently there in the faces of the children that were standing

2 As the end of the school year approached, the teachers scrambled to write final exams, review with their classes, and <u>finishing their grading</u>.

(A) finishing their grading
(B) to finish their grading
(C) finish their grading
(D) in finishing their grading
(E) they finished their grading

3 As we reached the final hill of the race, <u>I hear David's footsteps pounding rapidly behind me</u>.

(A) I hear David's footsteps pounding rapidly behind me
(B) I heard David's footsteps pounding rapidly behind me
(C) David's footsteps are pounding rapidly behind me
(D) I can hear the rapidly pounding footsteps of David behind me
(E) the rapid pounding of David's footsteps could be heard by me behind me

4 Jorge was unsure whether his recent success on the tennis court was <u>due to his new training regimen or because he was now more self-confident</u>.

(A) due to his new training regimen or because he was now more self-confident
(B) due to his new training regimen or his self-confidence had increased
(C) because of his new training regimen or that he had an increase in self-confidence
(D) due to his new training regimen or his greater self-confidence
(E) because of his new training regimen or due to a self-confidence increase

5 Valued for their loyalty and hunting skills, <u>breeders have been raising beagles</u> for nearly five hundred years.

(A) breeders have been raising beagles
(B) the raising of beagles by breeders has gone on
(C) beagles have been raised by breeders
(D) beagles are being raised by breeders
(E) breaders are raising beagles

GO ON TO THE NEXT PAGE

6 Two lanes of traffic were mysteriously closed, <u>and Fernando was nearly an hour late to work because of it</u>.

(A) and Fernando was nearly an hour late to work because of it
(B) causing Fernando to be nearly an hour late for work
(C) causing Fernando to be nearly an hour late for work because of it
(D) their causing Fernando to be nearly an hour late for work
(E) and this was what caused Fernando's being nearly an hour late for work

7 The story begins with the birth of Trepiste, <u>follows him through his difficult childhood and painful marriage, and ends</u> with his tragic death in Paris.

(A) follows him through his difficult childhood and painful marriage, and ends
(B) starts following him through his difficult childhood and painful marriage, and ending
(C) then following him through his difficult childhood and painful marriage, then ends
(D) then he is followed through his difficult childhood and painful marriage, and it ends
(E) following him through his difficult childhood and painful marriage, and it ends

8 Many professional baseball players are as <u>fit, if not more so, than</u> professional basketball players.

(A) fit, if not more so, than
(B) fit, if not fitter, than
(C) fit, if not more fit, than
(D) fit or even more so, than
(E) fit as, if not fitter than,

9 Perhaps the greatest resource in the world's rain forests <u>are the bounty of natural medicines they produce</u>.

(A) are the bounty of natural medicines they produce
(B) are the production of a bounty of natural medicines
(C) is the bounty of natural medicines they produce
(D) is the medicines that they produce in bountiful quantities
(E) are the bounty of medicines that are produced there

10 By this time next week, if all goes according to plan, we <u>will have completed the first project and begun</u> the second.

(A) will have completed the first project and begun
(B) will complete the first project and beginning
(C) would have completed the first project and be beginning
(D) will be completing the first project, beginning
(E) will have been completing the first project upon beginning

11 <u>Being that we were all seated</u>, the coach began analyzing the effectiveness of our game plan.

(A) Being that we were all seated
(B) Being seated
(C) Once we were all seated
(D) In being all seated
(E) Having been seated

12 Not until she started her first game as a pitcher <u>did Julia truly feel like a part of the team</u>.

(A) did Julia truly feel like a part of the team
(B) Julia truly felt like a part of the team
(C) was it that Julia truly felt like a part of the team
(D) was Julia feeling like a true part of the team
(E) Julia was truly feeling like a part of the team

GO ON TO THE NEXT PAGE

165

13 Scientists have defined many standard lengths in terms of the speed of light in a vacuum <u>being a remarkably stable quantity</u>.

(A) being a remarkably stable quantity
(B) as a remarkably stable quantity
(C) having remarkable stability as a quantity
(D) because this quantity is remarkably stable
(E) for its remarkable stability as a quantity

14 Too few readers understand that their task includes not only understanding the story, but also <u>should consider the manner in which the author chooses to reveal</u> that story.

(A) should consider the manner in which the author chooses to reveal
(B) considering the author's manner by which choosing to reveal
(C) to consider the manner in which the author chooses to reveal
(D) to consider the manner of the author's choosing to reveal
(E) considering the manner in which the author chooses to reveal

STOP You may check your work, on this section only, until time is called.

Section 2	Section 2	Section 3
☐ 1. C	☐ 25. E	☐ 1. D
☐ 2. D	☐ 26. A	☐ 2. C
☐ 3. E	☐ 27. B	☐ 3. B
☐ 4. E	☐ 28. B	☐ 4. D
☐ 5. C	☐ 29. A	☐ 5. C
☐ 6. B	☐ 30. D	☐ 6. B
☐ 7. A	☐ 31. C	☐ 7. A
☐ 8. D	☐ 32. C	☐ 8. E
☐ 9. B	☐ 33. E	☐ 9. C
☐ 10. B	☐ 34. C	☐ 10. A
☐ 11. E	☐ 35. E	☐ 11. C
☐ 12. C		☐ 12. A
☐ 13. D		☐ 13. D
☐ 14. A		☐ 14. E
☐ 15. E		
☐ 16. A		
☐ 17. A		
☐ 18. B		
☐ 19. D		
☐ 20. C		
☐ 21. B		
☐ 22. E		
☐ 23. A		
☐ 24. B		

Total number correct:

_____ (1 point each)

Total number incorrect:

_____ (−¼ point each)

Score Conversion Table

How to score your test

Use the answer key on the previous page to correct your test. Then use the worksheet below to determine your raw score for the multiple-choice portion. Then find the scaled score that corresponds to your essay score and multiple-choice raw score.

Total number of correct answers (Sections 1 and 2):   (A) _____

Total number of incorrect answers (Sections 1 and 2): _____ ÷ 4 =   (B) _____

Multiple-choice raw score: (A) – (B) = _____

Essay score (1–6):   _____

MC Raw Score	Essay Score						
	0	**1**	**2**	**3**	**4**	**5**	**6**
49	680	700	720	740	760	800	800
48	670	690	710	730	750	790	800
47	660	680	700	720	740	770	780
46	650	670	690	710	730	760	780
45	640	660	680	700	720	750	770
44	630	650	670	690	710	740	770
43	610	640	660	680	700	730	760
42	600	630	650	670	700	720	750
41	590	610	640	660	690	710	740
40	590	600	630	650	680	700	730
39	580	590	610	640	670	700	720
38	570	590	600	630	660	690	710
37	560	580	590	620	660	690	700
36	550	570	590	610	650	680	700
35	540	560	580	610	650	680	690
34	530	550	570	600	640	670	690
33	520	540	560	590	630	660	680
32	510	530	550	580	620	640	680
31	500	520	540	570	610	640	670
30	490	510	530	560	600	630	660
29	490	500	520	550	590	620	640
28	480	490	510	540	580	610	640
27	470	490	500	530	570	600	630
26	460	480	490	520	560	590	620
25	450	470	490	520	550	580	610
24	440	460	480	510	540	580	600
23	430	450	470	510	540	570	590
22	430	440	460	500	530	570	580
21	430	430	450	490	520	560	580
20	420	430	440	490	510	550	570
19	410	430	440	480	500	540	570
18	400	420	430	470	490	530	560
17	390	410	430	460	480	520	550
16	380	400	420	450	470	510	540
15	370	390	410	440	470	500	530

Practice Test 1—Sample Essays

> **Assignment:** What is the most important test of maturity?

The following passage received the highest possible score of 12. (Both readers gave it a 6.) This *outstanding* essay develops a clear and interesting point of view with appropriate examples. It demonstrates outstanding critical thinking and mastery of the standards of writing and organization.

Perhaps the most important test of one's maturity comes at that point when easy and self-righteous answers no longer suffice to help us make sense of the world. At such junctures, we are left without the comforting received wisdom of our elders, and must build our own ethical system. We can continue to delude ourselves that the world follows simple moral rules, we can try to make the world conform to our moral vision by destroying those who disagree with us, or we can try to make a part of the world better. The only mature response—the true moral response—is to make the world a little better, and not transform it into our image.

Holden Caulfield, the protagonist of "Catcher in the Rye," lived most of his young life in judgment of everything and everyone but himself. He failed out of four schools, continually picked fights and alienated those who loved him, but he remained arrogantly self-righteous. Only when the cloak of safety given to him by a sheltered adolescence was about to be removed did Holden realize that he had to actually live in the world, and not merely stand in judgment of it. When he arrived in New York City for the weekend, he asked his cabdrivers, "Where do the ducks go in the winter?" knowing that his own winter was coming, and he didn't know where to go to find his moral ballast. He only got some sense of his path when he finally did something unselfish. He took his sister on a carousel ride, and realized that, for all his judgmentalism, all he needed was to make one person happy.

Abraham Lincoln's dilemma was more profound. As the Civil War began in 1861 he was faced with holding a young nation together that seemed to be coming apart at the seams. He could have chosen the path of self-righteousness and domination, particularly when the North acquired the cause—belatedly—of abolitionism. Although some of Lincoln's generals, most notably Sherman, committed atrocities against the citizens of the South, Lincoln did not seek to humiliate the South. He knew that he could not make the citizens of the South agree with him completely, and that he would have to struggle to make the nation whole again. It could not be a simple matter of conquest, particularly if the nation were to maintain its ideals of equality and liberty. Both the ex-slave and the southern landowner would have to live together in a working nation.

Both Holden Caulfield and Abraham Lincoln realized that the problems of human existence could not be solved by holding the staff of righteousness over others. They passed the test of maturity by abandoning the need to be morally superior, and to heal what needed to be healed. This is what adults do. In an age when our leaders often mistake self-righteousness for the hard work of taking care of people, their lessons are welcome ones.

Practice Test 1—Sample Essays

Point of view. The thesis that maturity is marked by a willingness to accept problems without easy or self-righteous answers is a thoughtful and intelligent one. The author states this thesis clearly and maintains this point of view consistently throughout the essay.

Reasoning. The author analyzes the issues of maturity and self-righteousness effectively through the two examples of Holden Caulfield and Abraham Lincoln. With discussion of General Sherman's march and our current leadership, the author demonstrates an understanding of different sides and dimensions of the concepts of maturity and leadership.

Support. Although not very novel, the two examples of Holden Caulfield and Abraham Lincoln are relevant and effective. The author mentions specific relevant details, such as Holden's comments to the cabdrivers and Lincoln's duties as wartime president, to demonstrate their relevance to the concept of maturity.

Organization. The essay is well organized, with a clear introduction, development and conclusion. The conclusion does not merely repeat the thesis, but leaves the reader with a resonant note.

Use of language. The author shows particular strength in diction. The minor lapse into cliché with the phrase "coming apart at the seams" is more than made up for by original and effective phrases like "the cloak of safety given to him by a sheltered adolescence," "moral ballast" and "holding the staff of righteousness over others."

The following passage received a good score of 8. (Both readers gave it a 4.) This *competent* essay develops a point of view with adequate examples. It demonstrates competent critical thinking, adequate but inconsistent coherence and uses generally appropriate vocabulary.

A lot of teenagers complain that they are old enough to drive a car and even fight and die for our country, but they aren't old enough to have a drink. Many of my friends believe that this is intensely unfair, and spend a lot of their time trying to think of how they will get around it. But they do not realize that the real test of maturity is the ability to take care of another human being, to have that person rely totally upon you for their very existence.

One example of a literary character who had to care for another human being is George in the Steinbeck novel "Of Mice and Men" who has to take care of his friend Lennie, who has a mild mental disability. Lenny is very affectionate and loving and sincere but does not know his own strength and sometimes kills things that he loved like a pet mouse he was carrying around. George's passion for women who are "purty" gets him into deep trouble when he accidentally kills Curley's wife. George's love for Lennie is so deep that he is forced to make a horrible decision to protect Lennie from the punishment that surely awaited him.

Many of my friends who think that they are mature enough to drink don't fully realize that, when they get behind the wheel of a car, they are in fact taking responsibility for the lives of other human beings. They are stepping into a loaded weapon that could kill them, their friends, and even strangers. Three years ago, a friend of my older brother was home from college and decided to go to a party with his old friends. He decided to drive two of them home after the party, but after a night of drinking, he lost control of the car, sending it up an embankment where it rolled back down onto one of the passengers, killing her instantly. He spent six months in jail for vehicular manslaughter and must live the rest of his life knowing that he is responsible for the death of another person.

We really don't know whether we are mature human beings until we have had to take care of another human being. Maybe that is why so many young girls get pregnant when they feel unloved because they know that having a child means being mature and also that somebody loves you.

Reader's comments   **8 points out of 12**

Point of view. The thesis that the test of maturity is the ability to take care of another human being is thoughtful, if not unique. The author maintains this point of view fairly consistently throughout the essay.

Reasoning. The author examines the issue of maturity and caring through the two examples of George and Lennie and the author's brother's friend. These examples are connected somewhat to the thesis, although neither example is examined in great detail or with outstanding critical thinking.

Support. The two examples are somewhat but not exceptionally relevant. The author does not discuss in detail how George demonstrates maturity, and the second example does not illustrate maturity, but rather the lack of it, and only indirectly.

Organization. The essay is moderately well organized, with a clear, if slightly unfocused, introduction, two "example" paragraphs, and a conclusion. The conclusion is adequate and somewhat insightful.

Use of language. The author shows adequate facility with language, but also demonstrates occasional lapses in vocabulary and use of pronouns.

Section 2

1. **C**   This sentence compares the *attention that the media have given to* two different topics—*health care* and the *war*. To make the comparison clear, the sentence should use parallel structure. That is, it should compare one kind of *attention* to another kind of *attention*, and it should use similar phrasing to describe them. The original sentence is incorrect because it compares the *attention* to the *war*—an illogical comparison. Choice (C) parallels the phrasing of the first phrase most closely, and makes a logical comparison between one kind of *attention* and another, so it is the correct answer.
(Lesson 14, Parallelism)
(Lesson 15, Comparison problems)

2. **D**   The original sentence is a run-on sentence, or a comma splice. It joins two sentences into one with only a comma between them. This can be corrected by replacing the comma with a conjunction, a semicolon, or a colon, or by subordinating one of the clauses. Choice (D) corrects the problem by including the conjunction *and so*, which shows a logical cause and effect. Notice that choices (C) and (E) misuse the semicolon, because in both cases the phrase following the semicolon is not an independent clause. Choice (B) is awkward and illogical.
(Lesson 23, Awkwardness and coordination)

3. **E**   This sentence includes a list of the things that *Professor Ferril-Smith was*. Therefore, these things should be phrased in parallel. The first item in the list (which is not underlined and therefore must remain unchanged) is *a published author*, a simple noun phrase representing a person. Choice (E) provides parallel phrasing for the other two items: *a distinguished speaker* and *the winner of several prizes*.
(Lesson 14, Parallelism)

4. **E**   The original sentence is awkward because it uses the passive voice unnecessarily—*has been employed by him* (passive) instead of *he has employed* (active). The previous clause uses the active voice, and since the subjects of the two clauses are the same, parallelism requires the active voice be used in the main clause. Choices (C) and (E) both use the active voice with parallel phrasing, but only choice (E) uses the correct present perfect tense.
(Lesson 18, Tense and voice problems)

5. **C**   The opening phrase contains a participle, *presenting,* which requires a subject. Clearly, *the lawyer* is the one *presenting*, so the phrase *the lawyer* should follow the comma. Choices (C) and (E) fix this problem, but only choice (C) uses the correct verb tense.
(Lesson 17, Modifier problems)

6. **B**   The original sentence does not correctly convey the time and extent of events. The driving clearly took place over an extended time from the past to the present, so the perfect participle should be used to describe it—*having driven* instead of *driving*. Choice (D) uses the correct form of the participle, but the concept of *driving consecutively* is illogical.
(Lesson 18, Tense and voice problems)

7. **A**   The original sentence is correct. The semicolon is used properly because it joins two independent clauses that are closely related. The logical coordinator *however* is appropriate because the two ideas directly contrast each other. Lastly, the grammatical structure of the underlined phrase is parallel to the phrasing in the first clause.

8. **D**   The original sentence makes an illogical comparison between a shark's *eyesight*, on the one hand, and *other fish* on the other. The logical comparison is between the *eyesight of the shark* and the *eyesight of other fish*. Choice (D) makes the comparison logically, because the pronoun *that* takes the antecedent *eyesight*.
(Lesson 15, Comparison problems)

9. **B**   The original sentence uses an incorrect idiom *tuned for responding*. The correct idiom is *tuned to respond*. Otherwise, the sentence is fine. Choice (B) is therefore the correct answer. Notice that although choices (C) and (D) correct the first idiom problem, they contain other problems. Choice (C) uses the incorrect idiom *respond at* and choice (D) uses the vague gerund *being*.
(Lesson 19, Idiom problems)

10. **B**   In the original sentence, the gerund *being* is used in an awkward and vague way. What does it mean to *study something being something?* Choice (B) conveys a much clearer idea—the cells and stars are being studied *as computers*, that is, as if they were computing devices. This follows logically from the statement that *all physical systems store information*, since this suggests a comparison with computers.
(Lesson 23, Awkwardness and coordination)

11. **E**   The sentence begins with a participle *drawn*, which requires a subject. What is *drawn by the natural beauty of the wilderness?* The *campers and hikers*, not *safety*. Therefore, the underlined portion should be rephrased so that it begins with *campers and hikers*. Choices (B) and (E) both do this, but only choice (E) creates a complete sentence.
(Lesson 17, Modifier problems)

12. **C**   The past perfect tense requires the past participle. The past participle of *to take* is *taken*, not *took*.
(Lesson 22, Irregular verbs)

13. D The comparative *more easier* is redundant. The word *more* should be eliminated.
(Lesson 15, Comparison problems)

14. A This is an inverted sentence, in which the subject comes after the verb. Since *more than fifty students* is clearly a plural subject, the verb should be *are*, not *is*.
(Lesson 13, Subject-verb agreement)

15. E The sentence is correct.

16. A The pronoun *which* is being used to refer to people, so it should be changed to the personal pronoun *who*.
(Lesson 16, Pronoun problems)

17. A The phrase *persuaded to* uses improper idiom. The correct idiom is *persuaded by*.
(Lesson 19, Idiom problems)

18. B The word *data* is plural. This is reinforced by the use of the verb *were*, which is not underlined and therefore presumably correct. The correct conjugation of the verb is therefore *reveal*.
(Lesson 13, Subject-verb agreement)

19. D This comparison is illogical. It compares *challenges* to *modern wars*. Instead, it should compare the *challenges* of long ago to the *challenges of modern wars*.
(Lesson 15, Comparison problems)

20. C The pronoun *it* does not agree in number with its antecedent *large quantities*. It should be changed to *them*.
(Lesson 16, Pronoun problems)

21. B Since the sentence suggests that the *protective magnetic field* continues to exist, the present perfect *has provided* is required rather than the simple past *provided*. The second verb in the sentence, *has prevented*, confirms the need for the present perfect tense.
(Lesson 18, Tense and voice problems)

22. E This sentence is correct.

23. A The verb *are* does not agree with its singular subject *purpose,* and should be changed to *are*.
(Lesson 13, Subject-verb agreement)

24. B The phrase *Amanda and I* serves as the object of the preposition *of* and therefore must take the objective case *Amanda and me*.
(Lesson 16, Pronoun problems)

25. E The sentence is correct.

26. A This sentence is inverted; the subject follows the subject. The subject of the verb *was* does not agree with its plural subject *the local environmental action commit-* *tee and several dozen concerned citizens*, and should be changed to *were*.
(Lesson 13, Subject-verb agreement)

27. B The adjective *credulous* means *inclined to believe* or *gullible,* and therefore is improperly used in this context. A more appropriate word is *credible*.
(Lesson 21, Diction problems)

28. B The preposition *in* is not idiomatic in this context. The correct idiom is *concerned with*.
(Lesson 19, Idiom problems)

29. A The word *since* suggests a cause-and-effect relationship between the clauses, but the logic of the sentence, emphasized by the conjunction *but,* suggests a direct contrast instead. Therefore, the word *since* should be omitted.
(Lesson 23, Awkwardness and coordination)

30. D The pronoun *this* does not agree in number with its antecedent, because the previous sentence mentioned *two* things that e-mail writers tend to omit—*punctuation and capitalization*. Choices (C) and (D) both fix this problem, but choice (C) is illogical.
(Lesson 16, Pronoun problems)

31. C Sentence 3 suggests that the subsequent paragraph will discuss the *many aspects of e-mail that can cause grief*. Indeed, the next paragraph discusses one such aspect, so the phrase *for example* provides a logical transition.
(Lesson 23, Awkwardness and coordination)

32. C The phrase *I guess* does not fit with the objective tone maintained throughout the rest of the essay, and should be omitted.

33. E Since sentence 10 begins to discuss a new example, it is an appropriate opening sentence to a new paragraph.
(Lesson 23, Awkwardness and coordination)

34. C The pronoun *it* has an unclear reference, which must be clarified. Choices (C), (D), and (E) all correct this problem by specifying *the letter*, but choice (D) uses the past perfect tense illogically. The word *because* in choice (E) is redundant, because the conjunction *so* already indicates the cause-and-effect relationship.
(Lesson 16, Pronoun problems)
(Lesson 23, Awkwardness and coordination)

35. E The point of the final paragraph is that careful writing and punctuation, mentioned in line 14, are rare courtesies, so choice (E) is the most logical choice.

Section 3

1. **D**   The verb *were* does not agree with its singular subject *appeal*. Choices (C), (D), and (E) fix this problem, but choices (C) and (E) incorrectly use the impersonal pronoun *that* instead of the personal pronoun *who*.
(Lesson 13, Subject-verb agreement)
(Lesson 16, Pronoun problems)

2. **C**   The underlined phrase is not parallel with the previous two items in the list, *write final exams* and *review with their classes*. Since these phrases are both present tense verbs and their objects, choice (C) completes the list appropriately.
(Lesson 14, Parallelism)

3. **B**   The past tense verb *reached* in the opening phrase establishes that the main verb should also be in the past tense. Choice (E) is in the past tense, but is phrased awkwardly.
(Lesson 18, Tense and voice problems)
(Lesson 23, Awkwardness and coordination)

4. **D**   The phrasing of the original sentence is not parallel. The two parallel constructions from which to choose are *because of A or B* or *due to A or B*. Choice (D) is the only option that is parallel and uses the correct idiom. Notice that it is also the most concise choice.
(Lesson 14, Parallelism)

5. **C**   The subject of the participle *valued* is not *breeders* but rather *beagles*; therefore the underlined clause should begin with *beagles*. Notice that this requires using the passive voice, but this is preferable to misplacing the participle.
(Lesson 17, Modifier problems)
(Lesson 18, Tense and voice problems)

6. **B**   In the original sentence, the pronoun *it* lacks a clear antecedent. Choices (C) and (E) (the latter of which uses the pronoun *this*) have the same problem. Choice (D) is illogical because it is a noun phrase without a clear relationship with the main clause.
(Lesson 16, Pronoun problems)

7. **A**   The original sentence is clear and concise because it uses the parallel phrasing *begins…follows…and ends*. No other option provides parallel phrasing.
(Lesson 14, Parallelism)

8. **E**   In the original sentence, the phrase between the commas, *if not more so*, is an interrupter. A sentence should always remain logical and grammatical even if its interrupters are removed. The original sentence

would not be, because *as fit than* is improper idiom. Choice (E) is the only one that leaves a logical and grammatical sentence when the interrupter is removed.
(Lesson 13, Subject-verb agreement)
(Lesson 15, Comparison problems)

9. **C**   The verb *were* does not agree with its singular subject *resource*. Choices (C) and (D) correct this problem, but choice (D) commits a noun shift error, since *medicines* is plural.
(Lesson 13, Subject-verb agreement)

10. **A**   The original sentence is best. The future perfect subjunctive is required because the verb indicates an action that will be completed before some specified point in the future. The phrase *and begun* may seem odd at first, but it is understood to mean *and will have begun*, with the phrase *will have* omitted because it is implied by the parallel construction.
(Lesson 18, Tense and voice problems)

11. **C**   The phrase *being that* is a non-standard (that is, incorrect in formal written English) phrase that is usually taken to mean *because*. Choices (B), (D), and (E) are incorrect because they suggest that the coach spoke because he was seated. Choice (C) indicates a logical sequence of events.
(Lesson 21, Diction problems)

12. **A**   The original phrasing is best because the verb of the sentence is *did not feel*. These three words are separated because the sentence is inverted. Notice that uninverting the sentence makes the verb phrase more apparent: *Julia did not truly feel like a part of the team until she started her first game as a pitcher*. With the other options, uninverting the sentence leads to a nonsensical verb phrase.
(Lesson 13, Subject-verb agreement)

13. **D**   The original phrasing does not logically coordinate the ideas in the sentence. The sentence is indicating the reason for the scientists' choice, so a word like *because* is required.
(Lesson 23, Awkwardness and coordination)

14. **E**   The sentence uses the parallel construction *not only A but also B*. The phrase following *not only* begins with the gerund *understanding*, so parallelism requires that a gerund follow the phrase *but also* as well. Choices (B) and (E) both do this, but choice (B) uses an awkward and unidiomatic prepositional phrase *by which choosing*.
(Lesson 14, Parallelism)

Practice Test 2

Administering the Test

- **Remove these answer sheets** from the book and use them to record your answers to this test.
- This test, which consists only of the Writing portions of the SAT, will require **1 hour** to complete. Take this test in one sitting.
- Use a stopwatch to time yourself on each section. The time limit for each section is written clearly at the beginning of each section.
- Each multiple-choice response must **completely fill the oval. Erase all stray marks completely**, or they may be interpreted as responses.
- **You must stop ALL work on a section when time is called.**
- If you finish a section before the time has elapsed, check your work on that section. **You may NOT move on to the next section until time is called**.

Scoring the Test

- Your scaled score is based 70% on the multiple-choice section and 30% on the essay.
- On the multiple-choice section, you will receive one point toward your raw score for every correct answer.
- You will receive no points toward your raw score for an omitted question.
- For each wrong answer on a multiple-choice question, your raw score will be reduced by 1/4 point.

Time: 25 minutes Start: _____

Stop: _____

Write your essay for Section 1 in the space below and on the next page. Do not write outside the box.

SECTION 2

25 minutes
35 questions

1. Ⓐ Ⓑ Ⓒ Ⓓ Ⓔ
2. Ⓐ Ⓑ Ⓒ Ⓓ Ⓔ
3. Ⓐ Ⓑ Ⓒ Ⓓ Ⓔ
4. Ⓐ Ⓑ Ⓒ Ⓓ Ⓔ
5. Ⓐ Ⓑ Ⓒ Ⓓ Ⓔ
6. Ⓐ Ⓑ Ⓒ Ⓓ Ⓔ
7. Ⓐ Ⓑ Ⓒ Ⓓ Ⓔ
8. Ⓐ Ⓑ Ⓒ Ⓓ Ⓔ
9. Ⓐ Ⓑ Ⓒ Ⓓ Ⓔ
10. Ⓐ Ⓑ Ⓒ Ⓓ Ⓔ
11. Ⓐ Ⓑ Ⓒ Ⓓ Ⓔ
12. Ⓐ Ⓑ Ⓒ Ⓓ Ⓔ

13. Ⓐ Ⓑ Ⓒ Ⓓ Ⓔ
14. Ⓐ Ⓑ Ⓒ Ⓓ Ⓔ
15. Ⓐ Ⓑ Ⓒ Ⓓ Ⓔ
16. Ⓐ Ⓑ Ⓒ Ⓓ Ⓔ
17. Ⓐ Ⓑ Ⓒ Ⓓ Ⓔ
18. Ⓐ Ⓑ Ⓒ Ⓓ Ⓔ
19. Ⓐ Ⓑ Ⓒ Ⓓ Ⓔ
20. Ⓐ Ⓑ Ⓒ Ⓓ Ⓔ
21. Ⓐ Ⓑ Ⓒ Ⓓ Ⓔ
22. Ⓐ Ⓑ Ⓒ Ⓓ Ⓔ
23. Ⓐ Ⓑ Ⓒ Ⓓ Ⓔ
24. Ⓐ Ⓑ Ⓒ Ⓓ Ⓔ

25. Ⓐ Ⓑ Ⓒ Ⓓ Ⓔ
26. Ⓐ Ⓑ Ⓒ Ⓓ Ⓔ
27. Ⓐ Ⓑ Ⓒ Ⓓ Ⓔ
28. Ⓐ Ⓑ Ⓒ Ⓓ Ⓔ
29. Ⓐ Ⓑ Ⓒ Ⓓ Ⓔ
30. Ⓐ Ⓑ Ⓒ Ⓓ Ⓔ
31. Ⓐ Ⓑ Ⓒ Ⓓ Ⓔ
32. Ⓐ Ⓑ Ⓒ Ⓓ Ⓔ
33. Ⓐ Ⓑ Ⓒ Ⓓ Ⓔ
34. Ⓐ Ⓑ Ⓒ Ⓓ Ⓔ
35. Ⓐ Ⓑ Ⓒ Ⓓ Ⓔ

Time: 25 minutes

Start: _____

Stop: _____

SECTION 3

10 minutes
14 questions

1. Ⓐ Ⓑ Ⓒ Ⓓ Ⓔ
2. Ⓐ Ⓑ Ⓒ Ⓓ Ⓔ
3. Ⓐ Ⓑ Ⓒ Ⓓ Ⓔ
4. Ⓐ Ⓑ Ⓒ Ⓓ Ⓔ
5. Ⓐ Ⓑ Ⓒ Ⓓ Ⓔ

6. Ⓐ Ⓑ Ⓒ Ⓓ Ⓔ
7. Ⓐ Ⓑ Ⓒ Ⓓ Ⓔ
8. Ⓐ Ⓑ Ⓒ Ⓓ Ⓔ
9. Ⓐ Ⓑ Ⓒ Ⓓ Ⓔ
10. Ⓐ Ⓑ Ⓒ Ⓓ Ⓔ

11. Ⓐ Ⓑ Ⓒ Ⓓ Ⓔ
12. Ⓐ Ⓑ Ⓒ Ⓓ Ⓔ
13. Ⓐ Ⓑ Ⓒ Ⓓ Ⓔ
14. Ⓐ Ⓑ Ⓒ Ⓓ Ⓔ

Time: 10 minutes

Start: _____

Stop: _____

ESSAY
Time—25 minutes

Directions for Writing the Essay

Plan and write an essay that answers the question below. Do NOT write on another topic. An essay on another topic will receive a score of 0.

Two readers will grade your essay based on how well you develop your point of view, organize and explain your ideas, use specific and relevant examples to support your thesis, and use clear and effective language. How well you write is much more important than how much you write, but to cover the topic adequately you should plan to write several paragraphs.

Your essay must be written only on the lines provided on your answer sheet. You will have enough space if you write on every line, avoid wide margins, and keep your handwriting to a reasonable size. Your essay will be read by people who are not familiar with your handwriting, so write legibly.

You may use this sheet for notes and outlining, but these will not be graded as part of your essay.

Consider carefully the issue discussed in the following quotation; then write an essay that answers the question posed in the assignment.

> We will never be able to solve all of the problems that we encounter in our lives. We can and must choose our battles, but the key to a happy life is the ability to tolerate certain problems, lest we become possessed by them and fail to see the good things around us.

Assignment: **Is the ability to tolerate problems as important as the ability to fix them?** Write an essay in which you answer this question and explain your answer with reasoning and examples from literature, the arts, history, politics, science and technology, current events, or your experience or observation.

Write your essay on your answer sheet.

SECTION 2
Time—25 Minutes
35 Questions

Directions for Improving Sentences Questions

Each of the sentences below contains one underlined portion. The portion may contain one or more errors in grammar, usage, construction, precision, diction (choice of words), or idiom. Some of the sentences are correct.

Consider the meaning of the original sentence, and choose the answer that best expresses that meaning. If the original sentence is best, choose (A), because it repeats the original phrasing. Choose the phrasing that creates the clearest, most precise, and most effective sentence.

EXAMPLE:

The children <u>couldn't hardly believe their eyes</u>.

(A) couldn't hardly believe their eyes
(B) would not hardly believe their eyes
(C) could hardly believe their eyes
(D) couldn't nearly believe their eyes
(E) could hardly believe his or her eyes

ANSWER: C

1 A comprehensive program to protect the <u>environment, often difficult for developing countries to implement because</u> they lack sufficient governmental funds.

(A) environment, often difficult for developing countries to implement because
(B) environment, often difficult for developing countries to implement and
(C) environment is often difficult for developing countries to implement because
(D) environment, often difficult for developing countries to implement where
(E) environment is often difficult for developing countries to implement so

2 <u>The wrestlers, enduring weeks of practice, they</u> were well prepared for their first match.

(A) The wrestlers, enduring weeks of practice, they
(B) They, having endured weeks of practice, the wrestlers
(C) To endure weeks of practice, the wrestlers
(D) In enduring weeks of practice, the wrestlers
(E) Having endured weeks of practice, the wrestlers

3 Driving in light rain can sometimes be as treacherous as <u>that of</u> snow.

(A) that of
(B) it is in
(C) being in
(D) for
(E) for that of

4 Success in medical school requires not only intelligence <u>but also</u> dedication and hard work.

(A) but also
(B) it also includes
(C) one must also have
(D) and also
(E) not to mention

5 The president was committed to stimulating the economy through investment, decreasing the tax burden on corporations, and <u>he wanted to eliminate burdensome regulations</u>.

(A) he wanted to eliminate burdensome regulations
(B) the burdensome regulations were to be eliminated
(C) also to eliminate burdensome regulations
(D) to eliminate burdensome regulations
(E) eliminating burdensome regulations

6 <u>Without even consulting the teachers, the school board implemented their own</u> version of the science curriculum.

(A) Without even consulting the teachers, the school board implemented their own
(B) Without even consulting the teachers, the school board implemented its own
(C) Not even consulting the teachers, the school board implemented their own
(D) Without a consultation for the teachers, the school board implemented its own
(E) In not even consulting the teachers, the school board implemented its own

GO ON TO THE NEXT PAGE

7 Physicists can detect new subatomic particles by colliding nuclei at high <u>energies, they then analyze</u> the results of the collisions.

(A) energies, they then analyze
(B) energies by analyzing
(C) energies; analyzing
(D) energies and then analyzing
(E) energies who then analyze

8 Conventional capitalist theory holds that a country benefits most <u>when it focuses on those industries in which it has a natural advantage, and</u> trades freely for the other goods and services it needs.

(A) when it focuses on those industries in which it has a natural advantage, and
(B) when it focuses on those industries that it has a natural advantage, and
(C) in the focus on those industries to have a natural advantage for it, and
(D) focusing on those industries having a natural advantage for it, and
(E) from focusing on those industries in which it has a natural advantage, and

9 In some countries, choosing a leader is as much a religious ritual as <u>that of a civic duty</u>.

(A) that of a civic duty
(B) one's duty of a civic nature
(C) a civic duty
(D) in performing one's civic duty
(E) one of a civic duty

10 To promote new products, many companies prefer word-of-mouth campaigns <u>instead of the use of</u> traditional advertisements.

(A) instead of the use of
(B) but not
(C) and avoiding
(D) over that of
(E) to

11 Long criticized for his imperious leadership style, <u>the team hired the controversial coach over the objections of the fans</u>.

(A) the team hired the controversial coach over the objections of the fans
(B) the hiring of the controversial coach by the team was done over the objections of the fans
(C) the fans objected to the team's hiring of the controversial coach
(D) the controversial coach was hired by the team despite the objections of the fans
(E) the team's hiring of the controversial coach was done despite the fans' objections

GO ON TO THE NEXT PAGE

Directions for Identifying Sentence Errors Questions

The following sentences may contain errors in grammar, usage, diction (choice of words), or idiom. Some of the sentences are correct. No sentence contains more than one error.

If the sentence contains an error, it is underlined and lettered. The parts that are not underlined are correct.

If there is an error, select the part that must be changed to correct the sentence.

If there is no error, choose (E).

EXAMPLE:

By the time <u>they reached</u> the halfway point
          A

in the race, most <u>of the runners</u> <u>hadn't hardly</u>
  B   C   D

begun to hit their stride. <u>No error</u>
              E

ANSWER: D

12 The girls in the class <u>responded for</u> the teacher's
            A
suggestion <u>with</u> unmitigated glee, while the boys
         B
<u>muttered</u> under their breath and stared <u>at the floor</u>.
  C   D
<u>No error</u>
  E

13 Although the film was <u>well-received</u> overseas, and
            A
<u>was in fact</u> one of the top-grossing movies in the
  B
foreign market, <u>but</u> it did not fare <u>so well</u> in the
         C   D
United States. <u>No error</u>
         E

14 The variety <u>of species</u> in the islands off the western
          A
coast of South America <u>are</u> so rich <u>because</u>
         B   C
many profound evolutionary forces <u>have been</u> at
              D
work there for millions of years. <u>No error</u>
           E

15 Although her parents had never <u>heard of</u> the college,
              A
Angela <u>decided to apply</u> because it offered degree
      B
programs that were far <u>more flexible</u> than
          C
<u>other colleges</u>. <u>No error</u>
  D   E

16 We were very surprised that the topic of politics

<u>arose</u> again in the conversation, <u>especially</u> since
  A   B
Jie had just <u>spoke about</u> how unpleasant such
       C
discussions of divisive issues <u>can be</u>. <u>No error</u>
           D   E

17 The debate society has attracted <u>less</u> new students
              A
this year <u>than it did</u> last year, presumably <u>because</u>
      B   C
much of the funding for trips <u>has been eliminated</u>.
              D
<u>No error</u>
  E

GO ON TO THE NEXT PAGE

18 Sheila knew that the <u>opportunities for victory</u> were
                              A
dwindling, and that she <u>would have to act</u>
                              B
quickly or the championship would be <u>denied</u> to
                                          C
<u>her partner and she</u>. <u>No error</u>
___   D   E

19 The news <u>of the quarterback's injury</u> could not
                        A
<u>have come</u> at a worse time for the team, <u>because</u>
      B   C
the playoffs <u>were to begin</u> within two weeks.
                    D
<u>No error</u>
    E

20 Before the hurricane arrived, the villagers

<u>secure</u> their boats after <u>carrying them</u> nearly
  A   B
a mile inland, <u>far from</u> any <u>potential</u> ocean surge.
                    C   D
<u>No error</u>
    E

21 Our class <u>was extended</u> for an hour so that we could
                    A
see a film that offered insight <u>on</u> the origins of many
                                  B
of the tribal conflicts <u>that</u> are even <u>now raging</u> in
                          C   D
many parts of Africa. <u>No error</u>
                            E

22 John D. Rockefeller Jr., <u>like</u> the many philanthropists
                              A
who followed him, understood that <u>their wealth</u>
                                      B
<u>could be used</u> in many ways not only to improve the
      C
American economy, but also <u>to enhance</u> the
                              D
quality of life for ordinary citizens. <u>No error</u>
                                            E

23 Studying <u>for three hours</u> the night before a test <u>is</u>
                    A   B
usually not as <u>effective</u> as <u>to review</u> the major
                    C   D
concepts for ten minutes per night over the course of

several weeks. <u>No error</u>
                    E

24 Although fossils <u>provide</u> the strongest evidence for
                          A
the evolutionary progress <u>of our own species</u>,
                              B
scientists <u>are</u> still <u>far from unanimous</u> about the
              C   D
lineage of *Homo sapiens*. <u>No error</u>
                                E

25 Neither <u>the huge investment</u> in infrastructure
              A
<u>and not even</u> the beneficial weather, <u>which</u> kept fuel
      B   C
costs low, was <u>enough to bring</u> the region out of
                    D
the recession. <u>No error</u>
                    E

GO ON TO THE NEXT PAGE

26 Behind the protective walls of the castle was
       A   B
more than three hundred soldiers, each of whom
                                                 C
was trained to perform a specialized task.
                D
No error
   E

27 After the crash, the event officials had to ensure that
                                              A
the injured driver was safely evacuated and that the
                               B
track was free of debris before the race could
                    C
precede. No error
   D   E

28 The director was reluctant to giving any interviews
                    A   B
to reporters before the film was released, because she
did not want to reveal any information that
                C
might deflate audience anticipation. No error
    D   E

29 The government was alerted to deficiencies in
                        A
American science and math education by the rapid
progress of the Soviet space program and because of
           B   C
the fear of falling behind in the global economy.
        D
No error
   E

Directions for Improving Paragraphs Questions

The following passage is an early draft of an essay that may need revision.

Read the passage and select the best answers for the questions that follow. The questions may ask about the diction, logic, and structure of individual sentences. Other questions may ask you about the relationship among sentences or the cohesiveness of entire paragraphs. You are expected to follow the rules of standard written English.

Questions 30–35 are based on the following passage.

(1) When we think about the subject of philosophy, everybody imagines ancient thinkers the likes of Aristotle and Plato. (2) We don't imagine that there are professional philosophers in the modern age. (3) But there are many people who perform just that task, and not just on college campuses. (4) They work within diverse fields such as medicine, business, law, and government.

(5) Perhaps one of the most important places where philosophers are needed is in medicine. (6) We need highly trained scientists to create new drugs and medical therapies, but we also need professionals to help us to apply those new technologies in a fair and ethical way. (7) If doctors discover a promising medical therapy that seems to prevent cancer in mice, should they immediately start using it on people? (8) A lot of people would say yes if it works, but of course that is part of the problem. (9) A human being is not a mouse, so we have some work to do before we know if it works on humans. (10) This might mean subjecting some people to untested and potentially dangerous treatments.

(11) Modern medical breakthroughs in fields like cloning and stem-cell research have opened a Pandora's box of vexing philosophical questions. (12) Who owns medical knowledge? (13) Should a life-saving therapy be used if it derives from a procedure that some people consider morally wrong? (14) How do we reconcile potential conflicts of interest among doctors, patients, hospitals, insurance companies, and pharmaceutical corporations? (15) Without trained philosophers to help us to analyze these issues, the risk is committing horrible mistakes.

GO ON TO THE NEXT PAGE

30 In context, which of the following is the best revision of the underlined portion of sentence 1 (reproduced below)?

When we think about the subject of philosophy, everybody imagines ancient thinkers the likes of Aristotle and Plato.

(A) everybody imagines thinkers from the ancient world such as Aristotle and Plato

(B) what everyone imagines is ancient thinkers like Aristotle and Plato

(C) what we tend to imagine is that of ancient thinkers like Aristotle and Plato

(D) we tend to imagine ancient thinkers such as Aristotle and Plato

(E) everybody is likely to imagine Aristotle and Plato or some such ancient thinker

31 In context, which of the following is the best way to combine sentences 2 and 3?

(A) We don't imagine that there are professional philosophers in this day and age, that's why many people actually do it, and not just on college campuses.

(B) We often don't realize that there are professional philosophers at work today, and not just on college campuses.

(C) They aren't aware of the many professional philosophers working today not just on college campuses.

(D) It's not like we imagine people doing philosophy today, but they are, and not just on college campuses.

(E) In the modern age, though, people also are professional philosophers, but that isn't just on college campuses.

32 In context, which of the following is the best revision of the underlined portion of sentence 8 (reproduced below)?

A lot of people would say yes if it works, but of course that is part of the problem.

(A) that it should be used if it works, but without human testing, its effectiveness would be in doubt

(B) yes if it works, but that's the whole problem of the issue

(C) yes as long as it is effective, but that's a whole different issue

(D) that it should, but that it is uncertain

(E) yes but medical therapies have issues

33 Which of the following would best strengthen the argument in the second paragraph?

(A) a description of how cancer develops in mice

(B) an explanation of how doctors are portrayed in the media

(C) a discussion of an ethical dilemma in conducting medical experiments

(D) an account of how professional philosophers receive their training

(E) an example of how philosophy is applied in the law

GO ON TO THE NEXT PAGE

34 Which of the following questions would be best to insert after sentence 13?

(A) How should doctors treat a patient who cannot give his or her consent?
(B) How can philosophers best improve their status in the academic community?
(C) How can legislators implement fair and effective tax laws?
(D) How can we educate ordinary citizens to understand the deep issues in philosophy?
(E) How can we bring down the high cost of medication?

35 Which of the following is the best change to make to sentence 15?

(A) Change "Without" to "There being".
(B) Change "the risk is" to "we run the risk of".
(C) Change "to analyze" to "with".
(D) Omit "horrible".
(E) Insert "therefore" before "the risk".

STOP You may check your work, on this section only, until time is called.

SECTION 3
Time—10 Minutes
14 Questions

1 The main result of the three consecutive days of snow and sleet <u>were that the city was brought to a standstill</u>.

(A) were that the city was brought to a standstill
(B) were the standstill to which the city was brought
(C) was that the city was brought to a standstill
(D) was the standstill of the city that was brought
(E) was it brought the city to a standstill

2 The bulls ran through the streets of the village, knocking over kiosks, damaging buildings, and <u>the citizens were frightened</u>.

(A) the citizens were frightened
(B) the citizens being frightened
(C) frightened citizens
(D) frightening citizens
(E) they frightened citizens

3 As we came into the clearing, Alex <u>notices a small tent had been erected where none was before</u>.

(A) notices a small tent had been erected where none was before
(B) noticed that a small tent had been erected where none had been before
(C) was noticing that a small tent was erected where none would have been before
(D) had noticed that a small tent had been erected where none had been before
(E) noticed that a small tent had been erected where there would have been none before

4 It was clear <u>to Theo and I that our plan had not worked as we had hoped</u>.

(A) to Theo and I that our plan had not worked as we had hoped
(B) to Theo and I that our plan had not worked as we would have hoped
(C) to Theo and me that our plan had not worked as we had hoped
(D) for Theo and me that our plan had not worked as we had hoped
(E) to Theo and me that our plan had not worked as we would have hoped

5 The membership of the club had dropped to only three <u>people, this situation being indicative of the fact that we would need to recruit new members</u>.

(A) people, this situation being indicative of the fact that we would need to recruit new members
(B) people, which meant that we would need to recruit new members
(C) people, so we would have needed to recruit new members
(D) people, so we needed to recruit new members
(E) people, this indicating the fact that we would have needed to recruit new members

GO ON TO THE NEXT PAGE

6 Even the counselor's speech about safety could not convince the campers <u>from jumping off</u> the rocks.

- (A) from jumping off
- (B) to stop jumping off
- (C) instead of jumping off of
- (D) against jumping off
- (E) to fail to jump off of

7 <u>Mount Denali is part of the 600-mile-long Alaska range and rises 18,000 feet from its base, it is</u> taller from base to peak than even Mount Everest.

- (A) Mount Denali is part of the 600-mile-long Alaska range and rises 18,000 feet from its base, it is
- (B) Mount Denali is part of the 600-mile-long Alaska range, rises 18,000 feet from its base, making it
- (C) Mount Denali, being part of the 600-mile-long Alaska range, rises 18,000 feet from its base, it is therefore
- (D) Mount Denali, part of the 600-mile-long Alaska range, rises 18,000 feet from its base, and so is
- (E) Mount Denali is part of the 600-mile-long Alaska range, rises 18,000 feet from its base, and is made

8 The newly designed engine was not only more fuel efficient but also <u>it was far lighter than its predecessor</u>.

- (A) it was far lighter than its predecessor
- (B) being far lighter than its predecessor
- (C) its predecessor was not nearly as light
- (D) far lighter than its predecessor
- (E) far more light than its predecessor

9 Most so-called news programs should present <u>fewer partisan shouting matches and more</u> analyses of the problems our country faces.

- (A) fewer partisan shouting matches and more
- (B) less partisan shouting matches than
- (C) less partisan shouting matches and more
- (D) fewer partisan shouting matches but more
- (E) not so much partisan shouting matches as

10 Many politicians are not courageous enough to ask their constituents to sacrifice now for better security in the <u>future, consequently they cannot make</u> the right decisions for our country.

- (A) future, consequently they cannot make
- (B) future; and so cannot make
- (C) future, unable to make
- (D) future, and so cannot make
- (E) future, not making

11 The new film is at once stimulating because of its tight plot <u>but it entertains also because the dialogue is engaging</u>.

- (A) but it entertains also because the dialogue is engaging
- (B) although entertaining because of the engaging dialogue
- (C) and it is entertaining because its dialogue is engaging
- (D) while being entertaining because of its engaging dialogue
- (E) and entertaining because of its engaging dialogue

12 <u>Richard Feynman, a Nobel Prize-winning physicist, whose reputation as</u> a teacher and raconteur rivals his reputation as a scientific thinker.

- (A) Richard Feynman, a Nobel Prize-winning physicist, whose reputation as
- (B) Richard Feynman was a Nobel Prize-winning physicist whose reputation as
- (C) Richard Feynman, who was a Nobel Prize-winning physicist and whose reputation as
- (D) As a Nobel Prize-winning physicist, Richard Feynman, whose reputation as
- (E) Richard Feynman, a Nobel Prize-winning physicist, having a reputation as

GO ON TO THE NEXT PAGE

13 <u>Although its being even more expensive than</u> the original proposal, the new budget was unanimously approved by the committee.

(A) Although its being even more expensive than
(B) Despite being even more expensive than
(C) Whereas having a greater expense than
(D) In having a greater expense compared to
(E) Even with its being even more expensive than

14 Most ancient theories of biology were simply extensions of religious <u>myths, which ascribed most life functions</u> to spirits.

(A) myths, which ascribed most life functions
(B) myths in ascribing most life functions
(C) myths for the ascribing of most life functions
(D) myths; most life functions being ascribed
(E) myths; and these ascribed most life functions

STOP You may check your work, on this section only, until time is called.

Practice Test 2 Answer Key

Section 2	Section 2	Section 3
☐ 1. C	☐ 25. B	☐ 1. C
☐ 2. E	☐ 26. B	☐ 2. D
☐ 3. B	☐ 27. D	☐ 3. B
☐ 4. A	☐ 28. B	☐ 4. C
☐ 5. E	☐ 29. C	☐ 5. D
☐ 6. B	☐ 30. D	☐ 6. B
☐ 7. D	☐ 31. B	☐ 7. D
☐ 8. A	☐ 32. A	☐ 8. D
☐ 9. C	☐ 33. C	☐ 9. A
☐ 10. E	☐ 34. A	☐ 10. D
☐ 11. D	☐ 35. B	☐ 11. E
☐ 12. A		☐ 12. B
☐ 13. C		☐ 13. B
☐ 14. B		☐ 14. A
☐ 15. D		
☐ 16. C		
☐ 17. A		
☐ 18. D		
☐ 19. E		
☐ 20. A		
☐ 21. B		
☐ 22. B		
☐ 23. D		
☐ 24. E		

Total number correct:

_____ (1 point each)

Total number incorrect:

_____ (−¼ point each)

Score Conversion Table

How to score your test

Use the answer key on the previous page to correct your test. Then use the worksheet below to determine your raw score for the multiple-choice portion. Then find the scaled score that corresponds to your essay score and multiple-choice raw score.

Total number of correct answers (Sections 1 and 2):   (A) _____

Total number of incorrect answers (Sections 1 and 2): _____ ÷ 4 = (B) _____

Multiple-choice raw score: (A) – (B) = _____

Essay score (1–6):   _____

MC Raw Score	Essay Score						
	0	**1**	**2**	**3**	**4**	**5**	**6**
49	680	700	720	740	760	800	800
48	670	690	710	730	750	790	800
47	660	680	700	720	740	770	780
46	650	670	690	710	730	760	780
45	640	660	680	700	720	750	770
44	630	650	670	690	710	740	770
43	610	640	660	680	700	730	760
42	600	630	650	670	700	720	750
41	590	610	640	660	690	710	740
40	590	600	630	650	680	700	730
39	580	590	610	640	670	700	720
38	570	590	600	630	660	690	710
37	560	580	590	620	660	690	700
36	550	570	590	610	650	680	700
35	540	560	580	610	650	680	690
34	530	550	570	600	640	670	690
33	520	540	560	590	630	660	680
32	510	530	550	580	620	640	680
31	500	520	540	570	610	640	670
30	490	510	530	560	600	630	660
29	490	500	520	550	590	620	640
28	480	490	510	540	580	610	640
27	470	490	500	530	570	600	630
26	460	480	490	520	560	590	620
25	450	470	490	520	550	580	610
24	440	460	480	510	540	580	600
23	430	450	470	510	540	570	590
22	430	440	460	500	530	570	580
21	430	430	450	490	520	560	580
20	420	430	440	490	510	550	570
19	410	430	440	480	500	540	570
18	400	420	430	470	490	530	560
17	390	410	430	460	480	520	550
16	380	400	420	450	470	510	540
15	370	390	410	440	470	500	530

> **Assignment:** Is the ability to tolerate problems as important as the ability to fix them?

The following passage received the highest possible score of 12. **(Both readers gave it a 6.)** This *outstanding* essay develops a clear and interesting point of view with appropriate examples. It demonstrates outstanding critical thinking and mastery of the standards of writing and organization.

Reinhold Niebuhr's famous serenity prayer asks for "the serenity to accept the things that I cannot change, the courage to change the things I can, and the wisdom to know the difference." Without question, we must choose our battles carefully, for often a battle that seems worth fighting turns out to be very different from what we expected. When we decide to fight, we permit our more primitive, animalistic aspects to dominate our humane and rational qualities. Truly morality requires not only the wisdom to "know the difference," but also the intelligence and diligence to determine the nature of the problems we are trying to solve. If we do not choose wisely to tolerate certain problems as we attack others, we risk creating far more problems for ourselves and others.

There is no doubt that the United States is morally obligated to spread democracy and to defeat intolerance and murderous ideological terror wherever it exists. Yet, to do this correctly, we are obligated to learn the nature of this problem and to attack it competently from high moral grounds. Instead, George Bush has sent our soldiers to war without any moral vision or logistical competence from their commander-in-chief. Our president can proclaim many self-righteous platitudes, but he lacks the ability to solve problems intelligently and the ability to maintain moral leverage. He has wasted billions of dollars on politically expedient programs that make the public think that the government is keeping them safer, but which in fact are money pits of bureaucracy and political pork. For instance, in 2003, George Bush and his political handlers calculated that Americans would surely reelect a wartime president, but the real war against terror wasn't grabbing the favorable headlines they needed, and the president's approval ratings were sagging. They needed a new war. The president also calculated, correctly, that most American voters would not ask many questions about attacking an Arab country being run by an evil dictator, and would accept his judgment as our president.

When a president launches a war for political expedience rather than for moral and practical grounds, certain outcomes are predictable. Human rights will be violated, as they were with the torture and murder that occurred at Abu Ghraib. Innocent civilians will be murdered with no accountability from leadership. Of course, war is always a horrible thing, but a moral nation will at least take responsibility for its actions.

If George Bush had acted morally rather than politically, and had done his homework on the true nature of radical Islamic terrorism, he would have perhaps led this nation to victory over Al Qaida years ago. Instead, we have emboldened the terrorists and given them enormous targets. It is frightening beyond measure to imagine what would have happened if George Bush were in the White House during the Cuban missile crisis. His "shoot first, ask questions never" modus operandi would almost certainly have provoked full-scale nuclear war.

It is a mistake, however, to blame our leadership completely for our nation's poor performance in the war on terror. It is ultimately our fault, for allowing our leaders to shirk their duty to find the facts about Iraq's nuclear capability, as politically inexpedient as that may have been. We gave our political leaders a free pass, assuming they would make the right choices. We assumed that they would act in our best interests, rather than their own. We were wrong. Iraq was much less of a threat to us then than it is now. An Iraq, even under an evil dictator, was a problem that we could have tolerated for a while, until his government collapsed of its own incompetence and corruption. The problem that we should have fixed was the governmental incompetence and corruption right here at home.

Reader's comments   **12 points out of 12**

Point of view. Although the author's point of view is not necessarily one that the readers share, it is clear, substantial, consistent, and well supported with political and social analysis. Even a reader who supports the Iraq war must acknowledge that the author establishes an intelligent point of view.

Reasoning. The author analyzes the issues of domestic and foreign politics as well as political ethics with balance and insight. Although the author only discusses one example to support her point, it is analyzed so thoroughly that another example is scarcely needed.

Support. Although the essay discusses only one historical example in detail, it is substantial enough to support the author's thesis that "if we do not choose wisely to tolerate certain problems as we attack others, we risk creating far more problems for ourselves and others." Bonus points for knowing who wrote the "Serenity Prayer!"

Organization. The essay is well organized, with a clear introduction, development and conclusion. The conclusion offers the reader substantial "food for thought."

Use of language. The author shows a mastery of sentence variation and diction. Her twist on the cliché "shoot first, ask questions later" and use of vocabulary like "expedient," "animalistic," and "competence" are effective.

The following passage received a very good score of 10. (Both readers gave it a 5.) This *effective* essay develops a point of view with appropriate examples. It demonstrates strong critical thinking, coherence, and appropriate vocabulary.

I remember how it felt to wake up and feel my throat burning so I could barely swallow. That morning my mother, knowing that our forensics team was having its biggest debate of the year that afternoon, made me a big bacon and egg breakfast, but all I could do was sip hot tea. I seethed as I sat in my breakfast nook, knowing that I might be letting my team down. I wasn't necessarily our best debater, but I knew my team needed me. "The best thing you can do is rest and make sure you're ready for the next debate," my mother told me. "I know it's hard, but you'll make it worse worrying about it." She was trying to help, but I knew that I couldn't just sit at home. I could still be useful to my team, and just "accepting my fate" wasn't good enough.

Some problems should just be tolerated, such as if our intervention is unlikely to make a difference or even do harm, or when others are more qualified and motivated to solve the problem, or when the problem is likely to solve itself. For instance, during the Cold War, the United States had many opportunities, with its vast nuclear arsenal, to destroy the growing nuclear programs of many other countries, particularly those in the Soviet bloc. Our leaders correctly viewed nuclear proliferation as a dire problem, and one that could potentially spiral out of control. But our wiser leaders realized that direct intervention would be even worse than letting things run their course. It is remarkable that, in the nearly sixty years since nuclear weapons were first used aggressively, they have not been used since. This is because the horror of these weapons has deep roots in our conscience, and we have implemented international treaties and systems of oversight that keep them at bay. The problem, at least so far, has worked itself out because direct confrontation was avoided in favor of cool reasoning. Some problems work themselves out, but my debate team could not win without my help.

I loaded a thermos with hot water and lemon, and my mom reluctantly drove me to school. I would not have been allowed to go to the debate if I were absent from school, so I dozed through algebra, and outlined several debate strategies during English class. We had some idea of the topic of debate, but not which side we were on, so I had to plan to argue from all sides. I sat among my teammates, and handed them notes during the debate. I think my superior knowledge of the New Deal helped us to win the debate about Social Security and other entitlement programs.

When we are presented with problems, sometimes it is best to simply let others solve them or let them play themselves out, so to speak. At other times, however, it is very important for us to roll up our sleeves and meet the challenge head on. It's important for us to know the difference.

Reader's comments   **10 points out of 12**

Point of view. The narrative structure woven into the essay effectively establishes the author's point of view. The author's thesis that "sometimes it is best to tolerate problems, but at other times it is important to meet them head on" is articulated well, if not masterfully.

Reasoning. The reasoning presented in the second paragraph is exemplary. It insightfully and thoughtfully examines some conditions in which problems should be tolerated rather than attacked directly, and the example of the Cold War supports this reasoning effectively. The reasoning is somewhat less effective in the rest of the essay, but gives an overall impression of logical competence.

Support. The two examples of the Cold War and of the author's experience as a debate team member effectively support the thesis that direct intervention is necessary to solve some problems but not others. The author also explains the relationship between the examples and the thesis effectively, without overexplaining. The third paragraph, however, is a bit discursive, and would have been more effective if the author had maintained a focus on discussing the "problems" of the debate and the options for addressing them.

Organization. The overall organization is very good, but the conclusion is somewhat clichéd and insubstantial. The weaknesses in the final two paragraphs prevented this essay from receiving the highest possible score.

Use of language. Diction and sentence variation are a real strength of this essay. Phrases such as "vast nuclear arsenal," "viewed nuclear proliferation as a dire problem," and "has deep roots in our conscience" are precise and highly effective. The author demonstrates a lapse in diction in the final paragraph, but this is probably because he was rushing to finish the essay within the time constraints. Overall, the author impresses the reader as one with an excellent sense of diction.

Practice Test 2 Detailed Answer Key

Section 2

1. C The original is a sentence fragment because it lacks a main verb. Choices (C) and (E) both correct the problem by inserting the verb *is,* but choice (E) is illogical because it implies that the difficulty in implementing environmental protection measures *causes* the countries to run short of funds.
(Lesson 23, Awkwardness and coordination)

2. E The original phrasing contains two mistakes. First, the participle *enduring* is in the wrong form. Since the wrestlers had completed their *weeks of practice* before the first match, the participle should be in the perfect form, *having endured.* Also, the pronoun *they* is unnecessary in the original phrasing. Choice (E) makes both of these corrections concisely.
(Lesson 18, Tense and voice problems)
(Lesson 16, Pronoun problems)

3. B The original sentence contains a comparison error. The sentence should logically compare *driving in rain* with *driving in snow.* The pronoun *in* is required in both clauses to make the comparison parallel. Since *driving* is the subject of the sentence, it can be replaced with the pronoun *it* in the second clause, but not by *being* as it is in choice (C). Choice (B) is the only one that makes a logical comparison.
(Lesson 15, Comparison problems)

4. A The phrase *not only* suggests the parallel construction *not only A but also B.* Since *intelligence, dedication,* and *hard work* are grammatically parallel, the original sentence is correct.
(Lesson 14, Parallelism)

5. E The original sentence violates the law of parallelism. The sentence lists three things that the president *was committed to.* The first two were *stimulating* and *decreasing,* so the third should also be in gerund form. Choice (E) is the only one that provides a gerund, *eliminating,* to round off the list.
(Lesson 14, Parallelism)

6. B In the original sentence, the pronoun *their* does not agree in number with its antecedent *board.* Choices (B), (D), and (E) all correct this mistake, but choice (D) uses the non-idiomatic phrase *consultation for* and choice (E) uses an illogical prepositional phrase *in not even consulting.* Therefore, the best choice is (B).
(Lesson 16, Pronoun problems)

7. D The original sentence is a comma splice, joining two independent clauses with only a comma. This could be corrected with a semicolon or conjunction, but even this would not provide the parallelism that the sentence needs. The gerunds *colliding* and *analyzing* express what the physicists are doing in parallel form, and choices (B), (C), and (D) all provide the gerund

form. Choice (B) is illogical because it expresses an incorrect cause and effect, and choice (C) is incorrect because the phrase following the semicolon is not an independent clause. Choice (D) provides parallel phrasing as well as logical sequencing.
(Lesson 14, Parallelism)
(Lesson 23, Awkwardness and coordination)

8. A The original sentence is correct. Every other choice contains unidiomatic phrasing.

9. C The underlined phrase must be parallel to the noun phrase a *religious ritual.* Therefore, choice (C), *a civic duty,* is the best answer.
(Lesson 15, Comparison problems)

10. E In this context, the standard comparison idiom is *prefer A to B.* Therefore the correct answer is (E).
(Lesson 19, Idiom problems)

11. D The sentence begins with a participle, *criticized,* that requires a subject. Who is *criticized for his imperious leadership style?* The *coach,* not *the team.* Therefore, the underlined portion should be rephrased so that it begins with *the coach.* Choice (D) is the only option that keeps the participle from dangling. You may notice that (D) includes a verb in the passive voice, *was hired by the team.* Although you should avoid the passive voice when possible, it is the best option here.
(Lesson 17, Modifier problems)

12. A Choice (A) contains an incorrect idiom. The correct idiom is *responded to.*
(Lesson 19, Idiom problems)

13. C The word *but* is redundant, because the contrast is already conveyed by the word *although.*
(Lesson 23, Awkwardness and coordination)

14. B The subject of the verb is the singular *variety,* so the correct verb form is *is.*
(Lesson 13, Subject-verb agreement)

15. D This sentence makes an illogical comparison. It should compare the *degree programs* in one college with the *degree programs* in another. Therefore choice (D) should be changed to *those of other colleges.*
(Lesson 15, Comparison problems)

16. C The correct past participle form of *to speak* is *spoken,* not *spoke.*
(Lesson 22, Irregular verbs)

17. A Since students are countable, the correct comparative adjective is *fewer.*
(Lesson 15, Comparison problems)

18. D Since the phrase *her partner and she* is the object of the preposition *of,* it should take the objective case *her partner and her.*
(Lesson 16, Pronoun problems)

19. E The sentence is correct.

20. A The prepositional phrase *before the hurricane arrived* establishes that the main action of the sentence occurred in the past. Therefore the verb form should be *secured*.
(Lesson 18, Tense and voice problems)

21. B The correct idiom is *offered insight into*.
(Lesson 19, Idiom problems)

22. B The wealth is that of Mr. Rockefeller, not that of the *many philanthropists*; therefore choice (B) should be changed to *his wealth*.
(Lesson 16, Pronoun problems)

23. D The sentence makes a comparison, so the items being compared should have parallel form. The first item, *studying*, is a gerund, so choice (D) should be changed to *reviewing*.
(Lesson 14, Parallelism)

24. E The sentence is correct.

25. B The use of *neither* to start the sentence implies that choice (B) should be changed to *nor even*.
(Lesson 14, Parallelism)

26. B This sentence is inverted; the subject follows the subject. The subject of the verb *was* does not agree with its plural subject *more than three hundred soldiers*, and should be changed to *were*.
(Lesson 13, Subject-verb agreement)

27. D The word *precede* means *come before*, but this does not make sense in this context. The correct word here is *proceed*.
(Lesson 21, Diction problems)

28. B The correct idiom is *reluctant to give*, not *reluctant to giving*.
(Lesson 19, Idiom problems)

29. C Choice (C) should be changed to *by* to maintain parallel form with *by the rapid progress*.
(Lesson 14, Parallelism)

30. D The non-underlined portion of the sentence suggests that the subject of the sentence is *we*, not *everybody*. Choices (C) and (D) use the correct pronoun, but (C) is awkward and uses the illogical noun phrase *that of ancient thinkers*.
(Lesson 16, Pronoun problems)

31. B Choice (A) is vague because the two definite pronouns *that* and *it* lack clear antecedents. Choice (C) uses the incorrect pronoun *they*, choice (D) includes the vague and non-standard phrasing *it's not like*, and choice (E) is unclear because the definite pronoun *that* lacks a clear antecedent.
(Lesson 16, Pronoun problems)
(Lesson 23, Awkwardness and coordination)

32. A The original sentence is vague because the pronoun *that* lacks a clear antecedent. The sentence should make clear what the *problem* or *issue* is, and choice (A) does this most effectively.
(Lesson 7, Write the essay)

33. C Since this paragraph discusses philosophical issues in medicine, choice (C) is the only one that would be appropriate to the discussion.
(Lesson 6, Organize your essay)

34. A The final paragraph discusses *vexing philosophical questions* that are raised by *modern medical breakthroughs*. Choice (A) is the only one that addresses a philosophical concern relating to medicine. Choices (B), (C), and (D) are unrelated to medicine, and choice (E) is not a philosophical question.
(Lesson 6, Organize your essay)

35. B In the original sentence, the relationship is among *the risk*, the *philosophers,* and *the issues*. The change suggested in choice (B) corrects this problem. None of the other suggestions improves the sentence.

Section 3

1. C Since the subject *result* is singular, the proper verb form is *was*. Choices (C), (D), and (E) make this correction, but (D) is awkward and (E) includes a pronoun, *it*, that does not agree in number with its antecedent, *days*.
(Lesson 13, Subject-verb agreement)
(Lesson 16, Pronoun problems)

2. D The underlined phrase is not parallel with the previous two items in the list, *knocking over kiosks* and *damaging buildings*. Since these phrases both begin with gerunds, choice (D) completes the list appropriately.
(Lesson 14, Parallelism)

3. B The modifying phrase *as we came into the building* establishes that the main verb should also be in the past tense. Choices (B), (C), and (E) solve this problem, but choices (C) and (E) incorrectly use the subjunctive *would have been*.
(Lesson 20, Mood problems)
(Lesson 18, Tense and voice problems)

4. C The phrase *Theo and I* is the object of a prepositional phrase, and therefore must be in the objective case, *Theo and me*. Choices (C), (D), and (E) fix this problem, but (D) uses the incorrect idiom *clear for* and choice (E) incorrectly uses the subjunctive *would have hoped*. The sentence makes it clear that the two had an *actual* hope which was not met by reality, so the verb

expressing the hoping should be in the indicative mood rather than the subjunctive mood.
(Lesson 16, Pronoun problems)
(Lesson 20, Mood problems)

5. **D** The original sentence is wordy and awkward and misuses the subjunctive mood. (Since the need was actual, it must be expressed in the indicative mood.) Choice (D) provides a clear and logical phrasing that is also the most concise of the options.
(Lesson 20, Mood problems)
(Lesson 23, Awkwardness and coordination)

6. **B** The original sentence uses the unidiomatic phrase *convince from jumping*. The correct idiom is *convince to stop jumping*.
(Lesson 19, Idiom problems)

7. **D** The original sentence is a run-on, joining two independent clauses with only a comma. The correct sentence should join the two clauses in a way that shows their logical relationship. Since the ideas in the first clause serve to explain the second clause, the conjunction *so* is the most logical, so (D) is the best choice.
(Lesson 23, Awkwardness and coordination)

8. **D** This sentence uses the parallel construction *not only A but also B*. The underlined phrase must be parallel to the comparative adjective *more fuel efficient*, so the best option is (D) *far lighter than its predecessor*.
(Lesson 14, Parallelism)
(Lesson 15, Comparison problems)

9. **A** The original sentence is best. Since *shouting matches* are countable things, the comparative *fewer* should be used rather than *less*. Since the comparative adjectives *fewer* and *more* convey the relationship between the two noun clauses, the conjunction *but* in choice (D) is illogical.
(Lesson 15, Comparison problems)

10. **D** The original sentence is a run-on, joining two independent clauses with only a comma. Choice (B) misuses the semicolon, because the phrase following the semicolon is not an independent clause. In choice (C), the adjective *unable* has no clear referent, and in choice (E), the participle *making* has no clear subject.
(Lesson 17, Modifier problems)
(Lesson 23, Awkwardness and coordination)

11. **E** The phrase *at once* suggests that two things are true simultaneously. Therefore the contrasting conjunction *but* is illogical. Choices (C) and (E) fix this problem, but only choice (E) provides parallel phrasing.
(Lesson 14, Parallelism)

12. **B** The original is a sentence fragment, lacking a main verb. Choice (B) is the only option that corrects this problem.

(Lesson 23, Awkwardness and coordination)

13. **B** The subordinating conjunction *although* must be followed by a clause, but the original version lacks a conjugated verb, and so is not a clause. Choice (B) replaces the clause with a participial phrase that effectively modifies the main subject *budget*, and shows the logical relationship between the ideas in the sentence. Choice (C) repeats the problem in the original phrase, since *whereas* must also be followed by a clause. The prepositional phrases in choices (D) and (E) are illogical.
(Lesson 23, Awkwardness and coordination)

14. **A** The original phrasing is best, because the pronoun *which* has a clear antecedent, *myths*, and the phrasing shows a clear and logical relationship between the ideas in the sentence. Notice that choices (D) and (E) misuse the semicolon, and that choices (B) and (C) use illogical prepositional phrases.

Practice Test 3

Administering the Test

- **Remove these answer sheets** from the book and use them to record your answers to this test.
- This test, which consists only of the Writing portions of the SAT, will require **1 hour** to complete. Take this test in one sitting.
- Use a stopwatch to time yourself on each section. The time limit for each section is written clearly at the beginning of each section.
- Each multiple-choice response must **completely fill the oval. Erase all stray marks completely**, or they may be interpreted as responses.
- **You must stop ALL work on a section when time is called.**
- If you finish a section before the time has elapsed, check your work on that section. **You may NOT move on to the next section until time is called**.

Scoring the Test

- Your scaled score is based 70% on the multiple-choice section and 30% on the essay.
- On the multiple-choice section, you will receive one point toward your raw score for every correct answer.
- You will receive no points toward your raw score for an omitted question.
- For each wrong answer on a multiple-choice question, your raw score will be reduced by 1/4 point.

Time: 25 minutes Start: _____

Stop: _____

Write your essay for Section 1 in the space below and on the next page. Do not write outside the box.

SECTION 2

25 minutes
35 questions

1. Ⓐ Ⓑ Ⓒ Ⓓ Ⓔ
2. Ⓐ Ⓑ Ⓒ Ⓓ Ⓔ
3. Ⓐ Ⓑ Ⓒ Ⓓ Ⓔ
4. Ⓐ Ⓑ Ⓒ Ⓓ Ⓔ
5. Ⓐ Ⓑ Ⓒ Ⓓ Ⓔ
6. Ⓐ Ⓑ Ⓒ Ⓓ Ⓔ
7. Ⓐ Ⓑ Ⓒ Ⓓ Ⓔ
8. Ⓐ Ⓑ Ⓒ Ⓓ Ⓔ
9. Ⓐ Ⓑ Ⓒ Ⓓ Ⓔ
10. Ⓐ Ⓑ Ⓒ Ⓓ Ⓔ
11. Ⓐ Ⓑ Ⓒ Ⓓ Ⓔ
12. Ⓐ Ⓑ Ⓒ Ⓓ Ⓔ

13. Ⓐ Ⓑ Ⓒ Ⓓ Ⓔ
14. Ⓐ Ⓑ Ⓒ Ⓓ Ⓔ
15. Ⓐ Ⓑ Ⓒ Ⓓ Ⓔ
16. Ⓐ Ⓑ Ⓒ Ⓓ Ⓔ
17. Ⓐ Ⓑ Ⓒ Ⓓ Ⓔ
18. Ⓐ Ⓑ Ⓒ Ⓓ Ⓔ
19. Ⓐ Ⓑ Ⓒ Ⓓ Ⓔ
20. Ⓐ Ⓑ Ⓒ Ⓓ Ⓔ
21. Ⓐ Ⓑ Ⓒ Ⓓ Ⓔ
22. Ⓐ Ⓑ Ⓒ Ⓓ Ⓔ
23. Ⓐ Ⓑ Ⓒ Ⓓ Ⓔ
24. Ⓐ Ⓑ Ⓒ Ⓓ Ⓔ

25. Ⓐ Ⓑ Ⓒ Ⓓ Ⓔ
26. Ⓐ Ⓑ Ⓒ Ⓓ Ⓔ
27. Ⓐ Ⓑ Ⓒ Ⓓ Ⓔ
28. Ⓐ Ⓑ Ⓒ Ⓓ Ⓔ
29. Ⓐ Ⓑ Ⓒ Ⓓ Ⓔ
30. Ⓐ Ⓑ Ⓒ Ⓓ Ⓔ
31. Ⓐ Ⓑ Ⓒ Ⓓ Ⓔ
32. Ⓐ Ⓑ Ⓒ Ⓓ Ⓔ
33. Ⓐ Ⓑ Ⓒ Ⓓ Ⓔ
34. Ⓐ Ⓑ Ⓒ Ⓓ Ⓔ
35. Ⓐ Ⓑ Ⓒ Ⓓ Ⓔ

Time: 25 minutes

Start: _____

Stop: _____

SECTION 3

10 minutes
14 questions

1. Ⓐ Ⓑ Ⓒ Ⓓ Ⓔ
2. Ⓐ Ⓑ Ⓒ Ⓓ Ⓔ
3. Ⓐ Ⓑ Ⓒ Ⓓ Ⓔ
4. Ⓐ Ⓑ Ⓒ Ⓓ Ⓔ
5. Ⓐ Ⓑ Ⓒ Ⓓ Ⓔ

6. Ⓐ Ⓑ Ⓒ Ⓓ Ⓔ
7. Ⓐ Ⓑ Ⓒ Ⓓ Ⓔ
8. Ⓐ Ⓑ Ⓒ Ⓓ Ⓔ
9. Ⓐ Ⓑ Ⓒ Ⓓ Ⓔ
10. Ⓐ Ⓑ Ⓒ Ⓓ Ⓔ

11. Ⓐ Ⓑ Ⓒ Ⓓ Ⓔ
12. Ⓐ Ⓑ Ⓒ Ⓓ Ⓔ
13. Ⓐ Ⓑ Ⓒ Ⓓ Ⓔ
14. Ⓐ Ⓑ Ⓒ Ⓓ Ⓔ

Time: 10 minutes

Start: _____

Stop: _____

ESSAY
Time—25 minutes

Directions for Writing the Essay

Plan and write an essay that answers the question below. Do NOT write on another topic. An essay on another topic will receive a score of 0.

Two readers will grade your essay based on how well you develop your point of view, organize and explain your ideas, use specific and relevant examples to support your thesis, and use clear and effective language. How well you write is much more important than how much you write, but to cover the topic adequately you should plan to write several paragraphs.

Your essay must be written only on the lines provided on your answer sheet. You will have enough space if you write on every line, avoid wide margins, and keep your handwriting to a reasonable size. Your essay will be read by people who are not familiar with your handwriting, so write legibly.

You may use this sheet for notes and outlining, but these will not be graded as part of your essay.

Consider carefully the issue discussed in the following quotation; then write an essay that answers the question posed in the assignment.

> Most legal systems place a high value on intention. We do not hold someone as accountable for a terrible crime if the perpetrator did not fully intend its outcome. We also reserve the right to punish those who merely plan evil deeds, whether or not they actually carry out their plans.

Assignment: **Is the intention to do something ever as important as actually doing it?** Write an essay in which you answer this question and explain your answer with reasoning and examples from literature, the arts, history, politics, science and technology, current events, or your experience or observation.

Write your essay on your answer sheet.

SECTION 2
Time—25 Minutes
35 Questions

Directions for Improving Sentences Questions

Each of the sentences below contains one underlined portion. The portion may contain one or more errors in grammar, usage, construction, precision, diction (choice of words), or idiom. Some of the sentences are correct.

Consider the meaning of the original sentence, and choose the answer that best expresses that meaning. If the original sentence is best, choose (A), because it repeats the original phrasing. Choose the phrasing that creates the clearest, most precise, and most effective sentence.

EXAMPLE:

The children couldn't hardly believe their eyes.

(A) couldn't hardly believe their eyes
(B) would not hardly believe their eyes
(C) could hardly believe their eyes
(D) couldn't nearly believe their eyes
(E) could hardly believe his or her eyes

ANSWER: C

1 Neither the noise from the crowds nor there being many obstacles in the street seemed to slow the racers down.

(A) nor there being many obstacles in the street
(B) and the many obstacles in the street
(C) or even the many obstacles in the street
(D) nor the street having many obstacles
(E) nor the many obstacles in the street

2 Although Heinmann's latest book of poems has been lauded by the critics, the public has not as highly regarded it as them.

(A) the public has not as highly regarded it as them
(B) the public has not regarded it as highly as have those
(C) the regard by the public hasn't been as high
(D) it has not been as highly regarded by the public
(E) it was not regarded by the public as highly

3 Neither painting, when regarded at a distance, appears like the masterpieces they are.

(A) like the masterpieces they are
(B) to be the masterpiece that it is
(C) like they are masterpieces
(D) like a masterpiece
(E) to be the masterpieces they are

4 After Fernando and Julie had decided which historical era they would study, the research was begun by them for the project.

(A) the research was begun by them for the project
(B) the project's research was begun by them
(C) they began their research for the project
(D) they began in researching for the project
(E) the research for the project was begun by them

5 Many piano teachers believe that a student should learn to play Bach in order to master proper technique.

(A) Many piano teachers believe that a student should learn to play Bach in order to master proper technique.
(B) A student should learn to play Bach in order to master proper technique, this is what many piano teachers believe.
(C) To master proper technique, many piano teachers believe learning to play Bach is important for a student.
(D) Learning to play Bach in order to master proper technique is what many piano teachers believe.
(E) It is important for students to master proper technique by playing Bach, which is what many piano teachers believe.

6 Alicia, having practiced all summer to improve her shooting skills, and being disappointed that she was not chosen as a starter on the basketball team.

(A) and being disappointed that she was not
(B) and being disappointed in not being
(C) and was disappointed that she was not
(D) was disappointed that she was not
(E) disappointed that she was not

GO ON TO THE NEXT PAGE

7 Despite having committed to attracting more qualified teachers, <u>but the board did not allocate sufficient funds to pay them.</u>

(A) but the board did not allocate sufficient funds to pay them

(B) the board did not allocate sufficient funds to pay them

(C) sufficient funds to pay them were not allocated by the board

(D) the failure to allocate sufficient funds to pay them could be attributed to the board

(E) they were not allocated sufficient funds to pay them by the board

8 The climatological effect of a major volcanic eruption can be <u>as dramatic as that of cumulative emissions from cars and factories, if not more so.</u>

(A) as dramatic as that of cumulative emissions from cars and factories, if not more so

(B) as dramatic as, if not more so, cumulative emissions from cars and factories

(C) as dramatic as, if not more, than that due to cumulative emissions from cars and factories

(D) as dramatic as cumulative emissions from cars and factories, if not more so

(E) as dramatic, if not more, than cumulative emissions from cars and factories

9 Intrigued by the prospect of becoming a real author, <u>Lani eagerly signed the contract that the publishing company offered.</u>

(A) Lani eagerly signed the contract that the publishing company offered

(B) the contract that the publishing company offered was eagerly signed by Lani

(C) the publishing company offered Lani a contract, which she eagerly signed

(D) Lani was offered the contract by the publishing company, which she eagerly signed

(E) the publishing company offered Lani a contract and she eagerly signed it

10 As a mother of five adult children and a respected family therapist, <u>millions of readers have followed Dr. Krone's child rearing advice for more than twenty years.</u>

(A) millions of readers have followed Dr. Krone's child rearing advice for more than twenty years

(B) Dr. Krone's child rearing advice has been followed by millions of readers for more than twenty years

(C) Dr. Krone has offered child rearing advice that millions of readers are following for more than twenty years

(D) Dr. Krone's child rearing advice has been followed for more than twenty years by millions of readers

(E) Dr. Krone has offered child rearing advice that millions of readers have followed for more than twenty years

11 The evidence from the crime scene suggested that <u>the ones that had stole the jewelry were probably</u> employees at the store.

(A) the ones that had stole the jewelry were probably

(B) those that had stolen the jewelry probably being

(C) those who had stole the jewelry were probably

(D) those who had stolen the jewelry were probably

(E) those who had stolen the jewelry probably being

GO ON TO THE NEXT PAGE

Directions for Identifying Sentence Errors Questions

The following sentences may contain errors in grammar, usage, diction (choice of words), or idiom. Some of the sentences are correct. No sentence contains more than one error.

If the sentence contains an error, it is underlined and lettered. The parts that are not underlined are correct.

If there is an error, select the part that must be changed to correct the sentence.

If there is no error, choose (E).

EXAMPLE:

By the time <u>they reached</u> the halfway point
           A

<u>in the race,</u> most <u>of the runners</u> <u>hadn't hardly</u>
   B   C   D

begun to hit their stride. <u>No error</u>
                   E

ANSWER: D

12 Wilson's goal was <u>to transform</u> the very nature of
               A

the automobile engine, <u>this</u> had been <u>utilizing</u> the
              B   C

combustion <u>of fossil fuels</u> for nearly one hundred
          D

years. <u>No error</u>
       E

13 Anna and Sarah <u>were</u> both inspired <u>to become</u>
              A   B

<u>a performer</u> after seeing Kristen Chenoweth's
  C

performances as a <u>singer, dancer, and actress</u> in a
                D

wide variety of productions. <u>No error</u>
                 E

14 Although she was <u>intimidated</u> to be in the presence
              A

of <u>so many professionals</u>, Caroline impressed the
       B

interviewing committee <u>with</u> her knowledge,
              C

competence, and <u>the fact that she was patient</u>.
              D

<u>No error</u>
 E

15 Although she spent many years teaching high school

<u>and working</u> for a newspaper in Pittsburgh, Willa
  A

Cather <u>lived</u> most of her life in Nebraska, <u>where</u>
      B   C

many of her novels <u>are set</u>. <u>No error</u>
          D   E

16 The task of ensuring <u>that</u> new building designs
             A

<u>complied to</u> construction codes became increasingly
  B

difficult <u>because</u> new rules <u>were being established</u>
      C   D

at every meeting of the planning board. <u>No error</u>
                       E

17 Gregory <u>could not</u> concentrate on the morning
        A

lecture <u>because</u> he <u>stayed</u> up until 3 a.m. the previous
      B   C

night <u>talking</u> with his girlfriend. <u>No error</u>
    D   E

GO ON TO THE NEXT PAGE

18 The new ideas <u>about</u> the evolution of human
                    A
cognition and behavior, <u>as promoted by</u> such
                                    B
scientists as Steven Pinker, <u>has stimulated</u> a
                                        C
spirited debate <u>among psychologists</u>. <u>No error</u>
                            D   E

19 Preparing <u>to run</u> a marathon involves consistent
                        A
dedication and the <u>willingness to endure</u> long periods
                                B
of time <u>where</u> it seems no progress is <u>being made</u>.
                C   D
<u>No error</u>
    E

20 The blue whale <u>is</u> not only the largest mammal on
                            A
land or in the sea, but <u>they are</u> also quite likely the
                                    B
<u>largest</u> animal that <u>has ever lived</u> on the planet.
    C   D
<u>No error</u>
    E

21 The judges <u>deliberated</u> for nearly an hour about
                        A
<u>whether to award</u> first prize to Jenna or to Paulo,
        B
<u>then</u> decided that Jenna's painting was the <u>most</u>
    C   D
original of the two. <u>No error</u>
                            E

22 Many analysts <u>now believe</u> that the company could
                        A
not <u>have maintained</u> its dominance within the
            B
industry if it <u>had not made</u> such bold moves
                        C
<u>to acquire</u> its competitors. <u>No error</u>
    D   E

23 If you want <u>to maintain</u> your agility and range of
                        A
motion, <u>one</u> should take care to stretch <u>carefully</u> after
            B   C
<u>any vigorous exercise</u>. <u>No error</u>
    D   E

24 <u>Although</u> the dolphin and the whale both belong to
    A
the mammalian order Cetacea, <u>they belong</u> to
                                        B
different suborders, <u>reason being that</u> dolphins
                                C
have true teeth, <u>whereas</u> whales filter their food
                        D
through baleen. <u>No error</u>
                        E

25 <u>Regardless</u> of any fluctuations <u>in the cost</u> of oil due
    A   B
to changes in supply and demand, the company has

agreed <u>not to raise</u> the rate it charges <u>its</u> customers
            C   D
for at least six months. <u>No error</u>
                                E

GO ON TO THE NEXT PAGE

26 Immanuel Kant asserted that the mind <u>is</u> a
                                         A

sophisticated machine rather than <u>being</u> a "blank
                                       B

slate," <u>as</u> John Locke <u>had claimed</u> nearly one
        C   D

hundred years earlier. <u>No error</u>
                        E

27 <u>Being</u> a full-time student did not appeal to Kyra as
     A

much as taking an internship, <u>which</u> would allow <u>her</u>
                           B   C

to earn money <u>and to learn</u> about the professional
                 D

world. <u>No error</u>
         E

28 Once it is established, a stem cell line <u>can be</u>
                                    A

maintained <u>indefinitely</u>, and <u>they</u> can be used for
            B   C

treatment of diseases or <u>for transplantation</u>. <u>No error</u>
                         D   E

29 Directors have <u>long experimented</u> with such
                      A

temporal devices <u>as</u> flashbacks and time dilations,
                 B

but only recently <u>have</u> the viewing public become
                 C

<u>sophisticated</u> enough to appreciate films that eschew
     D

time sequence altogether. <u>No error</u>
                         E

Directions for Improving Paragraphs Questions

The following passage is an early draft of an essay that may need revision.

Read the passage and select the best answers for the questions that follow. The questions may ask about the diction, logic, and structure of individual sentences. Other questions may ask you about the relationship among sentences or the cohesiveness of entire paragraphs. You are expected to follow the rules of standard written English.

Questions 30–35 are based on the following passage.

(1) Although it has been historically associated with the dragon, the Chinese alligator, or *Alligator sinensis*, is actually very timid. (2) Because of its association with magical powers, it is one of the most endangered crocodilians in the world with its organs being thought to have magical medical powers. (3) Fortunately, the Chinese government has recently taken steps to preserve this magnificent creature. (4) Turning marshland into agricultural use has been the greatest threat to habitat for remaining populations. (5) Remaining alligators exist in areas which have already been modified for agricultural purposes, meaning that they frequently come into conflict with humans trying to raise food where Chinese farmers regard the alligator as nothing but a costly nuisance to be eliminated.

(6) The Law of Wildlife Conservation of the People's Republic of China has prohibited the sale of the alligator's organs as medicines, but such practices still continue. (7) Increased education of the status of the species could help to prevent this, but the main impetus must be to convince locals of their value in the wild. (8) Much work has been done in this regard, but recent updated surveys do not paint a promising picture. (9) Surveys in the 1980s revealed a significant decline in wild alligator numbers in the province of Anhui. (10) Recent surveys in 1999 by the Wildlife Conservation Society gave the alarming news that the wild population stood between 130 and 150 individuals. (11) The captive population is extremely healthy due to a successful breeding program, which has nurtured over 10,000 alligators in the Anhui research centre. (12) The breeding program at Anhui was initiated by professional biologists. (13) Although this is positive, despite the presence of the breeding program, human population pressure on the alligators is still severe as over one million people are living there.

GO ON TO THE NEXT PAGE

30 Which of the following is the best revision of sentence 2 (reproduced below)?

> *Because of its association with magical powers, it is one of the most endangered crocodilians in the world with its organs being thought to have magical medical powers.*

(A) By its association with magical powers, it is one of the most endangered crocodilians in the world by its organs being thought to have magical medical powers.

(B) In being associated with magical powers, it is one of the most endangered crocodilians in the world with its organs thought to have magical medical powers.

(C) Because its organs are thought to have magical medical powers, it has become one of the most endangered crocodilians in the world.

(D) Because its organs are thought to have magical medical powers, it being one of the most endangered crocodilians in the world.

(E) Because of the association of its organs with magical medical powers, so it is one of the most endangered crocodilians in the world.

31 Where is the most appropriate place to move sentence 3?

(A) after sentence 1
(B) after sentence 5
(C) after sentence 6
(D) after sentence 8
(E) after sentence 9

32 Which of the following best combines the underlined portion of sentences 4 and 5 (reproduced below)?

> *Turning marshland into agricultural use has been the greatest threat to habitat for remaining populations. Remaining alligators exist in areas which have already been modified for agricultural purposes, meaning that they frequently come into conflict with humans trying to raise food where* Chinese farmers regard the alligator as nothing but a costly nuisance to be eliminated.

(A) The greatest threat to the habitat of remaining wild populations has been the expansion of agricultural areas into marshlands, where

(B) The expansion of agricultural areas into marshlands being the greatest threat to remaining wild populations, where

(C) The greatest threat to the habitat of remaining wild populations has been where agricultural areas have expanded into marshlands, and where

(D) The expansion of agricultural areas into marshland habitats is the greatest threat to the remaining wild populations, in which

(E) The greatest threat to the habitat of remaining wild populations being where agricultural areas have expanded into marshlands, and

33 Which of the following sentences contributes the least relevant information to the second paragraph?

(A) sentence 9
(B) sentence 10
(C) sentence 11
(D) sentence 12
(E) sentence 13

GO ON TO THE NEXT PAGE

34 In context, which of the following is the best change to make to sentence 11?

(A) Change "nurtured" to "created".
(B) Remove the word "captive".
(C) Begin with "Furthermore,".
(D) Begin with "In contrast,".
(E) Change "which" to "and it".

35 In context, which of the following is the best revision of sentence 13 (reproduced below)?

Although this is positive, despite the presence of the reserve, human population pressure is still severe as over one million people are living there.

(A) Despite the breeding program's positive effects, it is the population of humans that has put severe pressure on the alligators, with over one million living there.
(B) Although the breeding program has had positive effects, the population of humans that has put severe pressure on the alligators, with over one million living there.
(C) Despite such positive developments as the breeding program, the human population, which now has reached over one million, has put severe pressure on the alligators.
(D) Although such positive developments as the breeding program have occurred, the human population, which now has reached over one million, putting severe pressure on the alligators.
(E) Despite the positive developments such as the breeding program, the human population now has reached over one million, putting severe pressure on the alligators.

STOP You may check your work, on this section only, until time is called.

SECTION 3
Time—10 Minutes
14 Questions

Directions for Improving Sentences Questions

Each of the sentences below contains one underlined portion. The portion may contain one or more errors in grammar, usage, construction, precision, diction (choice of words), or idiom. Some of the sentences are correct.

Consider the meaning of the original sentence, and choose the answer that best expresses that meaning. If the original sentence is best, choose (A), because it repeats the original phrasing. Choose the phrasing that creates the clearest, most precise, and most effective sentence.

EXAMPLE:

The children couldn't hardly believe their eyes.

(A) couldn't hardly believe their eyes
(B) would not hardly believe their eyes
(C) could hardly believe their eyes
(D) couldn't nearly believe their eyes
(E) could hardly believe his or her eyes

ANSWER: C

---

1 Audra McDonald demonstrated great emotional range, being a talented singer, she also has a magnetic stage presence.

(A) Audra McDonald demonstrated great emotional range, being a talented singer, she also has a magnetic stage presence.
(B) Audra McDonald, a talented singer, demonstrated a great emotional range and a magnetic stage presence.
(C) Audra McDonald demonstrated great emotional range, also a magnetic stage presence, and she is a talented singer.
(D) Audra McDonald, demonstrating great emotional range, is a talented singer, she has a magnetic stage presence.
(E) Audra McDonald, demonstrating a great emotional range and being a talented singer, in addition to having a magnetic stage presence.

2 Even professional baseball players have difficulty hitting the knuckle ball because of its tantalizing slowness and it is deceptively elusive.

(A) of its tantalizing slowness and it is deceptively elusive
(B) of the tantalizing slowness and deceptive elusiveness of it
(C) it is tantalizing in its slowness and deceptively elusive
(D) of the fact of its tantalizing slowness and that it is deceptively elusive
(E) it is tantalizingly slow and deceptively elusive

3 The committee chair wanted to adjourn the meeting, but the opportunity for doing so was not granted for her.

(A) but the opportunity for doing so was not granted for her
(B) despite her not being granted the opportunity for it
(C) but she was not granted the opportunity
(D) but not being granted the opportunity
(E) and was unable to because she was not granted the opportunity

4 Bottlenose dolphins weigh from 450 to 600 pounds, with its length being sometimes over 14 feet.

(A) with its length being
(B) and can reach lengths of
(C) and it can reach a length of
(D) their lengths being sometimes
(E) and their lengths being possibly

GO ON TO THE NEXT PAGE

5 As a teacher, <u>my attempt is always to challenge my students without frustrating them</u>.

(A) my attempt is always to challenge my students without frustrating them

(B) to challenge but not frustrate my students is always my goal

(C) I always try to challenge my students without the frustration of them

(D) I always try to challenge my students without frustrating them

(E) my attempt is always challenge without frustration of my students

6 <u>Las Vegas, being in the middle of a vast desert, while also being one of the fastest growing metropolitan areas in the United States.</u>

(A) Las Vegas, being in the middle of a vast desert, while also being one of the fastest growing metropolitan areas in the United States.

(B) Las Vegas is one of the fastest growing metropolitan areas in the United States, which is in the middle of a vast desert.

(C) Being in the middle of a vast desert, Las Vegas, one of the fastest growing metropolitan areas in the United States.

(D) Despite being in the middle of a vast desert, Las Vegas is one of the fastest growing metropolitan areas in the United States.

(E) Las Vegas is one of the fastest growing metropolitan areas in the United States, nevertheless being in the middle of a vast desert.

7 The arrangements of Rob <u>Mathes, like great classical composers, display</u> masterful instrumentation that blends the power and subtlety of dozens of instruments.

(A) Mathes, like great classical composers, display

(B) Mathes, like those of great classical composers, display

(C) Mathes, as with great classical composers displaying

(D) Mathes, as did those of the great classical composers, displays

(E) Mathes, like the great classical composers did, display masterful instrumentation

8 The habitats of the American mountain goat are usually covered with snow, <u>this not preventing them from wandering freely</u> at treacherously high altitudes.

(A) this not preventing them from wandering freely

(B) but this does not prevent them from wandering free

(C) but this does not prevent it from wandering free

(D) but this does not prevent it from wandering freely

(E) yet nevertheless can wander freely

9 Although cubism sought to break from traditional aesthetic forms, <u>but they did not emphasize the unconscious in the way that surrealism did</u>.

(A) but they did not emphasize the unconscious in the way that surrealism did

(B) but it did not emphasize the unconscious like surrealists

(C) it did not emphasize the unconscious like surrealists

(D) but it did not emphasize the unconscious in the way that surrealism did

(E) it did not emphasize the unconscious in the way that surrealism did

10 When we are hired to cater a party, <u>Dani is the one who does the menu planning, I organize the transportation, we do the cooking together</u>.

(A) Dani is the one who does the menu planning, I organize the transportation, we do the cooking together

(B) Dani plans the menu, I organize the transportation, and the cooking is done by us together

(C) Dani is the one who does the menu planning, I am the one who organizes the transportation, and the cooking we do together

(D) Dani plans the menu, I am the one to organize the transportation, and we do the cooking together

(E) Dani plans the menu, I organize the transportation, and we do the cooking together

GO ON TO THE NEXT PAGE

11 Sarah dominated yesterday's discussion about *Pride and Prejudice*; Jane Austen being her favorite author.

(A) *Prejudice*; Jane Austen being
(B) *Prejudice*, in that Jane Austen is
(C) *Prejudice* because Jane Austen is
(D) *Prejudice*, being that Jane Austen is
(E) *Prejudice*; since Jane Austen being

12 Data from radio telescopes suggests the universe is even older than astronomers previously believed.

(A) suggests the universe is even older than astronomers previously believed
(B) suggest that the universe is even older than astronomers previously believed
(C) suggests that the universe is even older than astronomers previously believed
(D) suggest that the universe is even older than astronomers would have previously believed
(E) suggest the universe would be even older than astronomers previously believed

13 Many people believe that nuclear power is dangerous, but the damage done to humanity and the environment is much greater in the burning of fossil fuels.

(A) but the damage done to humanity and the environment is much greater in the burning of fossil fuels
(B) but the damage done to humanity and the environment with the burning of fossil fuels is much greater than that
(C) but the burning of fossil fuels does much greater damage to humanity and the environment
(D) while burning fossil fuels does much greater damage with regard to humanity and the environment
(E) with the damage done to humanity and the environment by burning of fossil fuels being much greater

14 Although we had planned very carefully for the camping trip, we could hardly have anticipated the bizarre weather that we encountered.

(A) we could hardly have anticipated the bizarre weather that we encountered
(B) we could not hardly have anticipated the bizarre weather that we encountered
(C) we could hardly anticipate the bizarre weather which we encountered
(D) we could not hardly anticipate the bizarre weather we would have encountered
(E) the bizarre weather that we would have encountered could hardly have been anticipated by us

 STOP You may check your work, on this section only, until time is called.

Practice Test 3 Answer Key

Section 2	Section 2	Section 3
☐ 1. E	☐ 25. E	☐ 1. B
☐ 2. D	☐ 26. B	☐ 2. E
☐ 3. B	☐ 27. E	☐ 3. C
☐ 4. C	☐ 28. C	☐ 4. B
☐ 5. A	☐ 29. C	☐ 5. D
☐ 6. D	☐ 30. C	☐ 6. D
☐ 7. B	☐ 31. B	☐ 7. B
☐ 8. A	☐ 32. A	☐ 8. D
☐ 9. A	☐ 33. D	☐ 9. E
☐ 10. E	☐ 34. D	☐ 10. E
☐ 11. D	☐ 35. C	☐ 11. C
☐ 12. B		☐ 12. B
☐ 13. C		☐ 13. C
☐ 14. D		☐ 14. A
☐ 15. E		
☐ 16. B		
☐ 17. C		
☐ 18. C		
☐ 19. C		
☐ 20. B		
☐ 21. D		
☐ 22. E		
☐ 23. B		
☐ 24. C		

Total number correct:

_____ (1 point each)

Total number incorrect:

_____ (−¼ point each)

Score Conversion Table

How to score your test

Use the answer key on the previous page to correct your test. Then use the worksheet below to determine your raw score for the multiple-choice portion. Then find the scaled score that corresponds to your essay score and multiple-choice raw score.

Total number of correct answers (Sections 1 and 2):   (A) _____

Total number of incorrect answers (Sections 1 and 2): _____ ÷ 4 = (B) _____

Multiple-choice raw score: (A) − (B) = _____

Essay score (1–6):   _____

MC Raw Score	Essay Score						
	0	**1**	**2**	**3**	**4**	**5**	**6**
49	680	700	720	740	760	800	800
48	670	690	710	730	750	790	800
47	660	680	700	720	740	770	780
46	650	670	690	710	730	760	780
45	640	660	680	700	720	750	770
44	630	650	670	690	710	740	770
43	610	640	660	680	700	730	760
42	600	630	650	670	700	720	750
41	590	610	640	660	690	710	740
40	590	600	630	650	680	700	730
39	580	590	610	640	670	700	720
38	570	590	600	630	660	690	710
37	560	580	590	620	660	690	700
36	550	570	590	610	650	680	700
35	540	560	580	610	650	680	690
34	530	550	570	600	640	670	690
33	520	540	560	590	630	660	680
32	510	530	550	580	620	640	680
31	500	520	540	570	610	640	670
30	490	510	530	560	600	630	660
29	490	500	520	550	590	620	640
28	480	490	510	540	580	610	640
27	470	490	500	530	570	600	630
26	460	480	490	520	560	590	620
25	450	470	490	520	550	580	610
24	440	460	480	510	540	580	600
23	430	450	470	510	540	570	590
22	430	440	460	500	530	570	580
21	430	430	450	490	520	560	580
20	420	430	440	490	510	550	570
19	410	430	440	480	500	540	570
18	400	420	430	470	490	530	560
17	390	410	430	460	480	520	550
16	380	400	420	450	470	510	540
15	370	390	410	440	470	500	530

Practice Test 3—Sample Essays

> **Assignment:** Is the intention to do something ever as important as actually doing it?

The following passage received the highest possible score of 6. This *outstanding* essay develops a clear and interesting point of view with appropriate examples. It demonstrates outstanding critical thinking and mastery of the standards of writing and organization.

Johann Wolfgang von Goethe once said "It is not enough to have wishes, one must also accomplish." This focus on deeds, rather than intentions, is the bedrock of the American work ethic, which has created the most prosperous nation in the history of mankind. Without this emphasis on accomplishment, rather than mere thought, our forefathers and mothers would not have forged into unknown territories and made brave new discoveries that have made our world a better place.

For millenia, mankind has wanted to fly. And for the vast majority of that time, flight was only a wish. It was not until two courageous American minds, Orville and Wilbur Wright, decided to risk their lives and livelihood that humanity began to realize this wish. Their accomplishment inspired countless millions who since have taken to the sky, and have inspired as many to look beyond our planet to discoveries in other realms. Without this accomplishment, our dreams would have languished. We still may have looked at the stars in wonder, but we would hardly have been able to conceive of actually reaching them.

Those who regard intention as being as important as deed fail to appreciate the deep and wide chasm between intention and execution, which often can only be crossed by the bravest of souls. The thousands of years that humans tried unsuccessfully to fly only hints at the gulf between wishing and doing. This chasm provides us with our moral opportunities as well as our moral pitfalls. The punishment for announcing a wish to do harm to another must never approach the punishment that we exact on one who actually harms. Otherwise, we de-value the self-control that enables us to keep from acting on our wishes. Indeed, we assume that it does not even exist. Yet without such self-control, we cease to be human.

Unfortunately, modern societies tend to shield their leaders from responsibility for acting on their wishes, and so this crucible in which intention becomes forged into action becomes hidden. Corporate executives know that they need merely hint at the need to make their companies look more profitable, knowing that others will actually "cook the books." A president can declare war based on some abstract wish or principle, not having the slightest first-hand idea of the horrible events that will ensue. Such people live in a world of pure intention, without the essential responsibility for the actions that follow.

Without question, deeds are what cause the gears of history to turn. Intentions usually inspire these deeds, and so these intentions should be true and honorable. They cannot be honorable, however, if they are divorced from the responsibility of the actions that ensue.

Practice Test 3—Sample Essays

Reader's comments   **6 points out of 6**

Point of view. The thesis that "the focus on deeds, rather than intentions, is the bedrock of the American work ethic, which has created the most prosperous nation in the history of mankind" is interesting, well-articulated and consistently well-supported.

Reasoning. The author offers several deep insights in his analysis of action versus intention. The discussion of "the deep and wide chasm between intention and execution" shows a powerful analytical mind, as does the discussion of the "self-control that enables us to keep from acting on our wishes." These insights alone are strong, but the author follows with yet another meaningful path of analysis by discussing situations in which "the crucible in which intention becomes forged into action" becomes hidden to decision-makers.

Support. The examples of the first flight, mankind's yearning to fly, legal punishment, and executive decisions, while not discussed at great length, are marshalled to provide very effective support to the author's thesis.

Organization. The essay is well organized, with a clear introduction, development and conclusion. The conclusion does not merely repeat the original thesis, but rather provides an "expanded" thesis that draws upon the previous discussion. The author does not divert from the central line of reasoning, and does not succumb to repetition.

Use of language. The author shows exceptional strength in the use of language. Such metaphorical phrases as "the gears of history" and "the deep and wide chasm between intention and execution" serve to bring abstract concepts to life. The use of sophisticated diction like "ensue," "forged," "divorced," and "crucible" are used effectively without becoming overbearing or pedantic.

The following passage received a good score of 8. (Both readers gave it a 4.) This *competent* essay develops a point of view with adequate examples. It demonstrates competent critical thinking, adequate but inconsistent coherence, and uses generally appropriate vocabulary.

I think that a lot of times just intending to do something is almost as important as actually doing it. Just because a bomb that you planted on a bus didn't go off doesn't mean that you shouldn't be put away in prison for a long time. If you think long and hard about something and want it to happen, then you plan it out and anticipate that it will actually happen, then it is pretty much the same as if it actually did happen, even if it didn't.

If we don't punish criminals for intending to do horrible things, then the streets would be filled with people who are ticking time bombs. For instance there are many people who post their hatred of individuals or entire races on the internet, sometimes with bloody pictures and horrible disturbing images. These people should be put away someplace where they can at least get therapy and be kept away from the rest of the public.

I'm not saying that it isn't much worse to actually do a horrible thing than just to think about doing it, but what makes all the difference is whether you actually go through all of the steps to plan it. For instance, although Richard Reid's shoe bomb never actually detonated in an airplane over the Atlantic Ocean, he was still sentenced to life in prison, where hopefully he will rot in misery.

Lady Macbeth also shows how planning horrible deeds makes someone as guilty as the one who actually did it. She convinced her husband Macbeth to murder King Duncan, whom he respected, in order to gain the throne of Scotland. She tried to cover up her evil plot, but she could not wash the guilty blood from her hands and the pain of being hated by her subjects led to her descent into insanity and to her death.

No matter what area of life we are working in, our intentions matter. This is why we have a conscience, so that we can check our intentions before we actually act on them. But if we carry out a plan to do something, even if it doesn't happen, it is morally no different than if we actually did it.

Reader's comments   4 points out of 6

Point of view. The point of view, based on the thesis that "our intentions matter" is maintained consistently throughout the essay, even if the analysis of that point of view is weak in areas.

Reasoning. The author's reasoning is consistent and relevant, if not particularly strong. The discussions of intention and conscience show an attempt to analyze and provide insight on the topic.

Support. The examples of the shoe bomber and Lady Macbeth are appropriate to the discussion of intention as distinct from action. Each should have been explored in more depth, however.

Organization. The essay is moderately well organized, with a clear, if slightly unfocused, introduction, three "body" paragraphs, and a conclusion. Each paragraph contains a distinct line of thought, and the conclusion serves as an adequate summary.

Use of language. The author shows an adequate, but not masterful, use of language. The author occasionally uses imprecise pronouns, cliché, and self-conscious diction, but overall employs effective vocabulary.

Practice Test 3 Detailed Answer Key

Section 2

1. E The *neither A nor B* construction requires parallel phrasing. Since *the noise from the crowds* is not a gerund phrase, choices (A) and (D) violate parallelism. The phrasing that is most parallel to *neither the noise from the crowds* is (E) *nor the many obstacles in the street.* Choices (B) and (C) lack the *nor* required by idiom.
(Lesson 14, Parallelism)

2. D The pronoun *them* in the original sentence is unclear and in the wrong case. Furthermore, the two clauses share a subject but lack parallel phrasing. The most parallel option is (D), because its subject, *it*, refers to the subject of the first clause, *book*. Although (D) uses this same subject, it changes the verb tense from the present perfect to the past.
(Lesson 14, Parallelism)
(Lesson 16, Pronoun problems)

3. B Since the subject *neither painting* is singular, the noun with which it is compared should be singular as well. Choices (A), (C), and (E) compare it to the plural *masterpieces*. Choice (D) uses the incorrect idiom *appears like* instead of the correct idiom *appears to be*. Therefore the best choice is (B).
(Lesson 15, Comparison problems)

4. C The underlined clause in the original sentence is awkward, and the passive voice violates the law of parallelism. Choices (B) and (E) are also passive and therefore non-parallel, and choice (D) uses the incorrect idiom *began in researching*.
(Lesson 14, Parallelism)
(Lesson 18, Tense and voice problems)

5. A The original sentence is best. Choice (B) is a run-on sentence. In choice (C), the modifying infinitive phrase is misplaced. Choice (D) is illogical because it does not indicate *what many piano teachers believe*. Choice (E) is incorrect because the pronoun *which* lacks a clear antecedent.
(Lesson 16, Pronoun problems)
(Lesson 17, Modifier problems)

6. D The original sentence does not convey a complete thought because it lacks a main verb. Choices (C) and (D) both provide a main verb *was disappointed*, but the *and* in choice (C) is illogical. Therefore the best choice is (D).
(Lesson 23, Awkwardness and coordination)

7. B The sentence begins with a participial phrase, so what follows must be an independent clause whose subject is also the participial subject. The word *but* in the original phrasing is redundant, because the contrast of ideas is established by the word *despite*. The subject of

the participle *having committed* is *the board*, so choice (B) is the only one that prevents the dangling participle.
(Lesson 17, Modifier problems)

8. A The original sentence is best because it makes a clear and logical comparison between *the climatological effect of a major volcanic eruption* and *that of cumulative emissions from cars and factories*. Choices (B), (D), and (E) make an illogical comparison between the *effect* of the eruptions and the *emissions*, rather than the *effect* of the emissions. Choice (C) is incorrect because it is ungrammatical when the interrupter, *if not more*, is removed.
(Lesson 15, Comparison problems)

9. A The sentence begins with a participial phrase which must be followed by a clause whose subject is the participial subject. The logical subject of the participle *intrigued* is *Lani*, so the original sentence is best. Choice (D), although it begins with *Lani*, is illogical because it implies that she was *offered* the contract because she was *intrigued*, rather than that she *signed* the contract because she was intrigued. It is also awkward because the antecedent to the pronoun *which* is misplaced.
(Lesson 16, Pronoun problems)
(Lesson 17, Modifier problems)
(Lesson 23, Awkwardness and coordination)

10. E The prepositional phrase that begins the sentence serves much like an appositive, and so the clause that follows should have as its subject the *mother of five adult children*, which is clearly *Dr. Krone* and not her *advice* or her *readers*. Choices (C) and (E) both use the correct subject, but choice (C) is incorrect because, since the advice has been offered over an extended period in the past, the verb *are following* is in the wrong tense.
(Lesson 17, Modifier problems)
(Lesson 18, Tense and voice problems)

11. D The original sentence incorrectly uses the impersonal pronoun *that* to refer to people, and uses the incorrect past participle *stole* instead of the correct participle *stolen*. Choices (D) and (E) correct both problems, but choice (E) deprives the clause of its main verb by substituting *being*. The best choice is therefore (D).
(Lesson 16, Pronoun problems)
(Lesson 22, Irregular verbs)

12. B The original sentence is a comma splice. The simplest fix is to change *this* to *which*, thereby making the second clause subordinate.
(Lesson 23, Awkwardness and coordination)

13. **C**   Since Sarah and Anna are two people, they can only be inspired to be *performers*.
(Lesson 15, Comparison problems)

14. **D**   The phrase in choice (D) is not parallel to the others. It should be changed to *patience* so that it is parallel to *knowledge* and *competence*.
(Lesson 14, Parallelism)

15. **E**   The sentence is correct.

16. **B**   The correct idiom is *complied with*.
(Lesson 19, Idiom problems)

17. **C**   Since Gregory's talkfest was completed before the morning lecture, it should be in the past perfect tense, and (C) should be changed to *had stayed*.
(Lesson 18, Tense and voice problems)

18. **C**   Since the subject *ideas* is plural, the correct verb conjugation is *have stimulated*.
(Lesson 13, Subject-verb agreement)

19. **C**   Since *periods of time* are not places, the pronoun *where* is illogical, and should be changed to *when* or *in which*.
(Lesson 16, Pronoun problems)

20. **B**   The pronoun *they* does not agree in number with its antecedent *the blue whale*, so (C) should be changed to *it is*.
(Lesson 16, Pronoun problems)

21. **D**   Since there are only two paintings, the superlative *most* is illogical, and should be changed to the comparative *more*.
(Lesson 15, Comparison problems)

22. **E**   This sentence is correct.

23. **B**   The use of the pronoun *you* is established in the rest of the sentence, so (B) should be changed to *you* also.
(Lesson 16, Pronoun problems)

24. **C**   The phrase *reason being that* is a non-standard idiom, and should be changed to *because*.
(Lesson 21, Diction problems)

25. **E**   The sentence is correct.

26. **B**   The word *rather* indicates a comparison. The word *being* should be eliminated in order to maintain parallelism between *a sophisticated machine* and *a "blank slate."* Notice that, although Immanuel Kant's assertion is in the past, the *idea* in his assertion is timeless, so the verb *is* is correctly in the present tense.
(Lesson 14, Parallelism)
(Lesson 18, Tense and voice problems)

27. **E**   The sentence is correct. Notice that the gerunds *being* and *taking* are parallel, and the pronouns have clear antecedents.
(Lesson 14, Parallelism)

28. **C**   The antecedent of the plural pronoun *they* is the singular noun *stem cell line*, so the pronoun should be changed to *it*.
(Lesson 16, Pronoun problems)

29. **C**   The verb *have become* does not agree in number with the singular verb *public*, and should be changed to *has become*. This error is tough to catch for two reasons: the sentence is inverted, and the subject is a "collective" noun, that is, a singular term referring to a group. You should notice that the clause can be "univerted" by just rearranging the phrases: *the viewing public have only recently become sophisticated enough to appreciate films that eschew time sequence altogether.*
(Lesson 13, Subject-verb agreement)

30. **C**   The original sentence is redundant, mentioning *magical powers* twice, and uses an illogical prepositional phrase *with its organs being...* Choice (B) is redundant in the same way as the original, choice (D) lacks a main verb, and the use of the conjunction *so* in choice (E) is redundant. The most concise and effective phrasing is given in choice (C).
(Lesson 17, Modifier problems)
(Lesson 21, Diction problems)

31. **B**   Sentence 3 provides a transition from the less hopeful facts about the Chinese alligator to a more hopeful fact about how the Chinese government is trying to fix the problem. Since sentence (4) does not continue the more hopeful train of thought, the transition is misplaced. It logically belongs just before sentence 6, which discusses the *Law of Wildlife Conservation*.
(Lesson 23, Awkwardness and coordination)

32. **A**   Choice (A) most concisely and effectively combines these ideas. Choices (B) and (E) lack a main verb, choice (C) illogically equates the *threat* with a *place*, and choice (D) illogically suggests that the *farmers* are in the *wild populations*.
(Lesson 23, Awkwardness and coordination)

33. **D**   The fact that the program *was initiated by professional biologists* does not contribute to the main discussion of the paragraph, which centers on trends in the alligator population and their causes.
(Lesson 23, Awkwardness and coordination)

34. **D**   Since sentence 10 mentions *alarming news* about the wild population of alligators, but the next sentence gives positive news about the *captive population*, a transition is required to show the contrast of ideas.
(Lesson 23, Awkwardness and coordination)

35. C The ideas in the original sentence are coordinated awkwardly, and the pronoun *this* lacks a clear antecedent. Choice (C) coordinates the ideas logically and concisely, without any unclear references. Choices (A) and (E) are illogical. Choice (B) uses an illogical prepositional phrase *with over one million living there*, and *there* lacks a clear antecedent. Choice (D) lacks a main verb.
(Lesson 23, Awkwardness and coordination)

Section 3

1. B The original sentence is a run-on. Choice (C) is awkward and contains an illogical interrupter. Choice (D) is a run-on, and choice (E) lacks a main verb.
(Lesson 13, Subject-verb agreement)
(Lesson 23, Awkwardness and coordination)

2. E The underlined phrase lacks parallel phrasing. Choice (E) is the only one that provides a parallel structure.
(Lesson 14, Parallelism)

3. C The subject of the first clause is the subject of the second clause also, so the underlined clause should be parallel to, but in contrast to, the first. Choice (B) is illogical. Choice (D) is not a clause, and so does not convey a complete idea. Choice (E) is wordy and lacks a contrasting conjunction.
(Lesson 18, Tense and voice problems)
(Lesson 23, Awkwardness and coordination)

4. B The prepositional phrase in the underlined portion is illogical and uses a pronoun, *its*, which does not agree in number with its antecedent, *dolphins*. Choice (C) repeats the pronoun-antecedent disagreement. Choice (D) is awkward. Choice (E) does not follow the conjunction with a clause, as it should.
(Lesson 16, Pronoun problems)
(Lesson 17, Modifier problems)

5. D The prepositional phrase *as a teacher*, serves very much like an appositive, and should be followed by a noun phrase that represents *a teacher*. Only choices (C) and (D) do this, but (C) uses the illogical prepositional phrase *without the frustration of them*.
(Lesson 17, Modifier problems)

6. D The original phrasing is a sentence fragment, because it lacks a verb. Choice (C) has the same problem. Choice (B) incorrectly suggests that the United States, rather than Las Vegas, is in the middle of the desert. Choice (E) contains an illogical and awkward modifier, *nevertheless being in the middle*. The only choice that is clear, logical and complete is (D).
(Lesson 23, Awkwardness and coordination)

7. B Since the sentence is about Rob Mathes' *arrangements,* the comparison should be to the *arrangements of great classical composers*. Choice (C) lacks a main verb. Choice (D) uses a verb, *displays,* which does not agree with its subject *arrangements*. Choice (E) repeats the original comparison error.
(Lesson 15, Comparison problems)

8. D In the original sentence, the pronoun *them* does not agree in number with its presumable antecedent, *the American mountain goat*. In addition, the underlined clause contrasts the previous one, but lacks a contrasting conjunction. Choice (D) corrects these problems most concisely. Choice (B) repeats the pronoun-antecedent disagreement and misuses the adjective *free,* as does choice (C). Choice (E), although concise, is illogical, because parallelism suggests that its subject is *habitats,* which of course cannot *wander freely*.
(Lesson 16, Pronoun problems)
(Lesson 17, Modifier problems)
(Lesson 23, Awkwardness and coordination)

9. E The original sentence misuses the conjunction *but* because the contrast is already indicated by *although*. Also, the pronoun *they* lacks an antecedent. Choices (B) and (C) illogically compare *cubism* with the *surrealists*, rather than with *surrealism*. Choice (D) misuses the conjunction *but*, as in the original.
(Lesson 19: Idiom problems)

10. E The original sentence lacks parallel form. Choice (E), in addition to being the most concise option, is also the most parallel. Notice the consistency in phrasing: *Dani plans...I organize...we do...*
(Lesson 14, Parallelism)

11. C The original sentence misuses the semicolon, because what follows is not an independent clause. Choice (E) also commits this error. Choice (B) is illogical because it does not show the *fact-reason* relationship between the clauses. (D) is incorrect because it uses the non-standard idiom *being that* instead of the standard *because*.
(Lesson 23, Awkwardness and coordination)

12. B The subject *data* is plural, so the original verb *suggests* does not agree with its subject in number. Choice (C) repeats this error. Choices (D) and (E) are incorrect because they use the subjunctive mood for a verb that indicates a fact, and therefore should be in the indicative mood.
(Lesson 13, Subject-verb agreement)
(Lesson 20, Mood problems)

13. **C** The subject of the first clause is *nuclear power*, so the comparison is clearest if the subject of the second clause is what *nuclear power* is compared with, namely, *the burning of fossil fuels.* Choices (C) and (D) fix this problem, but choice (D) uses the incorrect idiom *does damage with regard to.*
(Lesson 14, Parallelism)
(Lesson 15, Comparison problems)
(Lesson 19, Idiom problems)
(Lesson 23, Awkwardness and coordination)

14. **A** The original sentence is best. Choices (B) and (D) use the double negative *could not hardly.* Choice (C) is incorrect because its tense sequence is illogical. The anticipation of problems could only happen before the problems occurred, so the past-tense *could hardly anticipate* should be changed to the past-perfect tense *could hardly have anticipated.* Choice (E), in addition to being awkward and needlessly passive, illogically suggests that the *encounter* did not occur, when in fact it did.
(Lesson 18, Tense and voice problems)
(Lesson 20, Mood problems)
(Lesson 21, Diction problems)

PRINTS on the MOON

Alexandra Siy

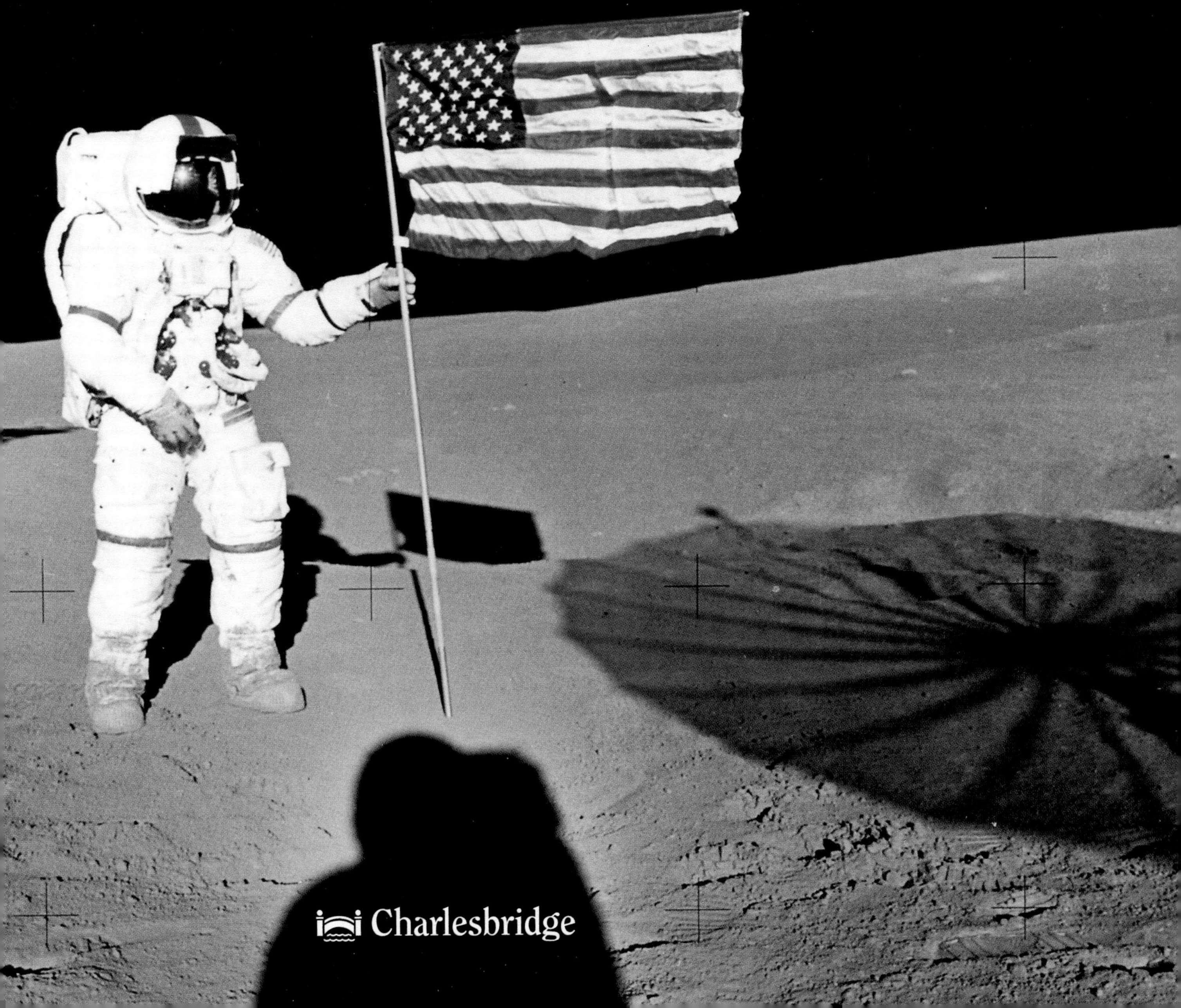

Charlesbridge

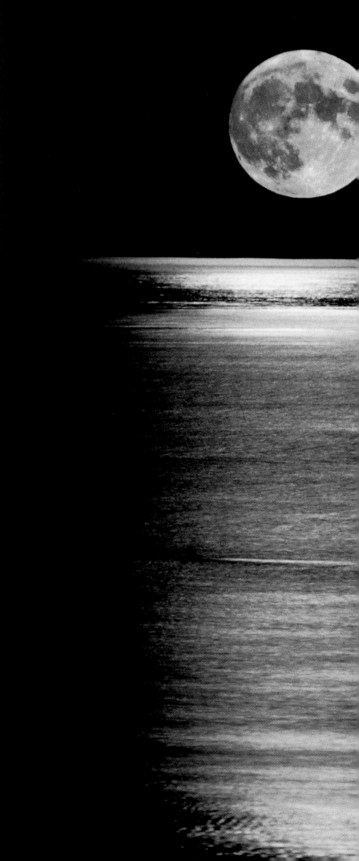

It's the brightest object in our night sky. A big yellow-white disk, it shrinks to a silver sliver and disappears. Then it's born again, growing full, bright, and mysterious. Throughout the centuries, the Moon's changing face has beckoned us silently. We have looked and wondered, imagined and dreamed.

Twenty-four astronauts have crossed the vast ocean of space that separates Earth and Moon. Twelve have left footprints.

As the Moon orbits Earth, we see the Moon's phases, or a changing portion of the Moon's sunlit surface visible from Earth. This crescent Moon is waxing, which means from day to day we see more of the Moon's sunlit area.

One half of the Moon's sunlit portion is visible in this first-quarter Moon, which has completed one fourth of its orbit.

This crescent Moon is waning, which means the portion of the sunlit surface we see is decreasing. Soon only the farside (the side that always faces away from Earth) will be lit, and the Moon will not be visible from Earth. That phase of the Moon is called a new Moon.

A full Moon occurs when the side of the Moon facing Earth is completely lit by the Sun.

Three quarters of the sunlit portion of the Moon is seen in this waxing gibbous Moon.

About four thousand years ago, prehistoric people watched the rising and setting Moon at Stonehenge, a temple built from massive stones that were arranged for keeping track of the motions of the Moon, the Sun, and the stars.

Nearly two thousand years later, the ancient Greeks thought that the Moon's dark areas were oceans and the bright spots were land.

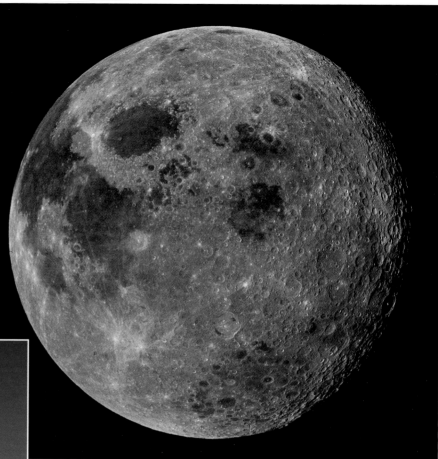

The Moon as photographed by *Apollo 17* astronauts. The bright, rugged highlands are *terrae*, which is Latin for "land." The dark areas are low, flat plains named *maria*, which is Latin for "seas."

Stonehenge, located on Great Britain's Salisbury Plain, at dusk.

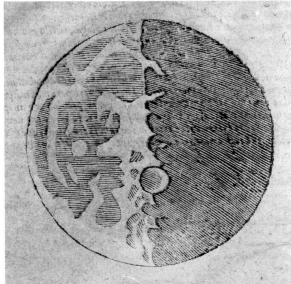

This woodcut print of the Moon as seen through a telescope was among the first published by Galileo.

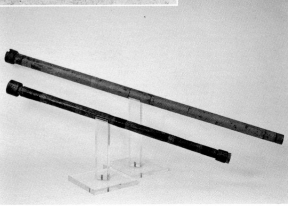

Galileo's telescopes made objects appear nearly one thousand times larger.

In 1610 the Italian scientist and inventor Galileo Galilei published a book called *The Starry Messenger*. The book described the Moon and stars as they appeared in his handmade spyglass, or telescope. Galileo was amazed to see that the Moon's surface was covered with tall mountains and deep craters.

Galileo Galilei (1564-1642) argued that Earth and the other planets circle the Sun. He was imprisoned for the final eight years of his life for contradicting the belief that Earth was the center of the universe.

Although the telescope made the heavens look closer, space travel was still just a dream. That dream suddenly seemed achievable at the dawn of the twentieth century. In 1903, Orville Wright piloted the first airplane, and in 1926 the inventor Robert H. Goddard launched the first liquid-fueled rocket.

Less than twenty years later, powerful rockets were used as weapons in World War II. After the war, scientists worked on rockets for space travel. Daring test pilots, who later became the world's first astronauts, pushed the limits of aviation by flying planes to the outer edge of Earth's atmosphere. Now space was within reach!

Robert H. Goddard stands next to his rocket, which was launched on March 16, 1926. The rocket accelerated upward for 2.5 seconds, reaching a height of 41 feet.

On December 17, 1903, at Kitty Hawk, North Carolina, Orville and Wilbur Wright's plane flew a distance of 120 feet and remained in the air for 12 seconds.

The desire to explore space became an intense competition between the United States and the Soviet Union (modern-day Russia and its former republics). The two countries were enemies in the "cold war," a conflict that threatened the world with nuclear destruction despite the lack of actual combat. One of the fiercest "battles" was the space race.

The Soviets took the lead in 1957 when they launched *Sputnik I*, the world's first artificial satellite. In 1961 a Soviet, Yuri Gagarin, became the first person in space. The American pilot Alan Shepard was the second. On May 25, 1961, President John F. Kennedy declared that before the end of the decade, the United States would try to send a man to the Moon and return him safely to Earth. The space race now had a finish line, and the United States was determined to get there first.

In 1958 the National Aeronautics and Space Administration (NASA) was created. NASA's Mercury project was formed to put humans into space. The first Mercury astronauts were (left to right): Walter M. Schirra Jr., Alan B. Shepard Jr., Donald K. Slayton, Virgil I. "Gus" Grissom, John H. Glenn, L. Gordon Cooper Jr., and M. Scott Carpenter.

In 1962 President Kennedy examines *Friendship 7*, in which John Glenn (standing behind Kennedy) became the first American to orbit the earth.

The crew of *Apollo 1* (left to right): Virgil I. Grissom, Edward H. White II, and Roger B. Chaffee.

Project Gemini (1964-1966) tested new equipment and skills such as rendezvous, the meeting of space vehicles while in Earth's orbit. Project Apollo was next; its mission was to fly men to the Moon.

The race to the Moon demanded the hard work and dedication of at least 400,000 people. The fast pace also took its toll. On January 27, 1967, the crew of *Apollo 1* died in a fire inside the command module during a practice countdown on the launchpad. The next command module was carefully redesigned to correct several fatal flaws, including a cabin door that was almost impossible to open from the inside.

After several unmanned test missions, *Apollo 7* was the first Apollo manned mission and the first U.S. spacecraft to carry three people. Less than two years after the *Apollo 1* tragedy, *Apollo 8* was aimed at the Moon. It was a bold plan: Three astronauts would orbit the Moon and return to Earth.

The *Apollo 7* commander, Wally Schirra, orbited Earth for ten days.

As a *Gemini 4* astronaut, Ed White became the first American to walk in space.

The *Apollo 8* crew trains inside a centrifuge, which simulates the feeling of traveling in space.

The *Apollo 8* astronauts, Commander Frank Borman, James A. Lovell Jr., and William A. Anders, were ready for the adventure. On December 21, 1968, they became the first people to blast off atop the 363-foot-tall Saturn V rocket.

It took sixty-nine hours to reach the Moon. On Christmas Eve, 1968, *Apollo 8* flew around the Moon. For the first time ever, humans saw the lunar farside, a view previously seen only in photographs taken by an unmanned probe. On the farside, radio transmissions to Earth were impossible, and the astronauts lost contact with Mission Control.

On the knee pad of his flight suit, Jim Lovell drew a picture that became the emblem for the first mission to the Moon.

BORMAN LOVELL ANDERS

A view of the lunar farside, which always faces away from Earth.

Back above the near side, the unexpected sight of Earth rising above the barren Moon stunned the astronauts.

"Oh, my God! Look at that picture over there," Commander Borman said, taking a black-and-white photograph. Bill Anders quickly loaded a roll of color film into the camera and took two more photographs of earthrise.

"This is *Apollo 8*, coming to you live from the Moon," Commander Borman announced.

The astronauts were broadcast on television to an audience of more than half a billion people. They took the awestruck world on a tour of the Moon, describing craters, mountains, and future landing sites. They talked about the long shadows, cast by the rising and setting Sun, that made the moonscape look jagged and sinister.

But Earth itself made the greatest impression on both the astronauts and the watching world. Jim Lovell said that Earth was a "grand oasis in the big vastness of space."

Apollo 8 crossed once again into silence behind the Moon. The spacecraft could return home only if the rocket engine fired. If it failed, the astronauts would remain in lunar orbit forever.

This is how earthrise actually looked
to Bill Anders from his spaceship as
he snapped the famous photo.
Usually the picture is printed so Earth
is seen above the Moon's horizon.

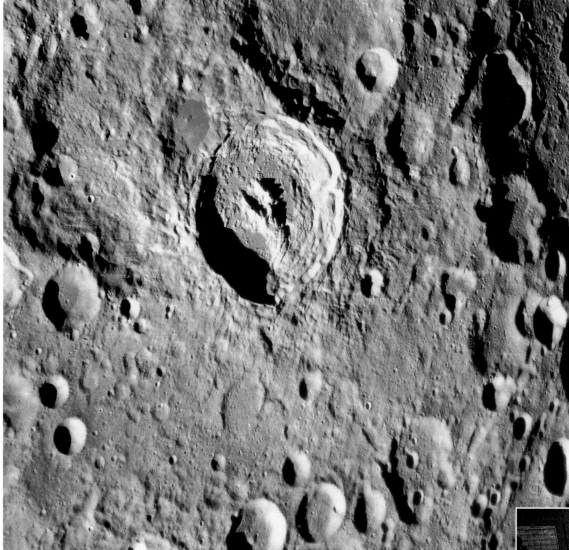

Scientists at Mission Control waited anxiously. Jim Lovell's voice broke the silence as the spaceship emerged from behind the moon.

"Please be informed," he exclaimed, "there is a Santa Claus!"

The engine had worked. On Christmas Day, *Apollo 8* headed for home—back to the little blue marble in space. The mission was a perfect success.

Apollo 8 had orbited the Moon ten times, photographing it and gathering information about its surface. In addition to these important scientific achievements, humans had seen an earthrise for the very first time.

The many craters on the farside are the result of billions of years of bombardment by meteors.

An *Apollo 8* flight director at his console in the Mission Control center.

Apollo 11 is launched from the Kennedy Space Center at 9:32 A.M. on July 16, 1969. Onboard are astronauts Neil A. Armstrong (commander), Michael Collins (command module pilot), and Edwin E. "Buzz" Aldrin Jr. (lunar module pilot).

Although the Soviets put the first man and woman into space and accomplished the first unmanned lunar landing, they ultimately lost the race to the Moon. On July 3, 1969, all hopes of a manned moon landing literally went up in smoke as the Soviet rocket exploded on the launchpad. For America, it was now simply a race against time.

It was July 20, 1969, 3:16 P.M. Houston time. *Apollo 11*'s computer-controlled lunar module, called *Eagle*, was headed straight for a field of boulders on the Moon. With less than sixty seconds' worth of fuel left, Commander Neil Armstrong took the controls and steered *Eagle* toward safer ground.

Moondust swirled under the engine. Then, all was quiet. Armstrong's voice broke the silence.

"Houston, Tranquility Base here. The *Eagle* has landed!"

A brilliant rising sun cast long shadows across the bleak landscape. Beyond the horizon there was only the blackness of space.

Flight controllers at Mission Control in Houston, Texas, celebrate the lunar landing.

Sixty-nine miles above the lunar surface, *Apollo 11* astronaut Michael Collins circled the moon in the command module *Columbia*. Traveling at 3,700 miles per hour, he searched the Moon's surface for *Eagle*. Even with the help of a computerized sextant, an instrument used in navigation, Collins never spotted *Eagle* during his twenty-two hours alone in *Columbia*.

While flying above the Moon's near side, Collins could hear his crewmates even though he couldn't see them. He listened spellbound as Armstrong and Aldrin prepared to leave the lunar module for the first-ever moon walk.

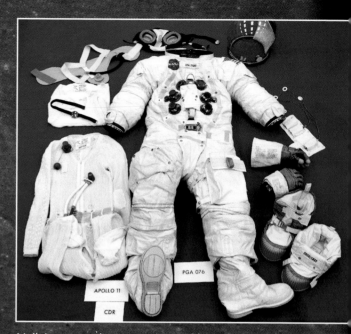

Neil Armstrong's space suit was fifteen layers thick and had five hundred parts. It carried oxygen, pumps, tubes, and cooling water to control the temperature inside the suit. It took Armstrong two hours to get dressed.

Columbia, as photographed from the lunar module.

Buzz Aldrin steps onto the Moon. "Magnificent desolation!" exclaimed Aldrin as he let go of the ladder.

Buzz Aldrin, with Neil Armstrong reflected in his visor. The small, repeating plus signs burned into the film are camera-lens grid marks used for measuring distances on the Moon.

As Buzz Aldrin opened the hatch and Neil Armstrong moved onto the ladder, *Columbia* flew behind the Moon's farside. Mike Collins couldn't hear Armstrong speak as he stepped onto the Moon, but millions of people back on Earth could:

"That's one small step for man, one giant leap for mankind."

Armstrong had planned to say, "That's one small step for *a* man, one giant leap for mankind," but he was so excited that he forgot to say the word *a* in the now-famous quote.

Armstrong took pictures and collected some powdery black soil before the amazed Aldrin joined him on the Moon's surface.

Six hundred million people watched and listened as Aldrin and Armstrong unfurled and raised an American flag on the Sea of Tranquility. The flag only looked like it was flying; wires stiffened the Stars and Stripes into a permanent flutter above the airless moonscape.

Throughout history, explorers have claimed newly discovered territory by flying their country's flag. But no one nation owns the Moon. It belongs to all people—past, present, and future. The astronauts did not claim the Moon for the United States. Instead, they celebrated their achievement with their fellow Americans and the world.

A remote-control camera shows the astronauts raising the flag. In 1967 the United Nations announced the Outer Space Treaty, which stated that "the Moon shall be the province of all mankind."

Buzz Aldrin faces the American flag and the rising Sun.

Buzz Aldrin sets up an experiment. *Eagle* is in the background. In the far left of the picture is the television camera that sent pictures back to Earth.

Now there was work to do. Aldrin and Armstrong set up a seismometer to detect moonquakes, as well as a laser reflector for measuring the distance between the Moon and Earth to within centimeters. They also collected twenty-two kilograms (about forty-seven pounds) of rocks and soil. Since the Moon's gravity is one sixth of Earth's, the astronauts felt lighter and described the way they walked on the Moon as "kangaroo hopping."

Aldrin and Armstrong spent less than one Earth day—just twenty-one hours and thirty-six minutes— on the Moon's surface. Their moon walk lasted for only two hours and thirty-one minutes. Despite their rush, the astronauts felt as if they were on a world where time almost stood still. One lunar day lasts about a month: It takes twenty-nine and a half days for the Moon to make one full spin on its axis. On any one place on the Moon, the sun shines for two weeks followed by another two weeks of dark night.

There on the Sea of Tranquility, during the brief early hours of that lunar morning, our universe was forever expanded. Our dream of touching the ancient, mysterious Moon had finally come true.

Because there are no major forces of erosion on the Moon, an astronaut's footprint could remain there for millions of years.

A tired, but happy, Commander Neil Armstrong inside *Eagle* after the first moon walk.

Mike Collins's biggest fear about the entire *Apollo 11* mission was that he might have to return to Earth alone:

> As *Eagle*'s liftoff time approached, I got really nervous. If their engine didn't work, there was nothing I could do to rescue them from the surface. I simply had to come home by myself, leaving Neil and Buzz to die on the surface of the moon.

—from *Flying to the Moon*, by Michael Collins. Farrar, Straus & Giroux, 1994.

The flag, photographed from inside the lunar module before liftoff. The astronauts had a hard time getting the flagpole to stand in the lunar soil, and during liftoff the flag was knocked over.

Michael Collins snapped this photograph of *Eagle*'s ascent, with Earth in the background. In that moment, Collins had captured all humanity on film except for himself.

The *Apollo 11* command module is hoisted out of the Pacific Ocean on July 24, 1969.

Fortunately, *Eagle* blasted off the Moon and was safely reunited with *Columbia*. Now the astronauts were on their way home to parades and parties. John F. Kennedy's goal had been achieved.

Apollo 11 fulfilled the dream of sending explorers to the Moon. It also answered important scientific questions. The seismometer proved that moonquakes are rare. Scientists learned from the rock samples that parts of the Moon were once hot with flowing volcanic lava. New minerals were also discovered. Armalcolite, a new type of titanium, was named after Armstrong, Aldrin, and Collins.

A ticker-tape parade for the *Apollo 11* astronauts.

From 1969 to 1972, six more Apollo spacecraft traveled to the Moon. Five missions actually got there. *Apollo 13* never landed because of an explosion in an oxygen tank.

Charles Conrad examines the TV camera on *Surveyor 3*, an unmanned probe that had landed on the Moon in 1967.

Apollo 12 lunar module pilot Alan Bean, with astronaut Charles Conrad Jr. reflected in his visor. The notebook on Bean's left wrist lists tasks to be completed.

Alan B. Shepard Jr., *Apollo 14*'s commander (and the first American in space ten years earlier in 1961), plants the third flag on the Moon in 1971. The second flag had been raised by the *Apollo 12* astronauts in 1969.

With each lunar landing, scientists discovered new information about the Moon. They learned that the Moon is ancient: about four and one-half billion years old.

The Apollo Moon rocks also suggested that the Moon was formed in a hot and violent crash after an early Mars-sized object collided with Earth. The Moon was formed from the dust and gas that flew into space after the crash.

Astronaut John Young kicks up moondust in the "grand prix" run of the lunar rover at the *Apollo 16* landing site. The rover's top speed was eleven miles per hour.

James Irwin scoops lunar soil during one of three moon walks. Long-duration backpacks allowed *Apollo 15* astronauts to spend extended periods of time exploring.

Apollo 16 was the first exploration of the Moon's central highlands. Here astronaut Charles M. Duke Jr. collects samples at the edge of a crater.

Apollo 16's commander, John W. Young, demonstrates the effect of one sixth of Earth's gravity by jumping three feet off the ground.

Apollo 17 astronaut Harrison "Jack" Schmitt was the first professional scientist to explore the Moon. Here he collects samples with a lunar rake.

Jack Schmitt discovered this orange soil, magnified here 160 times. The soil provided clues about the age, composition, and origin of the Moon.

The *Apollo 17* mission commander, Eugene A. Cernan, test-drives the lunar rover before loading it up with gear.

An *Apollo 17* photo of the rising crescent Earth above the lunar horizon.

Cernan, exhausted and filthy after his second of three moon walks. On December 13, 1972, he left the last footprints on the Moon.

After the *Apollo 17* mission, NASA focused on other projects, such as the space shuttle. In 1998 the United States returned to the Moon. For almost two years *Lunar Prospector,* an unmanned probe, orbited the Moon from sixty-three miles up. Information collected from *Prospector,* such as the size of the Moon's core and the amounts of gold, platinum, and iridium in moon rocks, supported the theory that the Moon was formed after an enormous object collided with Earth.

Prospector also discovered frozen water at the lunar poles and mapped the location of metals, such as aluminum and titanium, that might someday be mined for use on Earth. The probe also studied the Moon's magnetic fields and gravity.

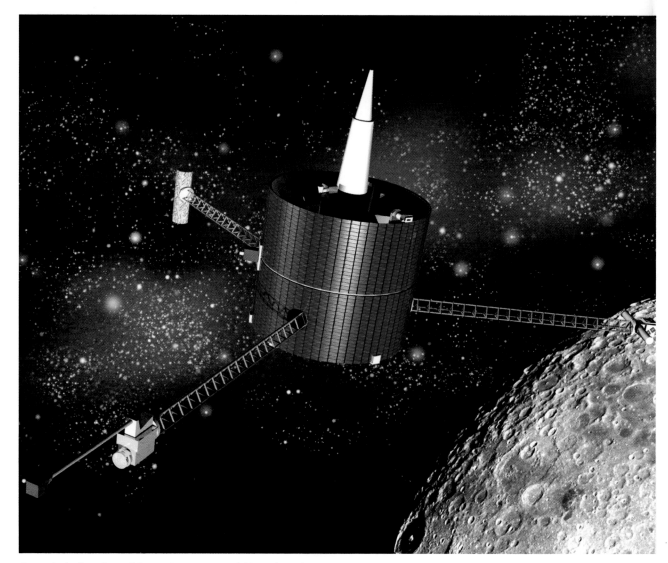

An artist's drawing of *Lunar Prospector* orbiting the Moon.

Today many astronauts and scientists think we should return to the Moon. Some astronomers believe that the Moon is the perfect place from which to study the universe. Moonquakes are a million times less likely than earthquakes, making the Moon a quiet, stable platform on which to build sensitive telescopes. The two weeks of nighttime on the Moon make it easier to study the stars, and with no atmosphere to blur the view, the stars are visible even in daylight.

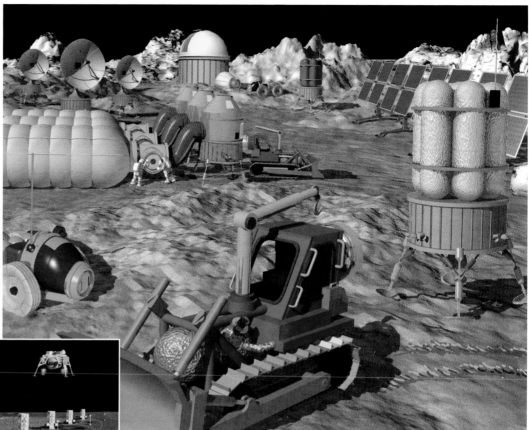

This drawing of a futuristic Moon camp includes inflatable living spaces, radio antennae, a telescope, storage tanks, and all-terrain vehicles.

An imagined lunar mining factory takes oxygen from rich volcanic soil.

Sending people back to the Moon would be very costly. If cheaper rocket-launching systems can be developed, then more scientific Moon missions could occur. Private businesses might also send workers to the Moon to mine minerals or operate solar power stations. Even tourist flights to the Moon could be in our future.

Many scientists believe that humans will visit Mars during the first half of the twenty-first century.

Only twelve humans have walked on the Moon. Others may follow. Now we dream of exploring more of our solar system. A round-trip mission to Mars could take two years or more. The challenges are great, but our need to explore, to discover, and to succeed is even greater.

When astronauts raise the flag once again, we will all experience the adventure as we share in the ancient desire to understand our place in the universe.

This solar system montage (not to scale) was created using photographs taken by five separate spacecraft. From top to bottom are images of Mercury (by *Mariner 10*), Venus (by *Magellan*), Earth, the Moon (both by *Galileo*), Mars (by *Viking*), Jupiter, Saturn, Uranus, and Neptune (all by *Voyager*). The *Voyager* probes did not visit Pluto.

MOON EXPLORATION TIME LINE

ca. 2000 B.C.

Stonehenge is built to keep track of celestial events.

ca. 270 B.C.

Greek astronomer Aristarchus estimates the distance between Earth and the Moon as 60 Earth radii. The true distance varies between 55 and 63 Earth radii (354,000–404,000 km, or about 220,000–251,000 miles).

1610

Galileo Galilei publishes *The Starry Messenger*.

1647

Polish astronomer Johannes Hevelius draws maps of the Moon and names many of its features in his book *Selenographia*.

1750

German astronomer Johann Tobias Mayer discovers the Moon's libration zones, or the edges of the farside that occasionally wobble into view.

1840s

Some of the first photographs ever taken are of the Moon.

1865

Author Jules Verne writes the science fiction novel *From the Earth to the Moon,* in which three space travelers are launched out of a cannon.

1903

(December 17) The Wright brothers pilot the first airplane.

1920s

Robert Goddard and other space enthusiasts build and launch rockets.

1957

(October 4) The Soviet Union launches the first satellite, *Sputnik I.*

1958

(January 31) The United States launches its first satellite, *Explorer 1.*
(July 28) The National Aeronautics and Space Administration (NASA) is created.

1959

(October) The Soviet unmanned mission *Luna 1* takes photographs of the lunar farside.

1961

(April 12) Soviet cosmonaut Yuri Gagarin pilots *Vostok,* the world's first spacecraft, becoming the first human in space and the first to orbit Earth.

1962

(February 20) John Glenn is the first American to orbit Earth.

1963

(June 16) Soviet cosmonaut Valentina Tereshkova is the first woman in space.

1965

(March 18) Soviet cosmonaut Aleksei Leonov is history's first space walker.
(June 3) Edward White is the first American to walk in space.

1966

(January 31) The unmanned Soviet *Luna 9* makes the first soft landing on the Moon. It lands gently, instead of crashing into the lunar surface.
(March 31) *Luna 10* is the first lunar orbiter.
(May 30) The first American soft lander is *Surveyor 1.*

1967

(January 27) A fire in *Apollo 1* kills three American astronauts.
(November 9) The unmanned *Saturn V* rocket is launched for the first time.

1968

(October 11-22) *Apollo 7* is the first manned Apollo mission.
(December 21-27) *Apollo 8* is the first manned flight to orbit the moon.

1969

(March 3-13) *Apollo 9* tests the Apollo spacecraft while in Earth's orbit.
(May 18-26) *Apollo 10* brings the lunar module to within 9.4 miles (15 km) of the Moon's surface.
(July 20) *Apollo 11* makes the first lunar landing. A plaque left on the Moon reads: "Here men from the planet Earth first set foot upon the Moon, July 1969 A.D. We came in peace for all mankind."
(November 14-24) *Apollo 12* makes the first pinpoint lunar landing when the lunar module touches down about 600 feet from the unmanned U.S. lander *Surveyor 3.*

1970

(April 13) An explosion cripples the *Apollo 13* command module, forcing the astronauts to use their lunar module as a lifeboat for the journey home.
(September 12) The Soviet *Luna 16* is the first unmanned mission to return lunar soil samples to Earth.

1971

(January 31-February 9) *Apollo 14* is the first mission devoted to scientific exploration of the Moon.
(July 26-August 7) *Apollo 15* is another scientific expedition and the first to use the lunar rover.

1972

(April 16-27) *Apollo 16* is the first exploration of the lunar highlands.
(December 7-19) *Apollo 17* is the final mission and the longest Apollo flight.

1990

Japan sends *Muses A,* an unmanned orbiter, around the Moon.

1994

The U.S. sends the unmanned orbiter *Clementine* to map the Moon.

1998-1999

The American unmanned probe *Lunar Prospector* orbits the Moon to map it and conduct scientific research.

For my sons: Sasha, Rory, and Leo;
and for everyone else who loves rockets, space suits, and flags.

Recommended Web Sites

NASA Sites

NASA Home Page
http://www.nasa.gov/
(The first step for navigating NASA's vast Internet resource. Of special note are links to a site for kids and a multimedia gallery of NASA's complete image archives.)

Apollo Lunar Surface Journal
http://www.hq.nasa.gov/alsj/main.html
(History, scientific information, links, photographs, and much more.)

Exploring the Moon
http://cass.jsc.nasa.gov/moon.html
(Information on the various NASA Moon missions, hosted by the Lunar and Planetary Institute.)

StarChild: A Learning Center for Young Astronomers
http://starchild.gsfc.nasa.gov/docs/StarChild/StarChild.html
(Information provided about the solar system, the universe, and space travel, with links to many resources.)

Other Web Sites

Kids Earth and Sky
http://www.earthsky.com/Kids/
(Web site of a daily science radio series; features articles, views of tonight's sky, sections for teachers and kids, and many links.)

Welcome to Heavens-Above
http://www.heavens-above.com/
(Explore the night sky from any location on Earth.)

Moon Phases
http://www.googol.com/moon/
(See the phase of the Moon for every day of the month.)

spaceKids.com
http://www.spacekids.com/
(Information, activities, and contests.)

Recommended Books

Collins, Michael. *Flying to the Moon: An Astronaut's Story.* New York: Farrar Straus Giroux, 1994.

Fraser, Mary Ann. *One Giant Leap.* New York: Henry Holt and Company, 1993.

Gibbons, Gail. *The Moon Book.* New York: Holiday House, 1997.

Light, Michael. *Full Moon.* New York: Alfred A. Knopf, 1999.

Sis, Peter. *Starry Messenger.* New York: Farrar, Straus & Giroux, 1996.

Text copyright © 2001 by Alexandra Siy
All rights reserved, including the right of reproduction in whole or in part in any form.

Published by Charlesbridge Publishing
85 Main Street, Watertown, MA 02472
(617) 926-0329
www.charlesbridge.com

Library of Congress Cataloging-in-Publication Data
Siy, Alexandra.
Footprints on the moon/Alexandra Siy.
p. cm.
Includes bibliographical references.
ISBN 1-57091-408-7 (reinforced for library use)
ISBN 1-57091-409-5 (softcover)
1. Project Apollo (U.S.)—History—Juvenile literature. 2. Space flight to the moon—History—Juvenile literature. 3. Space race—Juvenile literature. [1. Project Apollo (U.S.) 2. Space flight to the moon. 3. Space race.] I. Title.
TL789.8.U6 A5818   2001
629.45'4'0973—dc21   00-038370

Printed in the United States of America
(hc) 10 9 8 7 6 5 4 3 2 1
(sc) 10 9 8 7 6 5 4 3 2 1

Display type and text type set in Horizon, Garamond, and Stone Sans
Color separations by Eastern Rainbow, Derry, New Hampshire
Printed and bound by Phoenix Color, Rockaway, New Jersey
Production supervision by Brian G. Walker
Designed by Diane M. Earley

Acknowledgments

I extend special thanks to the *Apollo 16* commander, Captain John Young, for sharing his experiences and insights with me about Apollo, the Moon, and the future of space exploration. I am also indebted to my talented editors, Yolanda LeRoy and Harold Underdown, for their enthusiasm and wisdom; to book designer Diane Earley for her terrific work; and to R. Bruce Ward of the Harvard-Smithsonian Center for Astrophysics and Wally Schirra, the *Apollo 7* commander, for their expert readings.

I am grateful to the many people at NASA who helped me obtain photographs, especially Sherie Jefferson at the NASA Lyndon B. Johnson Space Center and Lisa Chu Thielbar at the NASA Ames Research Center. Thanks also to Roger Arno of the NASA Ames Research Center for his futuristic space art. For their photographic research assistance, thanks to James B. Hill of the John Fitzgerald Kennedy Library; Cathy Houghton at the English Heritage Photographic Library; Franca Principe of Istituto e Museo di Storia della Scienza; Robin Witmore at the UCO/Lick Observatory; and John Cunningham of Visuals Unlimited.

To my husband, Eric, thank you for your excellent critique and your extraordinary patience. To our daughter, Melissa, thanks for babysitting while I was far off in another world.

Photograph Credits

p. 2: © C. P. George, Visuals Unlimited; p. 3: (all images) UCO/Lick Observatory; p. 4: (bottom left) © English Heritage Photographic Library; p. 5: (top left) Library of Congress LC-USZ62-95171, (right) Library of Congress LC-USZ62-122699, (bottom left) Istituto e Museo di Storia della Scienza; p. 6: (background) Library of Congress LC-USZ62-6166-A; p. 7: (bottom left) Photo #ST-A13-60-62 in the John F. Kennedy Library; p. 26: NASA Ames Research Center/Roger Arno; p. 27: (right) NASA Ames Research Center/Roger Arno; p. 28: NASA Ames Research Center/Pat Rawlings; p. 29: photoNASA/jpl/caltech; all other photos are from NASA.